Global Perspectives in Business

A Pearson Custom Publication

Global Perspectives in Business

Compiled from:

International Business: The Challenges of Globalization
Fifth Edition
by John J. Wild, Kenneth L. Wild and Jerry C.Y. Han

*International Management: Managing Across Borders
and Cultures, Text and Cases*
Seventh Edition
by Helen Deresky

PEARSON
Custom
Publishing

Pearson Education Limited
Edinburgh Gate
Harlow
Essex CM20 2JE

And associated companies throughout the world

Visit us on the World Wide Web at:
www.pearsoned.co.uk

First published 2011

Compiled from:

International Business: The Challenges of Globalization
Fifth Edition
by John J. Wild, Kenneth L. Wild and Jerry C.Y. Han
ISBN 978 0 13 715375 6
Copyright © 2010, 2008, 2006, 2003, 2000, Pearson Education, Inc., publishing as
Prentice Hall, One Lake Street, Upper Saddle River, New Jersey.

International Management: Managing Across Borders and Cultures, Text and Cases
Seventh Edition
by Helen Deresky
ISBN 978 0 13 609867 6
Copyright © 2011, 2008, 2006, 2003, 2000, Pearson Education, Inc., publishing as
Prentice Hall, One Lake Street, Upper Saddle River, New Jersey 07458.

ISBN 978 0 85776 074 6

Printed and bound in Great Britain by Ashford Colour Press, Gosport, Hampshire

Contents

1

Globalization

Learning Objectives

After studying this chapter, you should be able to

1 Describe the process of globalization and how it affects markets and production.

2 Identify the two forces causing globalization to increase.

3 Summarize the evidence for each main argument in the globalization debate.

4 Identify the types of companies that participate in international business.

5 Describe the global business environment and identify its four main elements.

■ A LOOK **AT THIS CHAPTER**

This chapter defines the scope of international business and introduces us to some of its most important topics. We begin by presenting globalization—describing its influence on markets and production and the forces behind its growth. Each main argument in the debate over globalization is also analyzed in detail. We then identify the key players in international business today. This chapter closes with a model that depicts international business as occurring within an integrated global business environment.

▶ A LOOK **AHEAD**

Part 2, encompassing Chapters 2, 3, and 4, introduces us to different national business environments. Chapter 2 describes important cultural differences among nations. Chapter 3 examines different political and legal systems. Chapter 4 presents the world's various economic systems and issues surrounding economic development.

YouTube's Global Impact

S AN MATEO, California — YouTube (www.youtube.com) is the world's most popular service for sharing video clips through Web sites, mobile devices, blogs, and e-mail. YouTube officially launched in December 2005, and less than a year later was purchased by Google for $1.65 billion! YouTube's spectacular success illustrates the opportunities that globalization creates for entrepreneurs.

Pictured at right in Paris, France, YouTube founders Chad Hurley and Steve Chen introduce national versions of their service. YouTube localizes its service for 19 nations to capitalize on exploding global demand for user-created video content. "This is just the beginning," says Chen. "If we had the resources, we would be launching in 140 countries."

Most people visit YouTube's Web site to catch up on current events and find videos about their hobbies and interests. Wannabe pop stars and filmmakers also share their creative efforts with the world by uploading them to YouTube. And by creating CitizenNews (www.youtube.com/citizennews), YouTube has given a voice to citizen journalists and Vloggers (video bloggers) who report firsthand accounts of events where they live—whether their home is in Indiana or India.

Source: © Christoph Dernback/dpa/ CORBIS. All Rights Reserved.

Freedom sparks the creativity of artists and journalists, but it also draws the attention of heavy-handed governments. Nations that have at times blocked access to YouTube include China, Iran, Pakistan, Tunisia, and Turkey. YouTube and local providers of similar services must then employ their entrepreneurial creativity to overcome this government censorship.

As you read this chapter, consider how globalization is reshaping our personal lives and altering the activities of international companies. Also please visit this book's YouTube channel (www.youtube.com/myibvideos) to watch specially selected videos on international business topics.[1]

Globalization is reshaping our lives and leading us into uncharted territory. As *new technologies* drive down the cost of global communication and travel, we are increasingly exposed to the traits and practices of other cultures. As countries *reduce barriers to trade and investment*, globalization forces their industries to grow more competitive if they are to survive. And as multinationals from advanced countries and emerging markets seek out customers, *competition intensifies* on a global scale. These new realities of international business are altering our cultures and transforming the way companies do business.

International Business Involves Us All

The dynamic nature of international business affects each of us personally. In our daily communications we encounter terms such as outsourcing, innovation, emerging markets, competitive advantage, and social responsibility. And each of us experiences the result of dozens of international transactions every day.

The General Electric alarm clock/radio (www.ge.com) that woke you was likely made in *China*. The breaking news buzzing in your ears was produced by *Britain*'s BBC radio (www.bbc.co.uk). You slip on your Adidas sandals (www.adidas.com) made in *Indonesia*, Abercrombie & Fitch T-shirt (www.abercrombie.com) made in the *Northern Mariana Islands*, and American Eagle jeans (www.ae.com) made in *Mexico*. You pull the charger off your Nokia phone (www.nokia.com), which was designed in *Finland* and manufactured in the *United States* with parts from *Taiwan*, and head out the door. You hop into your Toyota (www.toyota.com) that was made in *Kentucky*, and pop in a CD performed by the *English* band Coldplay (www.coldplay.com). You swing by the local Starbucks (www.starbucks.com) to charge your own batteries with coffee brewed from a blend of beans harvested in *Colombia* and *Ethiopia*. Your day is just one hour old but in a way you've already taken a virtual round-the-world trip. A quick glance at the "Made in" tags on your jacket, backpack, watch, wallet, or other items with you right now will demonstrate the pervasiveness of international business transactions.

International business is any commercial transaction that crosses the borders of two or more nations. You don't have to set foot outside a small town to find evidence of international business. No matter where you live, you'll be surrounded by **imports**—goods and services purchased abroad and brought into a country. Your counterparts around the world will undoubtedly spend some part of their day using your nation's **exports**—goods and services sold abroad and sent out of a country. The total value of goods and services exported by all nations each year is a staggering $14,950,150,000,000 (nearly $15 trillion). That is nearly 40 times the annual revenue of the world's largest company, Wal-Mart Stores (www.walmart.com).[2]

Technology Makes It Possible

Technology is perhaps the most remarkable facilitator of societal and commercial changes today. Consumers use technology to reach out to the world on the Internet—gathering and sending information and purchasing all kinds of goods and services. Companies use technology to acquire materials and products from distant lands and to sell goods and services abroad.

When businesses or consumers use technology to conduct transactions, they engage in **e-business (e-commerce)**—the use of computer networks to purchase, sell, or exchange products, service customers, and collaborate with partners. E-business is making it easier for companies to make their products abroad, not simply import and export finished goods.

Consider how Hewlett-Packard (HP) (www.hp.com) designed and built a computer server for small businesses. Once HP identified the need for a new low-cost computer server, it seized the rewards of globalization. HP dispersed the design and production of its ProLiant ML150 server throughout a specialized manufacturing system across five Pacific Rim nations and India (see Figure 1.1). This helped the company minimize labor

---

international business
Commercial transaction that crosses the borders of two or more nations.

imports
Goods and services purchased abroad and brought into a country.

exports
Goods and services sold abroad and sent out of a country.

e-business (e-commerce)
Use of computer networks to purchase, sell, or exchange products, service customers, and collaborate with partners.

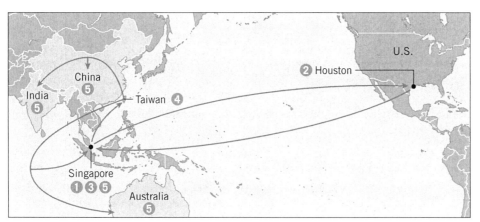

FIGURE 1.1

Global Production of an HP Server

Source: Rebecca Buckman, "H-P Outsourcing: Beyond China," *Wall Street Journal*, (www.wsj.com), February 23, 2004.

1 Idea for product hatched in **Singapore**

2 Concept approved in **Houston**

3 Concept design done in **Singapore**

4 Engineering design in **Taiwan**, where many computer components are made; initial manufacture by a Taiwanese contractor.

5 Final assembly in **Singapore**, **Australia**, **China**, and **India**. Products made in Australia, China, and India are primarily for those markets; machines made in Singapore go to all of Southeast Asia.

costs, taxes, and shipping delays yet maximize productivity when designing, building, and distributing its new product. Companies use such innovative production and distribution techniques to squeeze inefficiencies out of their international operations and boost their competitiveness.

Global Talent Makes It Happen

Media companies today commonly engage in a practice best described as a global relay race. Fox and NBC Universal created Hulu (www.hulu.com) as a cool venue for fans to watch TV shows online. Hulu employs two technical teams—one in the United States and one in China—to manage its Web site. Members of the team in Santa Monica, California, work late into the night detailing code specifications that it sends to the team in Beijing, China. The Chinese team then writes the code and sends it back to Santa Monica before the U.S. team gets to work in the morning.[3]

Some innovative companies use online competitions to tap global talent. InnoCentive (www.innocentive.com) connects companies and institutions seeking solutions to difficult problems using a global network of more than 145,000 creative thinkers. These engineers, scientists, inventors, and businesspeople with expertise in life sciences, engineering, chemistry, math, computer science, and entrepreneurship compete to solve some of the world's toughest problems in return for significant financial awards. InnoCentive is open to anyone, is available in seven languages, and pays cash awards that range from as little as $2,000 to as much as $1,000,000.[4]

This chapter begins by presenting globalization—we describe its powerful influence on markets and production and explain the forces behind its rapid expansion. Following coverage of each main point in the debate over globalization, we examine the key players in international business. We then explain why international business is special by presenting the dynamic, integrated global business environment. Finally, the appendix at the end of this chapter contains a world atlas to be used as a primer for this chapter's discussion and as a reference throughout the remainder of the book.

Quick Study

1. Define the term *international business* and explain how it affects each of us.
2. What do we mean by the terms *imports* and *exports*?
3. Explain how *e-business (e-commerce)* is affecting international business.

Globalization

Although nations historically retained absolute control over the products, people, and capital crossing their borders, economies are becoming increasingly intertwined. **Globalization** is the trend toward greater economic, cultural, political, and technological interdependence among national institutions and economies. Globalization is a trend characterized by *denationalization* (national boundaries becoming less relevant) and is different from *internationalization* (entities cooperating across national boundaries). The greater interdependence that globalization is causing means an increasingly freer flow of goods, services, money, people, and ideas across national borders.

globalization
Trend toward greater economic, cultural, political, and technological interdependence among national institutions and economies.

As its definition implies, globalization involves much more than the expansion of trade and investment among nations. Globalization embraces concepts and theories from political science, sociology, anthropology, and philosophy as well as economics. As such, it is not a term exclusively reserved for multinational corporations and international financial institutions. Nor is globalization the exclusive domain of those with only altruistic or moral intentions. In fact, globalization has been described as going "well beyond the links that bind corporations, traders, financiers, and central bankers. It provides a conduit not only for ideas but also for processes of coordination and cooperation used by terrorists, politicians, religious leaders, anti-globalization activists, and bureaucrats alike."[5]

For our purposes, this discussion focuses on the business implications of globalization. Two areas of business in which globalization is having profound effects are the globalization of *markets* and *production*.

Globalization of Markets

Globalization of markets refers to convergence in buyer preferences in markets around the world. This trend is occurring in many product categories, including consumer goods, industrial products, and business services. Clothing retailer L.L. Bean (www.llbean.com), shoe producer Nike (www.nike.com), and electronics maker Sony (www.sony.com) are just a few companies that sell *global products*—products marketed in all countries essentially without any changes. Global products and global competition characterize many industries and markets, including semiconductors (Intel, Philips), aircraft (Airbus, Boeing), construction equipment (Caterpillar, Mitsubishi), autos (Honda, Volkswagen), financial services (Citicorp, HSBC), air travel (Lufthansa, Singapore Airlines), accounting services (Ernst & Young, KPMG), consumer goods (Procter & Gamble, Unilever), and fast food (KFC, McDonald's). The globalization of markets is important to international business because of the benefits it offers companies. Let's now look briefly at each of these benefits.

Reduces Marketing Costs   Companies that sell global products can reduce costs by *standardizing* certain marketing activities. A company selling a global consumer good, such as shampoo, can make an identical product for the global market and then simply design different packaging to account for the language spoken in each market. Companies can achieve further cost savings by keeping an ad's visual component the same for all markets, but dubbing TV ads and translating print ads into local languages.

Creates New Market Opportunities   A company that sells a global product can explore opportunities abroad if the home market is small or becomes saturated. For example, China holds enormous potential for e-business with more than 240 million Internet users, but this represents just 18 percent of China's total population. By comparison, around 153 million people are online in the United States, about 70 percent of the popula-

An employee demonstrates the latest iPhone at a T-Mobile phone store in Cologne, Germany. The iPhone by Apple (www.apple.com) is a hugely successful global product that excites style-lovers the world over. The iPhone combines a music and video player, cell phone, and Web browser into a single handset. Apple standardized the iPhone to reduce production and marketing costs and to support the creation of a powerful global brand.

Source: © Nvennenbernd/epa/ CORBIS. All Rights Reserved.

tion. So, the battle for market share in the Middle Kingdom is raging between the top two online search engines—Google (www.google.cn) and Yahoo! (www.cn.yahoo.com).[6] Seeking sales growth abroad can be absolutely essential for an entrepreneur or small company that sells a global product but has a limited home market.

Levels Uneven Income Streams A company that sells a product with universal, but seasonal, appeal can use international sales to level its income stream. By supplementing domestic sales with international sales, the company can reduce or eliminate wide variations in sales between seasons and steady its cash flow. For example, a firm that produces suntan and sunblock lotions can match product distribution with the summer seasons in the northern and southern hemispheres in alternating fashion—thereby steadying its income from these global, yet highly seasonal, products.

Yet Local Needs Are Important Despite the potential benefits of global markets, managers must constantly monitor the match between the firm's products and markets to not overlook the needs of buyers. The benefit of serving customers with an adapted product may outweigh the benefit of a standardized one. For instance, soft drinks, fast food, and other consumer goods are global products that continue to penetrate markets around the world. But sometimes these products require small modifications to better suit local tastes. In southern Japan, Coca-Cola (www.cocacola.com) sweetens its traditional formula to compete with sweeter-tasting Pepsi (www.pepsi.com). In India, where cows are sacred and the consumption of beef is taboo, McDonald's (www.mcdonalds.com) markets the "Maharaja Mac"—two all-mutton patties on a sesame-seed bun with all the usual toppings.

Globalization of Production

Many production activities are also becoming global. *Globalization of production* refers to the dispersal of production activities to locations that help a company achieve its cost-minimization or quality-maximization objectives for a good or service. This includes the sourcing of key production inputs (such as raw materials or products for assembly) as well as the international outsourcing of services. Let's now explore the benefits companies obtain from the globalization of production.

Access Lower-Cost Workers   Global production activities allow companies to reduce overall production costs through access to low-cost labor. For decades, companies located their factories in low-wage nations to churn out all kinds of goods, including toys, small appliances, inexpensive electronics, and textiles. Yet whereas moving production to low-cost locales traditionally meant *production of goods* almost exclusively, it increasingly applies to the *production of services* such as accounting and research. Although most services must be produced where they are consumed, some services can be performed at remote locations where labor costs are lower. Many European and U.S. businesses have moved their customer service and other nonessential operations to places as far away as India to slash costs by as much as 60 percent.

Access Technical Expertise   Companies also produce goods and services abroad to benefit from technical know-how. Film Roman (www.filmroman.com) produces the TV series, *The Simpsons*, but it provides key poses and step-by-step frame directions to AKOM Production Company (www.akomkorea.com) in Seoul, South Korea. AKOM then fills in the remaining poses and links them into an animated whole. But there are bumps along the way, says animation director Mark Kirkland. In one middle-of-the-night phone call, Kirkland was explaining to the Koreans how to draw a shooting gun. "They don't allow guns in Korea; it's against the law," says Kirkland. "So they were calling me [asking]: 'How does a gun work?'" Kirkland and others put up with such cultural differences and phone calls at odd hours to tap a highly qualified pool of South Korean animators.[7]

Access Production Inputs   Globalization of production allows companies to access resources that are unavailable or more costly at home. The quest for natural resources draws many companies into international markets. Japan, for example, is a small, densely populated island nation with very few natural resources of its own—especially forests. But Japan's largest paper company, Nippon Seishi, does more than simply import wood pulp. The company owns huge forests and corresponding processing facilities in Australia, Canada, and the United States. This gives the firm not only access to an essential resource, but control over earlier stages in the papermaking process. As a result, the company is guaranteed a steady flow of its key ingredient (wood pulp) that is less subject to swings in prices and supply associated with buying pulp on the open market. Likewise, to access cheaper energy resources used in manufacturing, a variety of Japanese firms are relocating production to China, Mexico, and Vietnam where energy costs are lower.

Despite its benefits, globalization also creates new risks and accentuates old ones for companies. To read about several key risks that globalization heightens and how companies can better manage them, see this chapter's Global Challenges feature titled, "Investing in Security Pays Dividends."

Quick Study

1. Define *globalization*. How does denationalization differ from internationalization?
2. List each benefit a company might obtain from the globalization of markets.
3. How might a company benefit from the globalization of production?

Forces Driving Globalization

Two main forces underlie the globalization of markets and production: *falling barriers to trade and investment* and *technological innovation*. These two features, more than anything else, are increasing competition among nations by leveling the global business playing field; what author Thomas Friedman refers to in his book titled, *The World Is Flat*.[8] Greater competition is simultaneously driving companies worldwide into more direct confrontation *and* cooperation. Local industries once isolated by time and distance are increasingly

GLOBAL CHALLENGES
Investing in Security Pays Dividends

The globalization of markets and production creates new challenges for companies around the world. As well as the need to secure lengthier supply lines and distribution channels, companies must pay increased attention to their facilities, information systems, and reputations.

- **A Simple Plan.** Careful planning and a vulnerability assessment of facilities (around $12,000 for a midsized company; $1 million for a large firm) can be well worth the cost. For example, Wall Street firms with well-executed disaster plans had their employees working from hotel rooms, rented offices, and their homes the day after terrorists attacked New York City on September 11, 2001.

- **Digital Deterrence.** Computer viruses, software worms, malicious code, and cyber criminals cost the United States $55 billion a year in lost productivity. The usual suspects include disgruntled employees, dishonest competitors, and hackers. Upon quitting their jobs, some employees simply walk away with digital devices containing confidential memos, competitive data, and private e-mails.

- **Perception Is Reality.** News regarding the actions of today's largest corporations spreads worldwide quickly. Reputational risk is anything that can harm a firm's image, including accounting irregularities, product recalls, and workers' rights violations. Reputational risk is extremely important because a company's reputation can be its most valuable asset and be impossible to recover once tarnished.

- **The Challenge.** Like the risks themselves, the challenges are also varied. First, companies should identify all potential risks to their facilities and plan for business evacuation, continuity, and relocation. Second, employees should change passwords often, use software patches to guard computers and mobile devices, and return all company-owned digital devices when leaving the firm. Third, as they come under ever-increasing scrutiny, companies should act ethically and within the law to protect their reputations.

- **Want to Know More?** Visit leading risk consultancy Kroll (www.krollworldwide.com), leading Internet security firm Check Point Software Technologies (www.checkpoint.com), and Internet security agency CERT Coordination Center (www.cert.org).

Source: *The Economist*, (www.economist.com), January 22, 2004; "Living Dangerously," *The Economist*, (www.economist.com), January 22, 2004; "Your Jitters Are Their Lifeblood," *Business Week*, (www.businessweek.com), April 14, 2003.

accessible to large international companies based many thousands of kilometers away. Some small and medium sized local firms are compelled to cooperate with one another or with larger international firms to remain competitive. Other local businesses revitalize themselves in a bold attempt to survive the competitive onslaught. And on a global scale, consolidation is occurring in many industries as former competitors link-up to challenge others on a worldwide basis. Let's now explore in greater detail the pivotal roles of the two forces driving globalization.

Falling Barriers to Trade and Investment

In 1947, political leaders of 23 nations (12 developed and 11 developing economies) made history when they created the **General Agreement on Tariffs and Trade (GATT)**—a treaty designed to promote free trade by reducing both tariffs and nontariff barriers to international trade. *Tariffs* are essentially taxes levied on traded goods, and *nontariff barriers* are limits on the quantity of an imported product. The treaty was successful in its early years. After four decades, world merchandise trade had grown 20 times larger and average tariffs had fallen from 40 percent to 5 percent.

Significant progress occurred again with a 1994 revision of the GATT treaty. Nations that had signed on to the treaty further reduced average tariffs on merchandise trade and lowered subsidies (government financial support) for agricultural products. The treaty's revision also clearly defined *intellectual property rights*—giving protection to copyrights (including computer programs, databases, sound recordings, and films), trademarks and

General Agreement on Tariffs and Trade (GATT)
Treaty designed to promote free trade by reducing both tariffs and nontariff barriers to international trade.

service marks, and patents (including trade secrets and know-how). A major flaw of the original GATT was that it lacked the power to enforce world trade rules. Likely the greatest accomplishment of the 1994 revision was the creation of the *World Trade Organization*.

World Trade Organization   The **World Trade Organization (WTO)** is the international organization that enforces the rules of international trade. The three main goals of the WTO (www.wto.org) are to help the free flow of trade, help negotiate the further opening of markets, and settle trade disputes between its members. It is the power of the WTO to settle trade disputes that really sets it apart from its predecessor, the GATT. The various WTO agreements are essentially contracts between member nations that commit them to maintaining fair and open trade policies. Offenders must realign their trade policies according to WTO guidelines or face fines and, perhaps, trade sanctions (penalties). Because of its ability to penalize offending nations, the WTO's dispute settlement system truly is the spine of the global trading system. The WTO replaced the *institution* of GATT but absorbed all of the former GATT *agreements*. Thus the GATT institution no longer officially exists. The WTO recognizes 153 members and 30 "observer" members.

The WTO launched a new round of negotiations in Doha, Qatar, in late 2001. The renewed negotiations were designed to lower trade barriers further and help poor nations in particular. Agricultural subsidies that rich countries pay to their own farmers are worth $1 billion per day—more than six times the value of their combined aid budgets to poor nations. Because 70 percent of poor nations' exports are agricultural products and textiles, wealthy nations had intended to further open these and other labor-intensive industries. Poor nations were encouraged to reduce tariffs among themselves and were to receive help in integrating themselves into the global trading system. Although the Doha round was to conclude by the end of 2004, negotiations are proceeding more slowly than was anticipated.[9]

Regional Trade Agreements   In addition to the WTO, smaller groups of nations are integrating their economies as never before by fostering trade and boosting cross-border investment. For example, the *North American Free Trade Agreement (NAFTA)* gathers three nations (Canada, Mexico, and the United States) into a free-trade bloc. The more ambitious *European Union (EU)* combines 27 countries. The *Asia Pacific Economic Cooperation (APEC)* consists of 21 member economies committed to creating a free-trade zone around the Pacific. The aims of each of these smaller trade pacts are similar to those of the WTO, but are regional in nature. Moreover, some nations are placing greater emphasis on regional pacts because of resistance to worldwide trade agreements.

Trade and National Output   Together, the WTO agreements and regional pacts have boosted world trade and cross-border investment significantly. Trade theory tells us that openness to trade helps a nation to produce a greater amount of output. Map 1.1 illustrates that growth in national output over a recent 10-year period is significantly positive. Economic growth is greater in nations that have recently become more open to trade, such as China, India, and Russia, than it is in many other countries. Much of South America is also growing rapidly, while Africa's experience is mixed.

Let's take a moment in our discussion to define a few terms that we will encounter time and again throughout this book. **Gross domestic product (GDP)** is the value of all goods and services produced by a domestic economy over a one-year period. GDP excludes a nation's income generated from exports, imports, and the international operations of its companies. We can speak in terms of world GDP when we sum all individual nations' GDP figures. GDP is a somewhat narrower figure than **gross national product (GNP)**—the value of all goods and services produced by a country's domestic and international activities over a one-year period. A country's **GDP or GNP per capita** is simply its GDP or GNP divided by its population.

MAP 1.1

MAP 1.1

Growth in National Output

C OCEAN

NORWAY
SWEDEN
FINLAND
NMARK
ESTONIA
LATVIA
LITHUANIA
RUSSIA
ANDS
POLAND
BELARUS
ERMANY
1
CZECH
UKRAINE
ICHT
AUSTRIA
REP. SLOVAKIA
URG
HUNGARY
MOLDOVA
Z.
SLOVENIA
ROMANIA
CROATIA
BOSNIA
SERBIA AND
HERZEGOVINA
MONTENEGRO
ITALY
MACEDONIA
BULGARIA
ALBANIA
GEORGIA
GREECE
TURKEY
ARMENIA
AZERBAIJAN
CYPRUS
SYRIA
LEBANON
UNISIA
ISRAEL
IRAQ
JORDAN
KUWAIT

RUSSIA

KAZAKHSTAN

MONGOLIA

UZBEKISTAN
KYRGYZSTAN
TURKMENISTAN
TAJIKISTAN

NORTH
KOREA
SOUTH
KOREA

JAPAN

AFGHANISTAN
IRAN
PAKISTAN

CHINA

PACIFIC

OCEAN

LIBYA
EGYPT
QATAR
UNITED ARAB
EMIRATES
SAUDI
ARABIA
OMAN

NEPAL
BHUTAN
BANGLADESH

INDIA

MYANMAR
(BURMA)
LAOS

TAIWAN

GER
CHAD
ERITREA
YEMEN
SUDAN
DJIBOUTI
SOMALIA
ERIA
CENTRAL AFRICAN
REPUBLIC
ETHIOPIA
AMEROON

THAILAND
VIETNAM
CAMBODIA

PHILIPPINES

SRI
LANKA

INDIAN

OCEAN

BRUNEI
MALAYSIA
SINGAPORE

AL
CONGO
REPUBLIC
UGANDA
ABON
CONGO
DEMOCRATIC
REPUBLIC
(ZAIRE)
KENYA
RWANDA
BURUNDI
TANZANIA

INDONESIA

PAPUA
NEW
GUINEA

SOLOMON
ISLANDS

ANGOLA
ZAMBIA
MALAWI
MOZAMBIQUE
MAURITIUS
NAMIBIA
ZIMBABWE
MADAGASCAR
RÉUNION
BOTSWANA
SWAZILAND
SOUTH
AFRICA
LESOTHO

VANUATU
FIJI

NEW
CALEDONIA

AUSTRALIA

NEW
ZEALAND

**Average annual GDP growth
rate, 1998-2007, (%)**

negative
less than -2.5

-2.5 to 0

no data available

positive
0 to 1

1 to 2

2 to 3

3 to 4

4 to 5

over 5

Technological Innovation

Although falling barriers to trade and investment encourage globalization, technological innovation is accelerating the process. Significant advancements in information technology and transportation methods are making it easier, faster, and less costly to move data, goods, and equipment around the world. Let's examine several innovations that have had a considerable impact on globalization.

E-mail and Videoconferencing   Operating across borders and time zones complicates the job of coordinating and controlling business activities. But technology can speed the flow of information and ease the tasks of coordination and control. Electronic mail (e-mail) is an indispensable tool that managers use to stay in contact with international operations and to respond quickly to important matters. Videoconferencing allows managers in different locations to meet in virtual face-to-face meetings. Primary reasons for 25 to 30 percent annual growth in videoconferencing include lower-cost bandwidth (communication channels) used to transmit information, lower-cost equipment, and the rising cost of travel for businesses. Videoconferencing equipment can cost as little as $5,000 and as much as $340,000. A company that does not require ongoing videoconferencing can pay even less by renting the facilities and equipment of a local conference center.[10]

Internet and World Wide Web   Companies use the Internet to quickly and cheaply contact managers in distant locations to, for example, inquire about production runs, revise sales strategies, and check on distribution bottlenecks. They also use the Internet to achieve longer term goals, such as sharpen their forecasting, lower their inventories, and improve communication with suppliers. The lower cost of reaching an international customer base especially benefits small firms, which were among the first to use the Web as a global marketing tool. Further gains arise from the ability of the Internet to cut postproduction costs by decreasing the number of intermediaries a product passes through on its way to the customer. Eliminating intermediaries greatly benefits online sellers of books, music, and travel services, among others.

Company Intranets and Extranets   Internal company Web sites and information networks *(intranets)* give employees access to company data using personal computers. A particularly effective marketing tool on Volvo Car Corporation's (www.volvocars.com) intranet is a quarter-by-quarter database of marketing and sales information. The cycle begins when headquarters submits its corporate-wide marketing plan to Volvo's intranet. Marketing managers at each subsidiary worldwide then select those activities that apply to their own market, develop their marketing plan, and submit it to the database. This allows managers in every market to view every other subsidiary's marketing plan and to adapt relevant aspects to their own plan. In essence, the entire system acts as a tool for the sharing of best practices across all of Volvo's markets.

Extranets give distributors and suppliers access to a company's database to place orders or restock inventories electronically and automatically. These networks permit international companies (along with their suppliers and buyers) to respond to internal and external conditions more quickly and more appropriately.

Advancements in Transportation Technologies   Retailers worldwide rely on imports to stock their storerooms with finished goods and to supply factories with raw materials and intermediate products. Innovation in the shipping industry is helping globalize markets and production by making shipping more efficient and dependable. In the past, a cargo ship would sit in port up to 10 days while it was unloaded one pallet at a time. But because cargo today is loaded onto a ship in 20- and 40-foot containers that are quickly unloaded onto railcars or truck chassis at the final destination, a 700-foot cargo ship is routinely unloaded in just 15 hours.

Operation of cargo ships is now simpler and safer due to computerized charts that pinpoint a ship's movements on the high seas using Global Positioning System (GPS) satellites. Combining GPS with radio frequency identification (RFID) technology allows continuous monitoring of individual containers from port of departure to destination. RFID can tell whether a container's doors are opened and closed on its journey and can monitor the temperature inside refrigerated containers.[11]

Measuring Globalization

Although we intuitively feel that our world is becoming smaller, researchers have created ways to measure the extent of globalization. One of the most comprehensive indices of globalization is that created by A.T. Kearney (www.atkearney.com), a management consultancy, and *Foreign Policy* magazine (www.foreignpolicy.com).[12] The index ranks 72 nations, which altogether account for 97 percent of the world's GDP and 88 percent of its population. Each nation's ranking in the index comprises a compilation of over a dozen variables within four categories:

1. *Economic integration*—trade, foreign direct investment, portfolio capital flows, and investment income.
2. *Personal contact*—international travel and tourism, international telephone traffic, remittances, and personal transfers (including compensation to employees).
3. *Technological connectivity*—Internet users, Internet hosts, and secure servers.
4. *Political engagement*—memberships in international organizations, personnel and financial contributions to U.N. Security Council missions, international treaties ratified, and governmental transfers.

By incorporating a wide variety of variables, the index is apt to cut through cycles occurring in any one of the four areas listed above. And by encompassing social factors in addition to economic influences, it tends to capture the broad nature of globalization. Table 1.1 shows the 10 highest-ranking nations in the latest Globalization Index. It shows each nation's overall rank and its rank on each dimension described earlier: (1) economic integration, (2) personal contact, (3) technological connectivity, and (4) political engagement. Europe accounts for five of the top 10 spots and the United States appears in seventh place on the list. The United States is the first large nation to make it into the top ranks—due largely to its technological superiority. Large nations often do not make it into the higher ranks because they tend to depend less on external trade and investment.

TABLE 1.1 **Globalization's Top 10**

Country	Overall	Economic	Personal	Technological	Political
Singapore	1	2	3	15	40
Hong Kong	2	1	1	17	71
Netherlands	3	4	16	6	8
Switzerland	4	11	2	7	28
Ireland	5	6	4	13	5
Denmark	6	5	13	5	7
United States	7	71	40	1	51
Canada	8	34	11	2	13
Jordan	9	10	5	50	1
Estonia	10	3	10	21	25

Source: "The Globalization Index," *Foreign Policy*, November/December 2007, pp. 68–76.

The world's least-global nations also deserve mention. The least-global nations account for around half the world's population and are found in Africa, East Asia, South Asia, Latin America, and the Middle East. One remarkable commonality among these nations is their low levels of technological connectivity. These nations will likely have a difficult struggle ahead if they are to overcome their lack of global integration.

Some of the least-global nations are characterized by never-ending political unrest and corruption (Bangladesh, Indonesia, and Venezuela). Other nations with large agricultural sectors face trade barriers in developed countries and are subject to highly volatile prices on commodity markets (Brazil, China, and India). Still others are heavily dependent on oil exports but are plagued by erratic prices in energy markets (Iran and Venezuela). Kenya has suffered from recurring droughts, terrorism, and burdensome visa regulations that hurt tourism. Finally, Turkey and Egypt, along with the entire Middle East, suffer from continued concerns over terrorism, high barriers to trade and investment, and heavy government involvement in the economy. To deepen their global links, each of these nations will need to make great strides in their economic, social, technological, and political environments.

Quick Study

1. What two main forces underlie the expansion of globalization?
2. How have global and regional efforts to promote trade and investment advanced globalization?
3. How does technological innovation propel globalization?
4. What factors make some countries more global than others?

Untangling the Globalization Debate

Globalization means different things to different people. A businessperson may see globalization as an opportunity to source goods and services from lower-cost locations and to pry open new markets. An economist may see it as an opportunity to examine the impact of globalization on jobs and standards of living. An environmentalist may be concerned with how globalization affects our ecology. An anthropologist may want to examine the influence of globalization on the culture of a group of people. A political scientist may be concerned with the impact of globalization on the power of governments relative to that of multinational companies. And an employee may view globalization either as an opportunity for new work or as a threat to his or her current job.

It is because of the different lenses through which we view events around us that the globalization debate is so complex. Entrepreneurs, small business owners, and globetrotting managers need to understand globalization and the arguments of those who oppose it. In the pages that follow, we explain the main arguments of those opposed to globalization and the responses of those in favor of it. But before we address the intricacies of the debate, it is helpful to put today's globalization into its proper context.

Today's Globalization in Context

Many people forget that there was a first age of globalization that extended from the mid-1800s to the 1920s.[13] In those days, labor was highly mobile, with 300,000 people leaving Europe each year in the 1800s and one million people leaving each year after 1900.[14] Other than in wartime, nations did not even require passports for international travel before 1914. And like today, workers in wealthy nations back then feared competition for jobs from high- and low-wage countries.

Trade and capital flowed more freely than ever during that first age of globalization. Huge companies from wealthy nations built facilities in distant lands to extract raw materials and produce all sorts of goods. Large cargo ships plied the seas to deliver their manufactures to distant markets. The transatlantic cable (completed in 1866) allowed news between Europe and the United States to travel faster than ever before. The drivers of that first age of globalization included the steamship, telegraph, railroad, and later, the telephone and airplane.

That first age of globalization was abruptly halted by the arrival of the First World War, the Russian Revolution, and the Great Depression. A backlash to fierce competition in trade and unfettered immigration in the early 1900s helped usher-in high tariffs and barriers to immigration. The great flows of goods, capital, and people common before the First World War became a mere trickle. For 75 years from the start of the First World War to the end of the Cold War, the world remained divided. There was a geographic divide between East and West and an ideological divide between communism and capitalism. After the Second World War, the West experienced steady economic gains, but international flows of goods, capital, and people were confined to their respective capitalist and communist systems and geographies.

Fast-forward to 1989 and the collapse of the wall separating East and West Berlin. One by one, central and eastern European nations threw off the chains of communism, embraced freedom, and began a march toward democratic institutions and free-market economic systems. Although it took until the 1990s for international capital flows, in absolute terms, to recover to levels seen prior to the First World War, the global economy had finally been *reborn*. Lowering the cost of telecommunications and binding our world more tightly together are the drivers of this second age of globalization—communication satellites, fiber optics, microchips, and the Internet.

Introduction to the Debate

World Bank
Agency created to provide financing for national economic development efforts.

In addition to the World Trade Organization presented earlier, several other supranational institutions play leading roles in fostering globalization. The **World Bank** is an agency created to provide financing for national economic development efforts. The initial purpose of the World Bank (www.worldbank.org) was to finance European reconstruction following the Second World War. It later shifted its focus to the general financial needs of developing countries, and today it finances many economic development projects in Africa, South America, and Southeast Asia. The **International Monetary Fund (IMF)** is an agency created to regulate fixed exchange rates and enforce the rules of the international monetary system. Today the IMF (www.imf.org) has 185 member countries. Some of the purposes of the IMF include: promoting international monetary cooperation; facilitating expansion and balanced growth of international trade; avoiding competitive exchange devaluation; and making financial resources temporarily available to members.

International Monetary Fund (IMF)
Agency created to regulate fixed exchange rates and enforce the rules of the international monetary system.

A group of students order ice cream at a Dairy Queen (www.dq.com) outlet in Bangkok, Thailand. Dairy Queen is aggressively expanding abroad in response to rising incomes in Thailand and other emerging markets. In fact, Dairy Queen has 6,000 outlets worldwide, with Thailand home to the largest number outside the United States and Canada. Can you identify other emerging markets that are embracing globalization?

Source: © Andrew Holbrooke/ CORBIS. All Rights Reserved.

At this point we should note one caveat. Each side in the debate over globalization tends to hold up results of social and economic studies they say show "definitive" support for their arguments. Yet many organizations that publish studies on globalization have political agendas, such as decreasing government regulation or expanding government programs. This can make objective consideration of a group's claims and findings difficult. A group's aims may influence the selection of the data to analyze, the time period to study, the nations to examine, and so forth. It is essential to take into account such factors anytime we hear a group arguing the beneficial or harmful effects of globalization.

Let's now engage the debate over globalization by examining its effects on: (1) jobs and wages, (2) labor and environmental regulation, (3) income inequality, (4) national sovereignty, and (5) cultures.

Quick Study

1. How does this current period of globalization compare with the first age of globalization?

2. Explain the original purpose of the *World Bank* and its mandate today.

3. What are the main purposes of the *International Monetary Fund*?

Globalization's Impact on Jobs and Wages

We open our coverage of the globalization debate with an important topic for both developed and developing countries—the effect of globalization on jobs and wages. We begin with the arguments of those against globalization and then turn our attention to how supporters of globalization respond.

Against Globalization   Groups opposed to globalization blame it for eroding standards of living and ruining ways of life. Specifically, they say globalization: *eliminates jobs* and *lowers wages* in developed nations; and *exploits workers* in developing countries. Let's explore each of these arguments.

ELIMINATES JOBS IN DEVELOPED NATIONS   Some groups claim that *globalization eliminates manufacturing jobs in developed nations*. They criticize the practice of sending good-paying manufacturing jobs abroad to developing countries where wages are a fraction of the cost for international firms. It is argued that a label reading "Made in China" translates to "Not Made Here." Although critics admit that importing products from China (or another low-wage nation) lowers consumer prices for televisions, sporting goods, and so on, they say this is little consolation for workers who lose their jobs.

To illustrate their argument, globalization critics point to the activities of big-box retailers such as Costco (www.costco.com) and Wal-Mart (www.walmart.com). It is difficult to overstate the power of these retail giants and symbols of globalization. It is said that by relentlessly pursuing low-cost goods, these retailers force their suppliers to move to China and other low-wage nations.[15]

LOWERS WAGES IN DEVELOPED NATIONS   Opposition groups say *globalization causes worker dislocation that gradually lowers wages*. They allege that when a manufacturing job is lost in a wealthy nation, the new job (assuming new work is found) pays less than the previous one. Some evidence does suggest that a displaced manufacturing worker, especially an older one, receives lower pay in a subsequent job. Those opposed to globalization say this decreases employee loyalty, employee morale, and job security. They say this causes people to fear globalization and any additional lowering of trade barriers.

Big-box retailers come under fire in this discussion also. Globalization critics say powerful retailers continually force manufacturers in low-wage nations to accept lower profits so the retailers can slash prices to consumers. As a result of these business practices, critics charge, powerful retailers force down wages and working conditions worldwide.

EXPLOITS WORKERS IN DEVELOPING NATIONS   Critics charge that *globalization and international outsourcing exploit workers in low-wage nations*. One notable critic of globalization is Naomi Klein (www.naomiklein.org). She vehemently opposes the outsourced call center jobs of western companies, such as Victoria's Secret (www.victoriassecret.com) and Delta Airlines (www.delta.com). Klein says such jobs force young Asians to disguise their nationality, adopt fake mid-western accents, and work nights when their U.S. customers are awake halfway around the world. Klein maintains that free trade policies are "a highly efficient engine of dispossession, pushing small farmers off their land and laying off public-sector workers."[16]

For Globalization   Supporters of globalization credit it with improving standards of living and making possible new ways of life. They argue that globalization *increases wealth and efficiency in all nations*, *generates labor market flexibility in developed nations* and *advances the economies of developing nations*. Let's now examine each of these arguments.

INCREASES WEALTH AND EFFICIENCY IN ALL NATIONS   Some economists believe *globalization increases wealth and efficiency in both developed and developing nations.* Globalization supporters argue that openness to international trade (the ratio of trade to national output) increases national production (by increasing efficiency) and raises per capita income (by passing savings on to consumers). For instance, by squeezing inefficiencies out of the retail supply chain, powerful global retailers help restrain inflation and boost productivity. Some economists predict that removing all remaining barriers to free trade would significantly boost worldwide income and greatly benefit developing nations.

GENERATES LABOR MARKET FLEXIBILITY IN DEVELOPED NATIONS   Globalization supporters believe *globalization creates positive benefits by generating labor market flexibility in developed nations*. It is claimed that benefits derive from worker dislocation, or "churning" as it is called when there is widespread job turnover throughout an economy. Flexible labor markets allow workers to be redeployed rapidly to sectors of the economy where they are highly valued and in demand. This also allows employees, particularly young workers, to change jobs easily with few negative effects. For instance, a young person can gain experience and skills with an initial employer, then move to a different job that provides a better match between employee and employer.

ADVANCES ECONOMIES OF DEVELOPING NATIONS   Those in favor of globalization argue that *globalization and international outsourcing help to advance developing nations' economies*. India initially became attractive as a location for software-writing operations because of its low-cost, well-trained, English-speaking technicians. More recently, telephone call centers that provide all sorts of customer services offer bright futures to young graduates who will not become doctors and lawyers. Millions of young Indians view such a job as a ticket to working for an international firm at a good salary.

Today, the relentless march of globalization is making India a base for business process outsourcing—including financial, accounting, payroll, and benefits services. A bourgeoning back-office industry worth billions of dollars in India has significantly elevated living standards. As India's economy continues to develop, it will become an even greater attraction for professional occupations. Figure 1.2 illustrates why India is popular as a location to out-

FIGURE 1.2

Comparing Salaries of IT Workers

Source: Rachael King, "The New Economics of Outsourcing," *Business Week* (http://www.businessweek.com), April 7, 2008.

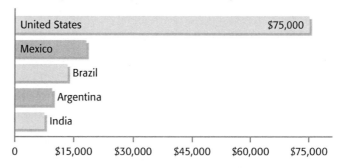

The average annual salary of an IT worker living in:

source information technology (IT) jobs, for instance. The salary of an IT worker in the United States is nearly 10 times that of an IT worker in India. So long as such economic disparities exist, international outsourcing will continue to grow more popular.[17]

SUMMARY OF THE JOBS AND WAGES DEBATE   All parties appear to agree that dislocation in labor markets is a byproduct of globalization. In other words, although globalization eliminates some jobs in a nation, it creates jobs in other sectors of the nation's economy. Yet while some people lose their jobs and find new employment, it can be very difficult for others to find new work. The real point of difference between the two sides in the debate, it seems, is whether overall gains that (may or may not) accrue to *national economies* are worth the lost livelihoods that *individuals* (may or may not) suffer. Those in favor of globalization say individual pain is worth the collective gain, whereas those against globalization say it is not.

Globalization's Impact on Labor, the Environment, and Markets

Critics of globalization say companies locate operations to where labor and environmental regulations are least restrictive and, therefore, least costly. They argue this puts downward pressure on labor and environmental protection laws in all countries as nations compete to attract international firms. Let's now examine these claims and the responses of globalization supporters.

Labor Standards   Trade unions claim globalization reduces labor's bargaining power and lowers global labor standards when international firms are permitted to continually move to nations with lower labor standards. One place to test this assertion is in developing nations' *export-processing zones (EPZs)*—special areas in which companies engage in tariff-free importing and exporting. More than 850 EPZs employ 27 million people worldwide. Yet a study by the International Labor Organization (www.ilo.org), hardly a pro-business group, found no evidence to support the claim that nations with a strong union presence suffered any loss of investment in their EPZs. In fact, another study by the World Bank found that the higher occupational safety and health conditions an EPZ had in place, the greater foreign investment it attracted.[18] The evidence fails to support critics' allegations that economic openness and foreign investment contribute to lower labor standards.

Environmental Protection   Some environmental groups say globalization causes a "race to the bottom" in environmental conditions and regulations. Yet studies show that pollution-intensive U.S. firms tend to invest in countries with stricter environmental standards. Many developing nations, including Argentina, Brazil, Malaysia, and Thailand, liberalized their foreign investment environment while simultaneously enacting *stricter* environmental legislation. If large international companies were eager to relocate to nations having poor environmental protection laws, they would not have invested in these countries for decades. Additional evidence that closed, protectionist economies are worse than open ones at protecting the environment includes Mexico before NAFTA, Brazil under military rule, and the former Warsaw Pact of communist nations—all of which had extremely poor environmental records. Again, the evidence does not support claims of lower environmental standards as a result of economic openness and globalization.

Future Markets   Opponents to globalization claim international firms exploit local labor markets and the environment to produce goods that are then exported back to the home country. Such claims may not only perpetuate a false image of corporations, but may have no factual basis. International firms today support reasonable labor and environmental laws because (if for no other reason) they want to expand future local markets for their goods and services. When analyzing a country prior to investing, companies today often examine a location for its potential as a future market as well as a production base. Less than 5 percent of U.S. firms invest in developing countries to obtain low-cost resources and then export finished products back to the United States. For additional insights into how managers today succeed by respecting unfamiliar markets, see the Global Manager's Briefcase titled, "The Keys to Global Success."

GLOBAL MANAGER'S BRIEFCASE
The Keys to Global Success

Making everything from 99-cent hamburgers (McDonald's) to $150 million jumbo jets (Boeing), managers of global companies must overcome obstacles when competing in unfamiliar markets. Global managers acknowledge certain common threads in their approaches to management and offer the following advice:

- **Communicate Effectively.** Cultural differences in values, attitudes, and business relationships are central to global business and require cross-cultural competency. Effective global managers tolerate ambiguity and demonstrate flexibility, respect, sensitivity, and empathy.
- **Know the Customer.** The successful manager has detailed knowledge of the different types of products that international customers require and ensures that the company is flexible enough to customize products to meet those needs.
- **Emphasize Global Awareness.** Good global managers ensure that the company designs and builds products and services for export from the beginning, not as an afterthought following the conquest of domestic markets.

- **Market Effectively.** The world can beat a path to your door to buy your "better mousetrap" only if it knows about it. A poor marketing effort can cause great products to fade into obscurity. Top global managers match quality products with excellent marketing.
- **Monitor Business Environments.** Successful managers watch global markets for shifting political, legal, and socioeconomic conditions. Among their most important tools is accurate information, whether it is freely available or confidential.
- **Know How to Analyze Problems.** Successful managers rarely start out with solutions. Instead, they employ creativity and knowledge to tackle their international business problems by experimenting and taking carefully calculated risks.

Source: John Saee, "Intercultural Awareness Is The Key To International Business Success," *Global Focus*, October 2007, pp. 56–59; Melissa Butcher, "Intercultural Competency A Key To Global Business Success," Inside Asia Web site (www.insideasia.com), March 3, 2006.

Quick Study

1. What are the claims of those who say globalization eliminates jobs, lowers wages, and exploits workers?
2. Identify the arguments of those who say globalization creates jobs and boosts wages.
3. Why do critics say globalization adversely affects labor standards, environmental regulations, and future markets?
4. How do supporters of globalization argue that it does not harm labor standards, environmental regulations, and future markets?

Globalization and Income Inequality

Perhaps no controversy swirling around globalization is more complex than the debate over its effect on income inequality. Here, we focus on three main branches of the debate: inequality within nations, inequality between nations, and global inequality.

Inequality within Nations   The first inequality debate is whether globalization is increasing income inequality among people *within* nations. Opponents of globalization argue that freer trade and investment allows international companies to close factories in high-wage developed nations and to move them to low-wage developing nations. They argue this increases the wage gap between white-collar and blue-collar occupations within rich nations.

Two studies of *developed and developing nations* find contradictory evidence on this argument. The first study of 38 countries over nearly 30 years supports the increasing inequality argument. The study finds that as a nation increases its openness to trade, income growth among the poorest 40 percent of a nation's population declines while income growth among other groups increases.[19] The second study of 80 countries over 40 years fails to support the increasing inequality argument. It finds that incomes of the poor rise one-for-one with overall economic growth and concludes that the poor benefit from international trade along with the rest of a nation.[20] The mixed findings of these two studies are typical of a large set of research examining inequality between developed *and* developing nations.

Two studies of *developing nations only* are more consistent in their findings. One study finds that an increase in the ratio of trade to national output of 1 percent raises average income levels by 0.5 to 2 percent. Another study shows that incomes of the poor keep pace with growth in average incomes in economies (and periods) of fast trade integration, but that the poor fall behind during periods of declining openness.[21] Results of these two studies suggest that by integrating their economies into the global economy, developing nations (by far the nations with the most to gain) can boost incomes of their poorest citizens.

Inequality between Nations   The second inequality debate is whether globalization is widening the gap in average incomes *between* rich and poor nations. If we compare average incomes in high-income countries to average incomes in middle- and low-income nations, we do find a widening gap. But *averages* conceal differences between nations.

On closer inspection, it appears the gap between rich and poor nations is not occurring everywhere: *one group of poor nations is closing the gap with rich economies, while a second group of poor countries is falling further behind*. For example, China is narrowing the income gap between itself and the United States as measured by GDP per capita, but the gap between Africa and the United States is widening. China's progress is no doubt a result of its integration with the world economy and annual economic growth rates of around 9 percent. Another emerging market, India, is also narrowing its income gap with the United States by embracing globalization.[22]

Developing countries that embrace globalization are increasing personal incomes, extending life expectancies, and improving education systems. In addition, post-communist countries that welcomed world trade and investment experienced high growth rates in GDP per capita. But nations that remain closed off from the world economy have performed far worse.[23]

Global Inequality   The third inequality debate is whether globalization is increasing *global inequality*—widening income inequality between all people of the world, no matter where they live. A recent study paints a promising picture of declining poverty. This study finds that the percent of world population living on less than a dollar a day (a common poverty gauge) fell from 17 percent to just 7 percent over a thirty-year period, which reduced the number of people in poverty by roughly 200 million.[24] Yet a widely cited study by the World Bank finds that the percent of world population living on less than a dollar a day fell from 33 percent to 18 percent over a twenty-year period, which reduced the number of people in poverty from 1.5 billion to 1.1 billion.[25]

For a variety of reasons, the real picture likely lies somewhere in between these two studies' estimates. For example, whereas the World Bank study used population figures for developing countries only, the first study used global population in its analyses, which lowered poverty estimates, all else being equal.[26] What is important is that most experts agree that global inequality has fallen, although they disagree on the extent of the fall.

What it must be like to live on less than a dollar a day in abject poverty in sub-Saharan Africa, South Asia, or elsewhere, is too difficult for most of us to comprehend. The continent of Africa presents the most pressing problem. Home to 13 percent of the world's population, Africa accounts for just 3 percent of world GDP. Rich nations realize they cannot sit idly by while so many of the world's people live under such conditions.

We see the result of embracing globalization in this photo of skyscrapers in the Lujiazui Financial and Trade Zone of the Pudong New Area in Shanghai, China. After years of stunning economic growth and expansion, Shanghai has emerged as a key city for companies entering China's marketplace. China developed Pudong to reinvigorate Shanghai as an international trade and financial center. The district is now ultra modern and very cosmopolitan.

Source: © Zhang Ming/Xinhua Press/CORBIS. All Rights Reserved.

What can be done to help the world's poor? First of all, rich nations could increase the amount of foreign aid they give to poor nations—foreign aid as a share of donor country GDP is at historically low levels. Second, rich nations can accelerate the process of forgiving some of the debt burdens of the most heavily indebted poor countries (HIPCs). The HIPC initiative is committed to reducing the debt burdens of the world's poorest countries. This initiative would enable these countries to spend money on social services and greater integration with the global economy instead of on interest payments on debt.[27]

SUMMARY OF THE INCOME INEQUALITY DEBATE   For the debate over inequality *within nations*, studies suggest that developing nations can boost incomes of their poorest citizens by embracing globalization and integrating themselves into the global economy. In the debate over inequality *between nations*, nations open to world trade and investment appear to grow faster than rich nations do. Meanwhile, economies that remain sheltered from the global economy tend to be worse off. Finally, for the debate over *global inequality*, although experts agree inequality has fallen in recent decades, they disagree on the extent of the drop.

Globalization and National Sovereignty

National sovereignty generally involves the idea that a nation-state: (1) is autonomous; (2) can freely select its government; (3) cannot intervene in the affairs of other nations; (4) can control movements across its borders; and (5) can enter into binding international agreements. Opposition groups allege that globalization erodes national sovereignty and encroaches on the authority of local and state governments. Supporters disagree, saying that globalization spreads democracy worldwide and that national sovereignty must be viewed from a long-term perspective.

Globalization: Menace to Democracy?

A main argument leveled against globalization is that it empowers supranational institutions at the expense of national governments. It is not in dispute that the World Trade Organization, the International Monetary Fund, and the United Nations are led by appointed, not democratically elected, representatives. What is debatable, however, is whether these organizations unduly impose their will on the citizens of sovereign nations. Critics argue that by undercutting the political and legal authority of national, regional, and local governments, such organizations undercut democracy and individual liberty.

Opponents of globalization also take issue with the right of national political authorities to enter into binding international agreements on behalf of citizens. Critics charge that such agreements violate the rights of subfederal (local and state) governments. For example, state and local governments in the United States had no role in creating the North American Free Trade Agreement (NAFTA). Yet WTO rules require the U.S. federal government to take all available actions (including enacting preemptive legislation or withdrawing funding) to force subfederal compliance with WTO terms. Protesters say such requirements directly attack the rights and authority of subfederal governments.[28]

Globalization: Guardian of Democracy?   Globalization supporters argue that an amazing consequence of globalization has been the spread of democracy worldwide. In recent decades, the people of many nations have thrown off the chains of authoritarianism and are now better educated, better informed, and more empowered. Supporters say globalization has not sent democracy spiraling into decline, but instead has been instrumental in spreading democracy to the world.

Backers of globalization also contend that it is instructive to take a long-term view on the issue of national sovereignty. Witnessing a sovereign state's scope of authority altered is nothing new, as governments have long given up trying to control issues that they could not resolve. In the mid-1600s, governments in Europe surrendered their authority over religion because attempts to control it undermined overall political stability. Also, Greece in 1832, Albania in 1913, and the former Yugoslavian states in the 1990s had to protect minorities in exchange for international recognition. And over the past 50 years, the United Nations has made significant progress on worthy issues such as genocide, torture, slavery, refugees, women's rights, children's rights, forced labor, and racial discrimination. Like the loss of sovereignty over these issues, globalization supporters say lost sovereignty over some economic issues may actually enhance the greater good.[29]

Globalization's Influence on Cultures

National culture is a strong shaper of a people's values, attitudes, customs, beliefs, and communication. Whether globalization eradicates cultural differences between groups of people or reinforces cultural uniqueness is a hotly debated topic.

Protesters complain that globalization is homogenizing our world and destroying its rich diversity of cultures. Critics say that in some drab, new world we all will wear the same clothes bought at the same brand-name shops, eat the same foods at the same brand-name restaurants, and watch the same movies made by the same production companies.

But supporters argue that globalization allows us all to profit from our differing circumstances and skills. Trade allows countries to specialize in producing the goods and services they can produce most efficiently. Nations can then trade with each other to obtain goods and services they desire but do not produce. In this way, France still produces many of the world's finest wines, South Africa yields much of the world's diamonds, and Japan continues to design some of the world's finest-engineered autos. Other nations then trade their goods and services with these countries to enjoy the wines, diamonds, and autos that they do not, or cannot, produce. To learn more about the interplay between culture and globalization, see this chapter's Culture Matters feature titled, "The Global Consumer."

Quick Study

1. What does the evidence suggest for each branch of the debate over globalization and income inequality?

2. What are each side's arguments in the debate over globalization's impact on national sovereignty?

3. Summarize the claims of each side in the debate over globalization's influence on cultures.

CULTURE MATTERS
The Global Consumer

The debate over globalization's influence on culture evokes strong opinions. Some say globalization promotes sameness among cultures while others say it fosters cultural individuality. Here are a few main arguments in this debate.

- **Material Desire.** Critics say globalization fosters the "Coca-Colanization" of nations through advertising campaigns that promote material desire. They also argue that global consumer-goods companies destroy cultural diversity (especially in developing nations) by putting local companies out of business.
- **Artistic Influence.** Evidence suggests that the cultures of developing nations are thriving and that the influence of their music, art, and literature has grown (not shrunk) throughout the past century. African cultures, for example, have influenced the works of artists including Picasso, the Beatles, and Sting.
- **Western Values.** Businesses reach far and wide through the Internet, global media, increased business travel, and local marketing by international companies. Critics say local values and traditions are being replaced by U.S. companies promoting "western" values.

- **A Force for Good.** Globalization tends to foster two important values: tolerance and diversity. Globalization advocates say nations should be more tolerant of opposing viewpoints and welcome diversity among their peoples. This view interprets globalization as a potent force for good in the world.
- **Deeper Values.** Globalization can cause consumer purchases and economic ideologies to converge, but these are rather superficial aspects of culture. Deeper values that embody the true essence of cultures may be more resistant to a global consumer culture.
- **Want to Know More?** Visit the globalization page of the Global Policy Forum (http://globalpolicy.igc.org), the Globalization Guide (www.globalisationguide.org), or The Globalist (www.theglobalist.com).

Source: "Economic Globalization and Culture: A Discussion with Dr. Francis Fukuyama," Merrill Lynch Forum Web site (www.ml.com); "Globalization Issues," The Globalization Web site (www.sociology.emory.edu/globalization); Cultural Diversity in the Era of Globalization," UNESCO Culture Sector Web site (www.portal.unesco.org/culture).

Key Players in International Business

Companies of all types and sizes and in all sorts of industries become involved in international business, yet they vary in the extent of their involvement. A small shop owner might only import supplies from abroad, while a large company may have dozens of factories located around the world. Large companies from the wealthiest nations still dominate international business, but firms from emerging markets (such as Brazil, China, and India) are increasingly important in international business activity. Small and medium-sized companies also account for a greater portion of international business largely because of advances in technology.

Multinational Corporations

multinational corporation (MNC)
Business that has direct investments abroad in multiple countries.

A **multinational corporation (MNC)** is a business that has direct investments (in the form of marketing or manufacturing subsidiaries) abroad in multiple countries. Multinationals generate significant jobs, investment, and tax revenue for the regions and nations they enter. Likewise, they can leave thousands of people out of work when they close or scale back operations. Mergers and acquisitions between multinationals are commonly worth billions of dollars and increasingly involve companies based in emerging markets.

Some companies have more employees than many of the smallest countries and island nations have citizens. Wal-Mart has 2,055,000 employees—the most of any company. We see the enormous economic clout of multinational corporations when we compare the revenues of the Global 500 ranking of companies to the value of goods and services that countries generate. Figure 1.3 shows the world's 10 largest companies (measured in revenue) inserted into a ranking of nations according to their national output (measured in GDP). If Wal-Mart (www.walmart.com) were a country, it would weigh in

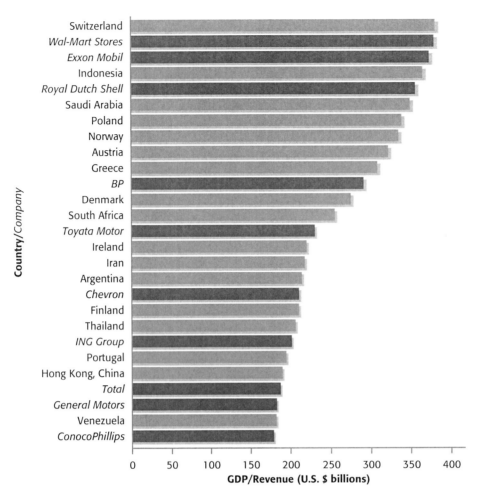

FIGURE 1.3

**Comparing the Global
500 with Selected
Countries**

Source: Data obtained from "Global
500," *Fortune*, July 21, 2008, pp.
156–182; *World Development
Indicators 2008* (Washington, D.C.:
World Bank, April 2008),
(www.worldbank.org).

as a rich nation and rank just below Switzerland. Even the nearly $17 billion in revenue generated by the 500th largest firm in the world, Fluor (www.fluor.com), exceeds the output of many countries.[30]

Entrepreneurs and Small Businesses

In this age of globalization, small companies are increasingly active in international trade and investment. Companies are exporting earlier and growing faster, often with help from technology. Whereas traditional distribution channels often gave only large companies access to distant markets, electronic distribution is a cheap and effective alternative for small businesses that sell digitized products. Small companies that sell traditional products also benefit from technology that lowers the cost and difficulties of global communication.

Globalization has given rise to a new international entity, the **born global firm**—a company that adopts a global perspective and engages in international business from or near its inception. Key characteristics of born global firms are an innovative culture and knowledge-based organizational capabilities. Although these firms first appeared in nations having small domestic markets, today they arise from all major trading nations. Remarkably, many of these companies rise to the status of international competitor in less than three years.

Perhaps the extreme example of a born global firm is one that reaches out to customers around the world solely through the Internet. Alessandro Naldi's *Weekend a Firenze* (Weekend in Florence) Web site (www.firenze.waf.it) offers global villagers more authentic Florentine products than they'll find in the scores of overpriced tourist shops in downtown Florence. A Florentine himself, Naldi established his site to sell high-quality, authentic Italian merchandise made only in the small factories of Tuscany. *Weekend a Firenze* averages 20,000 visitors each month, with 40 percent coming from Japan, 30 percent from the United States, and the remainder from Greece, Australia, Canada, Mexico, Saudi Arabia, and Italy.[31]

born global firm
Company that adopts a global
perspective and engages in
international business from or near
its inception.

Debunking the Myths of Small Business Exporting

- **Myth 1:** Only large companies can export successfully. **Fact:** Most exporters are small and medium-sized enterprises with fewer than 50 employees. Exporting can reduce the dependency of small firms on domestic markets and can help them avoid seasonal sales fluctuations. A product popular domestically, or perhaps even unsuccessful at home, may be wanted elsewhere in the global market.
- **Myth 2:** Small businesses can find little export advice. **Fact:** Novice and experienced exporters alike can receive comprehensive export assistance from federal agencies (www.export.gov). International trade specialists can help small businesses locate and use federal, state, local, and private-sector programs. They are also an excellent source of market research, trade leads, financing, and trade events.
- **Myth 3:** Licensing requirements needed to export are too complicated. **Fact:** Most products do not need export licenses. Exporters need only to write 'NLR' for 'no license required' on their Shipper's Export Declaration. A license is generally needed only for high-tech or defense-related goods or when the receiving country is under a U.S. embargo or other restriction.
- **Myth 4:** Small businesses cannot obtain export financing. **Fact:** The Small Business Administration (www.sba.gov) and the Export-Import Bank (www.exim.gov) work together in lending money to small businesses. Whereas the SBA is responsible for loan requests below $750,000, the Ex-Im Bank handles transactions over $750,000. The Trade and Development Agency (www.tda.gov) also helps small and medium-sized firms obtain financing for international projects.

Source: Shannon McRae, "Debunking Small-Business Myths," National Federation of Independent Business Web site (www.nfib.com), September 26, 2007; "Myths About Exporting," BuyUSA Web site (www.buyusa.gov).

Unfortunately, many small businesses capable of exporting have not yet begun to do so. By some estimates, only 10 percent of U.S. companies with fewer than 100 employees export—the number is twice as high for companies of all sizes. Although there are certain real obstacles to exporting for small businesses, such as a lack of investment capital, some common myths create artificial obstacles. To explore some of these myths and the facts that dispute them, see this chapter's Entrepreneur's Toolkit titled, "Debunking the Myths of Small Business Exporting."

Why International Business Is Special

As we've already seen in this chapter, international business differs greatly from business in a purely domestic context. The most obvious contrast is that nations can have entirely different societies and commercial environments. Let's now take a moment to examine what makes international business special by introducing a model unique to this book—a model we call the *global business environment*.

The Global Business Environment

International business is special because it occurs within a dynamic, integrated system that weaves together four distinct elements:

1. The forces of *globalization*
2. Many *national* business environments
3. The *international* business environment
4. International *firm* management

The model in Figure 1.4 identifies each of these main elements and their subparts that together comprise the *global business environment*. Thinking about international business as occurring within this global system helps us understand its complexities and the interrelations between its distinct elements. Let's now preview each of the four main components in the global business environment.

FIGURE 1.4

The Global Business Environment

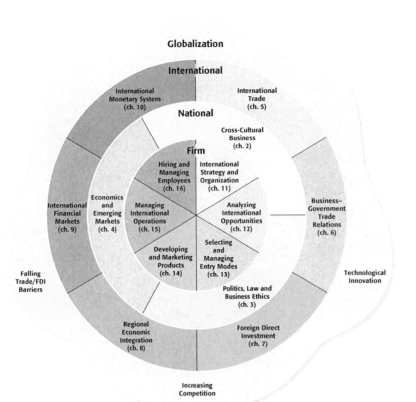

Globalization is a potent force transforming our societies and commercial activities in countless ways. Globalization, and the pressures it creates, forces its way into each element shown in Figure 1.4. In this way, the drivers of globalization (technological innovation and falling trade and investment barriers) influence every aspect of the global business environment. The dynamic nature of globalization also creates increasing competition for all firms everywhere, as managers begin to see the entire world as an opportunity. At home and abroad, firms must remain vigilant to the fundamental societal and commercial changes that globalization is causing.

Each *national business environment* is composed of unique cultural, political, legal, and economic characteristics that define business activity within that nation's borders. This set of national characteristics can differ greatly from country to country. But as nations open up and embrace globalization, their business environments are being transformed. Globalization can cause powerful synergies and enormous tensions to arise within and across various elements of a society. Company managers must be attentive to such nuances, adapting their products and practices as needed.

The *international business environment* influences how firms conduct their operations in both subtle and not-so-subtle ways. No business is entirely immune to events in the international business environment, as evidenced by the long-term trend toward more porous national borders. The drivers of globalization are causing the flows of trade, investment, and capital to grow and become more entwined—often causing firms to search simultaneously for production bases *and* new markets. Companies today must keep their finger on the pulse of the international business environment to see how it may affect their business activities.

International firm management is vastly different from managing a purely domestic business. Companies must abide by the rules in every market in which they choose to operate. Therefore, the context of international business management is defined by the characteristics of national business environments. Because of widely dispersed production and marketing activities today, firms commonly interact with people in distant locations within the international business environment. Finally, managers and their firms are compelled to be knowledgeable about the nations in which they operate because of the integrating power of globalization. Businesses should try to anticipate events and forces that can affect their operations by closely monitoring globalization, national business environments, and the international business environment.

The Road Ahead for International Business

The coverage of international business in this book follows the model of the global business environment displayed in Figure 1.4. In this chapter, we learned how *globalization* is transforming our world and how elements of the global business environment are becoming increasingly intertwined. As globalization penetrates deeper into the national context, every aspect of international business management is being affected.

In Part 2 (Chapters 2 through 4), we explore how *national business environments* differ from one nation to another. We examine how people's attitudes, values, beliefs, and institutions differ from one culture to another and how this affects business. This section also covers how nations differ in their political, legal, and economic systems. This material is placed early in the text because such differences between countries help frame subsequent topics and discussions, such as how companies modify business practices and strategies abroad.

We describe major components of the *international business environment* in Part 3 (Chapters 5 through 8) and Part 4 (Chapters 9 and 10). Our coverage begins with an examination of trade and investment theories and why governments encourage or discourage these two forms of international business. We explore the process of regional economic integration sweeping the globe and outline its implications for international business. Finally, we discuss how events in global financial markets affect international business and how the global monetary system functions.

In Part 5 (Chapters 11 through 16), our coverage turns to ways in which *international business management* differs from management of a purely domestic firm. We explain how a company creates an international strategy, organizes itself for international business, and analyzes and selects the markets it will pursue. We explore different potential entry modes and then discuss how a firm develops and markets products for specific nations, regions, or the entire world. We then cover how international companies manage their sometimes far-flung international operations. The book closes by discussing how international firms manage their human resources in the global business environment.

Quick Study

1. Why do large *multinational corporations* dominate international business?
2. Explain why small companies and *born global firms* are increasingly involved in international business.
3. Describe the global business environment and how its main elements interact.

Bottom Line FOR BUSINESS

The main theme of this chapter is that the world's national economies are becoming increasingly intertwined through the process of globalization. Cultural, political, legal, and economic events in one nation increasingly affect the lives of people in other countries. Companies must pay attention to how changes in nations where they do business can affect operations. In this section, we briefly examine several important business implications of globalization.

Harnessing Globalization's Benefits

People opposed to globalization say it negatively impacts wages and environmental protection, reduces political freedom, increases corruption, and inequitably rewards various groups. Yet there is evidence that the most global nations have the strongest records on equality, the most robust protection of natural resources, the most inclusive political systems, and the lowest levels of corruption. People in the most global nations also live the healthiest and longest lives, and women there have achieved the most social, educational, and economic progress.

One thing the debate over globalization has achieved is a dialogue on the merits and demerits of globalization. What has emerged is a more sober, less naïve notion of globalization. Those on each side of the debate understand that it can have positive effects on people's lives, but globalization cannot, by itself, alleviate the misery of the world's poor. Both sides in the debate are now working together to harness the benefits of globalization while minimizing its costs.

Intensified Competition

The two driving forces of globalization (lower trade and investment barriers and increased technological innovation) are taking companies into previously isolated markets and increasing competitive pressures worldwide. And innovation is unlikely to slow any time soon.

As the cost of computing power continues to fall and new technologies are developed, companies will find it easier and less costly to manage widely dispersed marketing activities and production facilities. Technological developments may even strengthen the case for outsourcing more professional jobs to low-cost locations. As competition intensifies, international companies will increase their cooperation with suppliers and customers.

Wages and Jobs

Some labor groups in wealthy nations contend that globalization is forcing companies to join the "race to the bottom" in terms of wages and benefits. But to attract investment, a location must offer low-cost, adequately skilled workers in an environment with acceptable levels of social, political, and economic stability.

Rapid globalization of markets and production is making delivery a complex engineering task. And as companies cut costs by outsourcing activities, supply and distribution channels grow longer and more complex. Corporate logistics departments and logistics specialist firms are helping international players respond to such challenges. Logistic experts are helping companies untangle lengthy supply chains, monitor shipping lanes, and forecast weather patterns. High-wage logistics jobs represent the kind of high-value-added employment that results from the "churning" in labor markets caused by globalization.

The Policy Agenda

Countless actions could be taken by developed and developing nations to lessen the negative effects of globalization. The World Bank calls on rich countries to: (1) open their markets to exports from developing countries; (2) slash their agricultural subsidies that hurt poor-country exports; and (3) increase development aid, particularly in education and health. It calls on poor countries to improve their investment climates and improve social protection for poor people in a changing economic environment.

The Institute for International Economics (www.iie.com) proposed a policy agenda for rich nations on two fronts. On the *domestic front*, it proposes: (1) establishing on-the-job training to help workers cope with globalization; (2) offering "wage insurance" to workers forced by globalization to take a lower-paying job; (3) subsidizing health insurance costs in case of lost work; and (4) improving education and lifetime learning. On the *international front*, it proposes: (1) better enforcing labor standards; (2) clarifying the relation between international trade and environmental agreements; and (3) reviewing the environmental implications of trade agreements.

This chapter has only introduced you to the study of international business—we hope you enjoy the rest of your journey!

Chapter Summary

1. Describe the process of globalization and how it affects markets and production.
   - *Globalization* is the trend toward greater economic, cultural, political, and technological interdependence among national institutions and economies.
   - It is marked by "denationalization," in which national borders are becoming somewhat less relevant.
   - The globalization of *markets* helps a company to: (1) reduce costs by standardizing marketing activities, (2) explore international markets if the home market is small or saturated, and (3) level income streams, especially for makers of seasonal products.
   - The globalization of *production* helps a company to: (1) access low-cost labor and become more price-competitive, and (2) access technical know-how or natural resources nonexistent or too expensive at home.
2. Identify the two forces causing globalization to increase.
   - *Falling barriers to trade and investment* is one major force behind globalization.
   - Trade barriers have been drastically reduced through institutions such as the *General Agreement on Tariffs and Trade* and the *World Trade Organization.*
   - Groups of several or more nations are reducing trade barriers by creating regional trade agreements.
   - *Technological innovation* is a second main force driving globalization.
   - Companies can manage global business activities with the use of e-mail, videoconferencing, intranets, and extranets.
   - Technology increases the speed and ease with which companies can manage far-flung operations.
   - Innovations in transportation technologies are making the shipment of goods between nations more efficient and dependable.
3. Summarize the evidence for each main argument in the globalization debate.
   - Regarding *jobs and wages*, both sides agree that globalization causes dislocation in labor markets: those supporting globalization believe overall gains of national economies are worth lost jobs for individuals, but globalization critics do not.
   - Labor unions argue globalization causes a "race to the bottom" in *labor and environmental regulation*, though they lack supporting evidence.
   - Regarding inequality *within nations*, developing nations can boost incomes of their poorest citizens by integrating themselves into the global economy.
   - In the debate over *inequality between nations*, nations that embrace world trade and investment grow faster than rich nations, whereas sheltered economies become worse off.
   - Groups agree that *global inequality* has fallen in recent decades but differ on the extent of the drop.
   - In terms of *national sovereignty*, globalization has helped spread democracy worldwide and aided progress on many global issues.
   - Evidence suggests that *cultures* of developing nations are thriving in an age of globalization and that deeper elements of culture are not easily abandoned.
4. Identify the types of companies that participate in international business.
   - Entrepreneurs and small firms are increasingly active in international business because the Internet and other technologies help them overcome high advertising and distribution costs.
   - Large *multinational corporations (MNCs)* still conduct most international business transactions.
   - MNCs have great economic and political muscle and their deals are often worth billions of dollars.
   - Globalization has given rise to the *born global firm*—a company that adopts a global perspective and engages in international business from or near its inception.
   - Born global firms tend to have an innovative culture and knowledge-based organizational capabilities.
   - Many born global firms rise to the status of international competitor in less than three years.
5. Describe the global business environment and identify its four main elements.
   - International business occurs within an integrated, *global business environment* consisting of four elements.
   - *Globalization* is transforming business and society and increasing competition for all firms.
   - Separate *national business environments* comprise unique cultural, political, legal, and economic characteristics that define business activity within a nation.
   - The *international business environment* influences how firms conduct operations, while globalization further entwines the flows of trade, investment, and capital.
   - *International business management* differs from management of a purely domestic firm in nearly all respects.

Talk It Over

1. Today, international businesspeople must think globally about production and sales opportunities. Many global managers will eventually find themselves living and working in cultures altogether different from their own. Many entrepreneurs will find themselves booking flights to places they had never heard of. What do you think companies can do now to prepare their managers for these new markets? What can entrepreneurs and small businesses with limited resources do?

2. In the past, national governments greatly affected the pace of globalization through agreements to lower barriers to international trade and investment. Is the pace of change now outpacing the capability of governments to manage the global economy? Will national governments become more or less important to international business in the future? Explain your answer.

3. Information technologies are developing at a faster rate than ever before. How have these technologies influenced globalization? Give specific examples. Do you think globalization will continue until we all live in one "global village"? Why or why not?

4. Consider the following statement: "Globalization and the resulting increase in competition harm people, as international companies play one government against another to get the best deal possible. Meanwhile, governments continually ask for greater concessions from their citizens, demanding that they work harder and longer for less pay." Do you agree? Why or why not?

Teaming Up

1. **Research Project.** Imagine that you and a group of your fellow classmates own a company that manufactures cheap sunglasses. To lower production costs, you want to move your factory from your developed country to a more cost-effective nation. Choose a prospective country to which you will move production. What elements of the national business environment might affect your move? Are there obstacles to overcome in the international business environment? How will managing your company be different when you undertake international activities? What challenges will you face in managing your new employees?

2. **Market Entry Strategy Project.** This exercise corresponds to the *MESP* online simulation. With a group of classmates, select a country that interests you. Describe its national flag: what do its colors and any symbols represent? Identify neighbors with which it shares borders. Give some important facts about the country, including its population, population density, land area, topography, climate, natural resources, and the locations of main industries. What does the nation produce? Do any aspects of the natural environment help explain why it produces what it does? Integrate your findings into your completed *MESP* report.

Key Terms

born global firm
e-business (e-commerce)
exports
GDP or GNP per capita
General Agreement on Tariffs and
   Trade (GATT)

globalization
gross domestic product (GDP)
gross national product (GNP)
imports
international business

International Monetary Fund (IMF)
multinational corporation (MNC)
World Bank
World Trade Organization (WTO)

Take It to the Web

1. **Video Report.** Visit this book's channel on YouTube (YouTube.com/MyIBvideos). Click on "Playlists" near the top of the page and click on the set of videos labeled "Ch 01: Globalization." Watch one video from the list and summarize it in a half-page report. Reflecting on the contents of this chapter, which aspects of globalization can you identify in the video? How might a company engaged in international business act on the information contained in the video?

2. **Web Site Report.** In this chapter, we've seen how globalization is fundamentally changing business and society. Managers can be more effective if they know what drives globalization and are familiar with its positive and negative aspects.

Select a controversial globalization topic that interests you, and visit the Web sites of two organizations that have opposing views on this topic. (Hint: You might begin by visiting an organization noted in this chapter.) For the topic you've chosen, report on the: (1) specific argument(s) of each side, (2) evidence each side uses to support its position(s), and (3) policy agenda, if any, each side promotes.

Which argument(s) do you agree with most? Have your views on this topic changed as a result of your research? If yes, explain how. Which types of firms/industries do you think this topic affects most? Explain. Write a short summary of your findings and include key Web sites you found helpful.

Ethical Challenges

1. You recently started a new job in a foreign country as manager of distribution for a busy seaport. On your first day of work, you are asked to sign for a shipment at the dock. Normally, there would be an official shipping fee of $1,000 for the delivery. The captain of the ship says that he is willing to forget about the official shipping paperwork and split the cost with you in exchange for a "tip." This situation makes you feel uncomfortable, as you know that bribery is illegal and could easily cost you your job. What do you tell the ship captain? Do you take your half of the money and keep quiet, tell the captain that you cannot participate in such a deal and leave it at that, or do you report the captain to higher authorities?

2. You are the president of a Japanese textile manufacturer. Your company has recently decided to outsource production to a developing country to save on labor costs. Complaints have been arising from workers in the foreign plant that supervisors are verbally and sometimes even physically abusive. You have yet to visit the plant but have been hearing rumors that working conditions are poor and that plant safety is not up to the company standard. When you confront the managers in charge of this plant, they claim that labor conditions are acceptable and that the workers are only complaining in the hopes of receiving higher payment for their work. A local labor-advocacy group has made claims that your managers at the plant have threatened workers with incarceration and bodily harm if they reveal the conditions of the plant. How do you handle this situation? Do you take steps to improve working conditions, or do you simply shut down the plant? How might your actions affect your relations with officials in this country and your future ability to do business there?

3. You are the newly elected president of a developing country. In the past, your economic foreign policy did not favor importing goods from the global market. However, you feel that encouraging trade with foreign nations will benefit your country. What steps do you take to convince the public that this is the best policy? If you encounter public resistance to your plan, will you go ahead with it anyway? Why or why not?

MTV Goes Global with a Local Beat

As goes the Buggles song, did "video kill the radio star"? Well, perhaps not, but no company has been more successful at getting teenagers around the world to tune in to music television than MTV Networks International (www.mtv.com/mtvinternational). Applying the maxim "Think globally, act locally," the company beams its irreverent mix of music, news, and entertainment to 340 million homes in over 140 countries. Although style and format are largely driven by the U.S. youth culture, content is tailored to suit local markets. MTV has never grown old with its audience and has remained true to young people between the ages of 18 and 24.

In 1987, MTV (www.mtv.com) commanded an audience of 61 million in the United States. But to counteract slowing demand, the company took the music revolution global by starting MTV Europe (www.mtv.tv) and MTV Australia (www.mtv.com.au). Through its experiences in Europe, MTV refined its mix of programming to become a "global national brand with local variations." At first, it took a pan-European approach, marketing the same product to all European countries. MTV broadcast primarily British and U.S. music (both of which were topping the charts throughout Europe) and used European "veejays" who spoke English. The European network was a huge overnight success.

Seven years later, however, MTV had become the victim of its own success. It suddenly had to compete with a new crop of upstart rivals that tailored content to language, culture, and current events in specific countries. One successful competitor was Germany's VIVA (www.viva.tv), launched in 1993 and featuring German veejays and more German artists than MTV Europe. Managers at MTV Networks were not overly concerned because MTV was still extremely popular. But they did realize they were losing their edge (and some customers) to the new national networks. So, the company's top managers had to reassess the company's strategy.

Because they had spent almost two decades building a global brand identity, MTV executives initially rejected the idea of splitting MTV into national stations. But the company gradually decided to go ahead with a national strategy because a new technology made it possible for MTV to think globally and act locally at little cost. The breakthrough was digital compression technology, which allows multiple services to be offered on a single satellite feed. "Where there were three or four services," explained one MTV official, "now we can broadcast six or eight."

Today, teens all over the world have their MTV cake and eat it, too. German teens see German-language programs that are created and produced there and shown on MTV Germany (www.mtv.de)—along with the usual generous helpings of U.S., British, and international music and the ever-popular duo Beavis and Butthead. European nations that still share an MTV channel are those that share cultural similarities—such as the Nordic nations (www.mtve.com). Likewise, while much of Latin America receives MTV Latin America (www.mtvla.com), Brazilian teens see Portuguese-language programs that are created there and shown on MTV Brazil (www.mtv.uol.com.br). An added side benefit for MTV of its strategy is that national advertisers who shunned the channel during its pan-European days have returned to beam targeted ads to teenage consumers.

Now, nearly 30 years after MTV planted its flag on the pop-culture moon in 1981, the beat goes on for the MTV generation. As Robert Thompson, professor of media and popular culture at Syracuse University says, "It's the only television entity of any kind that ever had a generation named after it."

Thinking Globally

1. Some say globalization is homogenizing the attitudes and spending habits of young consumers worldwide. As one journalist puts it, "It may still be conventional wisdom to 'think globally and act locally,' but in the youth market, it is increasingly a case of one size fits all." Do you agree or disagree? Why or why not?

2. Some people outside the United States say teens exposed to large doses of U.S. culture on MTV will identify less with their own societies and that teens in developing countries will want Western goods they cannot afford. MTV's response: "It's just fun, it's only TV," says one executive. What do you think? Are there dangers in broadcasting U.S.-style programs and ads to developing countries?

3. Digital compression technology made it possible for MTV to program over a global network. Can you think of other technological innovations that have helped companies to think globally and act locally?

4. Advances in technology often spur evolution in the entertainment industry. How might new products and services, such as the iPhone and YouTube, affect entertainment in years to come?

Source: George Winslow, "Q&A With MTV Networks International Managing Director Bhavneet Singh," *Multichannel News* (www.multichannel.com), January 2, 2008; Peter Grant, "Coming to Your TV—Homemade Hamster Videos?" *Wall Street Journal* (www.wsj.com), November 8, 2006; Marc Gunther, "MTV's Passage To India," *Fortune* (www.fortune.com), August 9, 2004; Kenny Santana, "MTV Goes to Asia," Yale Center for the Study of Globalization, (www.yaleglobal.yale.edu), August 12, 2003; Kerry Capell et al., "MTV's World," *Business Week*, February 18, 2002, pp. 81–84.

Appendix World Atlas

As globalization continues its march across the globe, we must maintain a thorough grasp of world geography. By knowing the locations of countries and the distances between them, international business managers can make more informed decisions. This atlas presents the world in a series of maps and is designed to assist you in understanding the global landscape of business.

Familiarize yourself with each of the maps in this appendix, and then try to answer the following 20 questions. We encourage you to return to this atlas frequently to refresh your memory of the global landscape, especially when you encounter the name of an unfamiliar city or country.

Map Exercises

1. Which of the following countries border the Atlantic Ocean?
   a. Bolivia
   b. Australia
   c. South Africa
   d. Japan
   e. United States

2. Which of the following countries are found in Africa?
   a. Guyana
   b. Morocco
   c. Egypt
   d. Pakistan
   e. Niger

3. Which one of the following countries does not border the Pacific Ocean?
   a. Australia
   b. Venezuela
   c. Japan
   d. Mexico
   e. Peru

4. Prague is the capital city of:
   a. Uruguay
   b. Czech Republic
   c. Portugal
   d. Tunisia
   e. Hungary

5. If transportation costs for getting your product from your market to Japan are high, which of the following countries might be good places to locate a manufacturing facility?
   a. Thailand
   b. Philippines
   c. South Africa
   d. Indonesia
   e. Portugal

6. Seoul is the capital city of:
   a. Vietnam
   b. Cambodia
   c. Malaysia
   d. China
   e. South Korea

7. Turkey, Romania, Ukraine, and Russia border the body of water called the _____ Sea.

8. Thailand shares borders with:
   a. Cambodia
   b. Pakistan
   c. Singapore
   d. Malaysia
   e. Indonesia

9. Which of the following countries border no major ocean or sea?
   a. Austria
   b. Paraguay
   c. Switzerland
   d. Niger
   e. all of the above

10. Oslo is the capital city of:
    a. Germany
    b. Canada
    c. Brazil
    d. Australia
    e. Norway

11. Chile is located in:
    a. Africa
    b. Asia
    c. the Northern Hemisphere
    d. South America
    e. Central Europe

12. Saudi Arabia shares borders with:
    a. Jordan
    b. Kuwait
    c. Iraq
    d. United Arab Emirates
    e. all of the above

13. The body of water located between Sweden and Estonia is the _____ Sea.

14. Which of the following countries are located on the Mediterranean Sea?
    a. Italy
    b. Croatia
    c. Turkey
    d. France
    e. Portugal

15. The distance between Sydney (Australia) and Tokyo (Japan) is shorter than that between:
    a. Tokyo and Cape Town (South Africa)
    b. Sydney and Hong Kong (China, SAR)
    c. Tokyo and London (England)
    d. Sydney and Jakarta (Indonesia)
    e. all of the above

16. Madrid is the capital city of (capitals are designated with red dots):
    a. Madagascar
    b. Italy
    c. Mexico
    d. Spain
    e. United States

17. Which of the following countries is not located in central Asia?
    a. Afghanistan   d. Kazakhstan
    b. Uzbekistan   e. Suriname
    c. Turkmenistan

18. If you were shipping your products from your production facility in Pakistan to market in Australia, they would likely cross the _____ Ocean.

19. Papua New Guinea, Guinea-Bissau, and Guinea are alternative names for the same country.
    a. true
    b. false

20. Which of the following countries are island nations?
    a. New Zealand   d. Australia
    b. Madagascar   e. all of the above
    c. Japan

Answers

(1.) c. South Africa, e. United States; (2.) b. Morocco, c. Egypt, e. Niger; (3.) b. Venezuela; (4.) b. Czech Republic; (5.) a. Thailand, b. Philippines, d. Indonesia; (6.) e. South Korea; (7.) Black; (8.) a. Cambodia, d. Malaysia; (9.) e. all of the above; (10.) e. Norway; (11.) d. South America; (12.) e. all of the above; (13.) Baltic; (14.) a. Italy, c. Turkey, d. France; (15.) a. Tokyo and Cape Town (South Africa), c. Tokyo and London (England); (16.) d. Spain; (17.) e. Suriname; (18.) Indian; (19.) b. false; (20.) e. all of the above.

Self-Assessment

If you scored 15 correct answers or more, well done! You seem well prepared for your international business journey. If you scored fewer than 8 correct answers, you may wish to review this atlas before moving on to Chapter 2.

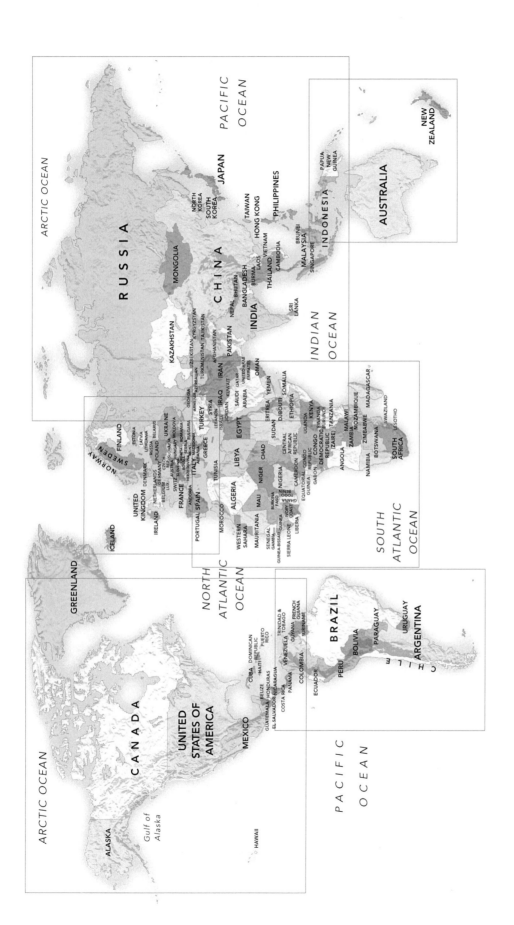

MAP A.1

The World in 2009

This global view identifies each continent and acts as a reference for the six maps that follow.

North America

MAP A.3

South America

MAP A.4

Europe

MAP A.5

Asia

Africa

Cross-Cultural Business

Learning Objectives

After studying this chapter, you should be able to

1. Describe culture and explain the significance of both national culture and subcultures.

2. Identify the components of culture and describe their impact on international business.

3. Describe cultural change and explain how companies and culture affect each other.

4. Explain how the physical environment and technology influence culture.

5. Describe the two main frameworks used to classify cultures and explain their practical use.

◀ A LOOK **BACK**

Chapter 1 introduced us to international business. We examined the impact of globalization on markets and production, the forces behind its expansion, and each main argument in the debate over globalization. We also profiled the kinds of companies engaged in international business.

■ A LOOK **AT THIS CHAPTER**

This chapter introduces the important role of culture in international business. We explore the main elements of culture and how they affect business policies and practices. We learn different methods of classifying cultures and how these methods can be applied to business.

▶ A LOOK **AHEAD**

Chapter 3 describes the political and legal systems of nations. We will learn how different national systems affect international businesses and how managers can reduce political risk. We also will discover how ethics and social responsibility impact international business.

Connecting Cultures

HELSINKI, Finland—Nokia Corporation (www.nokia.com) is the world's number one manufacturer of mobile handsets. The company's 112,000 employees in more than 150 countries generate $79 billion in sales annually. Nokia uses its knowledge of cultures to control 40 percent of the global handset market.

Nokia is especially talented at detecting consumer needs in emerging markets. China and India represent Nokia's first and second largest markets ahead of third-place United States. Nokia knows that in India a buyer selects a handset that has the right look and style and projects the right image. But for a consumer in China, a handset needs to be the right bargain. And Nokia recently finished a year-long study of the handset needs of people who live in Accra, capital city of the African nation Ghana.

Source: Jeffrey Barbee.

Nokia spends around $8 billion a year on research and development. Anthropologists and psychologists first travel the globe for Nokia to learn how people behave and communicate. Personnel at Nokia's headquarters in Finland then blend these unique insights with emerging global trends to design new handsets. Finally, the company develops phones suitable for a variety of markets but localizes each one with colors, surface textures, services, and ring-tones.

Nokia maintains its competitive edge through careful cultural research. For example, company anthropologists learned that people in rural areas of emerging markets need a phone that can be shared among many users. So Nokia added the capability to save each person's contacts separately and installed a call tracker that imposes a time or cost limit on each call. Handsets designed for emerging markets also feature menus in local languages, a one-touch flashlight in case of power outages, and a demo program for those who have never used a mobile phone. As you read this chapter, consider how culture influences international business and how company actions affect cultures.[1]

This chapter is the first of three that describe the links between international business activity and a nation's business environment. We introduce these topics early because of their strong influence on how commerce is conducted in different countries. In fact, success in international business can often be traced directly to a deep understanding of some aspect of a people's commercial environment. This chapter explores the influence of *culture* on international business activity. Chapter 3 presents the roles of *political and legal systems*, and Chapter 4 examines the impact of *economic systems and emerging markets* on international business.

An assessment of any nation's overall business climate is typically the first step in analyzing its potential as a host for international commercial activity. This means addressing some important questions, such as the following: What language(s) do the people speak? What is the climate like? Are the local people open to new ideas and new ways of doing business? Do government officials and the people want our business? Is the political situation stable enough so that our assets and employees are not placed at unacceptable levels of risk? Answers to these kinds of questions—plus statistical data on items such as income level and labor costs—allow companies to evaluate the attractiveness of a location as a place for doing business.

We address culture first in our discussion of national business environments because of its pivotal role in all international commercial activity. Whether we are discussing an entrepreneur running a small import/export business or a huge global firm directly involved in over 100 countries, *people* are at the center of all business activity. When people from around the world come together to conduct business, they bring with them different backgrounds, assumptions, expectations, and ways of communicating—in other words, *culture*.

We begin this chapter by exploring the influence of nation-states and subcultures on a people's overall cultural image. Next we learn the importance of values, attitudes, manners, and customs in any given culture. We then examine ways in which social institutions, religion, language, and other key elements of culture affect business practices and national competitiveness. We close this chapter with a look at two alternative methods for classifying cultures.

What Is Culture?

When traveling in other countries, we often perceive differences in the way people live and work. In the United States dinner is commonly eaten around 6:00 p.m.; in Spain it's not served until 8:00 or 9:00 p.m. In the United States most people shop in large supermarkets once or twice a week; Italians tend to shop in smaller local grocery stores nearly every day. Essentially, we are experiencing differences in **culture**—the set of values, beliefs, rules, and institutions held by a specific group of people. Culture is a highly complex portrait of a people. It includes everything from high tea in England to the tropical climate of Barbados, to Mardi Gras in Brazil, to segregation of the sexes in Saudi Arabian schools.

Before we learn about the individual components of culture, let's look at one important concept that should be discouraged and one that should be fostered.

Avoiding Ethnocentricity   **Ethnocentricity** is the belief that one's own ethnic group or culture is superior to that of others. Ethnocentricity can seriously undermine international business projects. It causes people to view other cultures in terms of their own and, therefore, disregard the beneficial characteristics of other cultures. Ethnocentricity played a role in many stories, some retold in this chapter, of companies that failed when they tried to implement a new business practice in a subsidiary abroad. The failures occurred because managers ignored a fundamental aspect of the local culture, which provoked a backlash from the local population, their government, or nongovernmental groups. As suppliers and buyers increasingly treat the world as a single, interconnected marketplace, managers should eliminate the biases inherent in ethnocentric thinking. For more information on how companies can foster a non-ethnocentric perspective, see this chapter's Culture Matters feature titled, "Creating a Global Mind-set."

culture
Set of values, beliefs, rules, and institutions held by a specific group of people.

ethnocentricity
Belief that one's own ethnic group or culture is superior to that of others.

CULTURE MATTERS
Creating a Global Mind-set

In this era of globalization, companies need employees who function without the blinders of ethnocentricity. Here are some ways managers can develop a *global mind-set*:

■ **Cultural Adaptability.** Managers need the ability to alter their behavior when working with people from other cultures. The first step in doing this is to develop one's knowledge of unfamiliar cultures. The second step is to act on that knowledge to alter behavior appropriately in response to cultural expectations. This can help managers to evaluate others in a culturally unbiased way and to motivate and lead multicultural teams.

■ **Bridging the Gap.** A large gap can emerge between theory and practice when Western management ideas are applied in Eastern cultures. "U.S. management principles may be accepted throughout the world, but Anglo-Saxon business customs and practices [on which they are based] may not be," says management adviser Kim Tae Woo. In Asia, Western managers may try implementing "collective leadership" practices more in line with Asian management styles.

■ **Building Global Mentality.** Companies can apply personality-testing techniques to measure the global aptitude of managers. The Global Mentality Test evaluates an individual's openness and flexibility in mind-set, understanding of global principles and terminology, and strategic implementation abilities. It also identifies areas in which training is needed and generates a list of recommended programs.

■ **Flexibility Is Key.** The more behavioral are the issues, the greater is the influence of local cultures. Japanese and Korean managers are more likely than U.S. managers to wait for directions and consult peers on decisions. And Western managers posted in the Middle East must learn to work within a rigid hierarchy to be successful. Although showing respect for others is universally valued, respect is defined differently from country to country.

■ **Want to Know More?** Visit the Center for Creative Leadership (www.ccl.org), Intercultural Business Center (www.ib-c.com), and Transnational Management Associates (www.tmaworld.com).

Developing Cultural Literacy As globalization continues, people directly involved in international business increasingly benefit from a certain degree of **cultural literacy**— detailed knowledge about a culture that enables a person to function effectively within it. Cultural literacy improves people's ability to manage employees, market products, and conduct negotiations in other countries. Global brands such as Procter & Gamble (www.pg.com) and Sony (www.sony.com) provide a competitive advantage because consumers know and respect these highly recognizable names. Yet cultural differences often dictate alterations in some aspect of a business to suit local tastes and preferences. The culturally literate manager who compensates for local needs and desires brings his or her company closer to customers and improves the firm's competitiveness.

cultural literacy
Detailed knowledge about a culture that enables a person to function effectively within it.

As you read through the concepts and examples in this chapter, try to avoid reacting with *ethnocentricity* while developing your own *cultural literacy*. Because these two concepts are central to the discussion of many international business topics, you will encounter them throughout this book. In the book's final chapter (Chapter 16), we explore specific types of cultural training that companies use to develop their employees' cultural literacy.

National Culture and Subcultures

Rightly or wrongly, we tend to invoke the concept of the *nation-state* when speaking of culture. In other words, we usually refer to British and Indonesian cultures as if all Britons and all Indonesians were culturally identical. We do this because we are conditioned to think in terms of *national culture*. But this is at best a generalization. In Great Britain, campaigns for greater Scottish and Welsh independence continue to make progress. And people in remote parts of Indonesia build homes in treetops even as people in the nation's developed regions pursue ambitious economic development projects. Let's now take a closer look at the diversity that lies beneath the veneer of national culture.

National Culture   Nation-states *support* and *promote* the concept of national culture by building museums and monuments to *preserve* the legacies of important events and people. Nation-states also intervene in business to preserve national culture. Most nations, for example, regulate culturally sensitive sectors of the economy, such as film-making and broadcasting. France continues to voice fears that its language is being tainted with English and its media with U.S. programming. To stem the English invasion, French laws limit the use of English in product packaging and storefront signs. At peak listening times, at least 40 percent of all radio station programming is reserved for French artists. Similar laws apply to television broadcasting. The French government even fined the local branch of a U.S. university for failing to provide a French translation on its English-language Web site.

Cities, too, get involved in enhancing national cultural attractions, often for economic reasons. Lifestyle enhancements to a city can help it attract companies, which benefit by having an easier task retaining top employees. The Guggenheim Museum in Bilbao, Spain (www.guggenheim-bilbao.es), designed by Frank Gehry, revived that old Basque industrial city. And Hong Kong's government enhanced its cultural attractions by building a Hong Kong Disney to lure businesses that may otherwise locate elsewhere in Asia.

Subcultures   A group of people who share a unique way of life within a larger, dominant culture is called a **subculture**. A subculture can differ from the dominant culture in language, race, lifestyle, values, attitudes, or other characteristics.

Although subcultures exist in all nations, they are often glossed over by our *impressions* of national cultures. For example, the customary portrait of Chinese culture often ignores the fact that China's population includes more than 50 distinct ethnic groups. Decisions regarding product design, packaging, and advertising should consider each group's distinct culture. Marketing campaigns also need to recognize that Chinese dialects in the Shanghai and Canton regions differ from those in the country's interior; not everyone is fluent in the official Mandarin dialect.

A multitude of subcultures also exists within the United States. Of 300 million U.S. residents, around 80 million are black, Hispanic, and Asian. Frito Lay (www.fritolay.com) was initially disheartened that 46 million U.S. Hispanics were not buying its Latin-flavored versions of Lay's and Doritos chips. The company looked south of the border

subculture
A group of people who share a unique way of life within a larger, dominant culture.

Subculture members define themselves by their style (such as clothing, hair, tattoos) and rebel against mass consumerism. London, England's Camden district is famous for its historic markets and as a gathering place for alternative subcultures such as goth, punk, and emo. Businesses like YouTube help subcultures to spread quickly worldwide. Can you think of a company that targets an international subculture with its products?

Source: © Hemis/CORBIS. All Rights Reserved.

to its Mexican subsidiary, Sabritas, and brought four popular brands into the U.S. market, including Sabritones Chile & Lime Puffed Wheat Snacks. The gamble paid off as sales of Frito's Sabritas brand doubled to more than $100 million over a two-year period.[2]

Cultural boundaries do not always correspond to political boundaries. In other words, subcultures sometimes exist across national borders. People who live in different nations but who share the same subculture can have more in common with one another than with their fellow nationals. Arab culture, for example, extends from northwest Africa to the Middle East, with pockets of Arabs in many European countries and the United States. Because Arabs share a common language and tend to share purchasing behaviors related to Islamic religious beliefs, marketing to Arab subcultures can sometimes be accomplished with a single marketing campaign.

Quick Study

1. Define *culture*. How does ethnocentricity distort one's view of other cultures?
2. What is *cultural literacy*? Why should businesspeople understand other cultures?
3. How do nation-states and *subcultures* influence a nation's cultural image?

Components of Culture

The actions of nation-states and the presence of subcultures help define the culture of a group of people. But a people's culture also includes what they consider beautiful and tasteful, their underlying beliefs, their traditional habits, and the ways in which they relate to one another and their surroundings. Let's take a detailed look at each main component of culture: *aesthetics*, *values* and *attitudes*, *manners* and *customs*, *social structure*, *religion*, *personal communication*, *education*, and *physical* and *material environments*.

Aesthetics

What a culture considers "good taste" in the arts (including music, painting, dance, drama, and architecture), the imagery evoked by certain expressions, and the symbolism of certain colors is called **aesthetics**.

Aesthetics are important when a company does business in another culture. The selection of appropriate colors for advertising, product packaging, and even work uniforms can improve the odds of success. For example, green is a favorable color in Islam and adorns the national flags of most Islamic nations, including Jordan, Pakistan, and Saudi Arabia. Companies take advantage of the emotional attachment to the color green in these countries by incorporating it into a product, its packaging, or its promotion. Across much of Asia, on the other hand, green is associated with sickness. In Europe, Mexico, and the United States, the color of death and mourning is black; in Japan and most of Asia, it's white.

Shoe manufacturer Nike (www.nike.com) experienced firsthand the importance of imagery and symbolism in international marketing. The company emblazoned a new line of shoes with the word "Air" written to resemble flames or heat rising off blacktop. The shoes were given various names, including *Air Bakin'*, *Air Melt*, *Air Grill*, and *Air B-Que*. But what Nike did not realize was that the squiggly lines of the "Air" logo resembled Arabic script for "Allah," the Arabic name for God. Under threat of a worldwide boycott by Muslims, who considered it a sacrilege, Nike apologized and recalled the shoes.

Music is deeply embedded in culture and, when used correctly, can be a clever and creative addition to a promotion; if used incorrectly, it can offend the local population. The architecture of buildings and other structures should also be researched to avoid making cultural blunders attributable to the symbolism of certain shapes and forms.

aesthetics
What a culture considers "good taste" in the arts, the imagery evoked by certain expressions, and the symbolism of certain colors.

The importance of aesthetics is just as great when going international using the Internet. Many companies exist that teach corporations how to globalize their Internet presence. These companies often provide professional guidance on how to adapt Web sites to account for cultural preferences such as color scheme, imagery, and slogans.[3] The advice of specialist firms can be particularly helpful for entrepreneurs and small businesses because they rarely have in-house employees well-versed in other cultures. To read how small business owners can tailor a Web site to suit local aesthetics and other cultural variables, see the Entrepreneur's Toolkit titled, "Localize Your Web Site."

Values and Attitudes

values
Ideas, beliefs, and customs to which people are emotionally attached.

Ideas, beliefs, and customs to which people are emotionally attached are called **values**. Values include concepts such as honesty, marital faithfulness, freedom, and responsibility. Values are important to business because they affect a people's work ethic and desire for material possessions. For example, whereas people in Singapore value hard work and material success, people in Greece value leisure and a modest lifestyle. The United Kingdom and the United States value individual freedom; Japan and South Korea value group consensus.

The influx of values from other cultures can be fiercely resisted. Many Muslims believe drugs, alcohol, and certain kinds of music and literature will undermine important Islamic values. This is why nations under Islamic law (including Iran and Saudi Arabia) exact severe penalties against anyone possessing illegal items such as drugs and alcohol. Deeply held conservative values are why the Arab world's reality TV programs tend to be short-lived. In Bahrain, the local version of "Big Brother" was canceled after people objected to the program's format, which involved young unmarried adults of both sexes

ENTREPRENEUR'S TOOLKIT

Localize Your Web Site

When going global with an Internet presence, the more a company localizes, the better. Online customers want an experience corresponding to their cultural context offline. Here are a few tips for entrepreneurs launching an online presence.

- **Choosing Colors.** A black-and-white Web site is fine for many countries, but in Asia visitors may think you are inviting them to a funeral. In Japan and across Europe, Web sites in pastel color schemes often work best.
- **Selecting Numbers.** Many Chinese-speaking cultures consider the number four unlucky, although eight and nine symbolize prosperity. Be careful that your Web address and phone numbers do not send the wrong signal.
- **Watching the Clock.** If marketing to countries that use the 24-hour clock, adjust times stated on the site so it reads, "Call between 9:00 and 17:00" instead of "Call between 9 a.m. and 5 p.m."

- **Avoiding Slang.** English in Britain is different from that in the United States, Spanish in Spain is different from that in Mexico, and French in France is different from that in Quebec. Avoid slang to lessen the potential negative impact of such differences.
- **Waving the Flag.** Using national flags as symbols for buttons that access different language versions of your site should be done carefully. Mexican visitors to your site may be put off by a Spanish flag to signify the site's Spanish-language version, for example.
- **Doing the Math.** Provide conversions into local currencies for buyer convenience. For online ordering, be sure your site calculates any shipping costs, tax rates, tariffs, and so on. Also allow enough blanks on the order form to accommodate longer international addresses.
- **Getting Feedback.** Finally, talk with customers to know what they want to accomplish on your Web site. Then thoroughly test the site to ensure it functions properly.

living under the same roof. The Lebanon-based program "Hawa Sawa" (*"On Air Together"*) was shut down because its "elimidate" format (in which a young man would gradually eliminate young women to finally select a date) was perceived by many people as too Western.[4]

Attitudes are positive or negative evaluations, feelings, and tendencies that individuals harbor toward objects or concepts. Attitudes reflect underlying values. For example, a Westerner would be expressing an attitude if he or she were to say, "I do not like the Japanese purification ritual because it involves being naked in a communal bath." The Westerner quoted here might hold conservative beliefs regarding exposure of the body.

Similar to values, attitudes are learned from role models, including parents, teachers, and religious leaders. Attitudes also differ from one country to another because they are formed within a cultural context. But unlike values (which generally concern only important matters), people hold attitudes toward both important and unimportant aspects of life. And whereas values remain quite rigid over time, attitudes are more flexible.

It seems a "European" attitude has sunk into the psyche of young people there as companies from different countries merge, industries consolidate, and nations grow closer together in the European Union. Many young people in Europe today consider themselves to be "European" as much as they identify with their individual national identities. Still, the underlying values of young Europeans tend to remain similar to those of their parents. Such cultural knowledge can help managers decide whether to adapt promotions to local attitudes for maximum effectiveness.

Let's now look at how people's attitudes differ toward three important aspects of life that directly affect business activities: time, work and achievement, and cultural change.

Attitudes Toward Time   People in many Latin American and Mediterranean cultures are casual about their use of time. They maintain flexible schedules and would rather enjoy their time than sacrifice it to unbending efficiency. Businesspeople, for example, may arrive after the scheduled meeting time and prefer to build personal trust before discussing business. Not surprisingly, it usually takes longer to conduct business in these parts of the world than in the United States or northern Europe.

By contrast, people in Japan and the United States typically arrive promptly for meetings, keep tight schedules, and work long hours. The emphasis on using time efficiently reflects the underlying value of hard work in both these countries. Yet people in Japan and the United States sometimes differ in how they use their time at work. For example, U.S. employees strive toward workplace efficiency and may leave work early if the day's tasks are done, reflecting the value placed on producing individual results. But in Japan, although efficiency is prized, it is equally important to look busy in the eyes of others even when business is slow. Japanese workers want to demonstrate their dedication to superiors and coworkers—an attitude grounded in values such as the concern for group cohesion, loyalty, and harmony.

Attitudes Toward Work   Whereas some cultures display a strong work ethic, others stress a more balanced pace in juggling work and leisure. People in southern France like to say they work to live, while people in the United States live to work. They say work is a means to an end for them, whereas work is an end in itself in the United States. Not surprisingly, the lifestyle in southern France is slower-paced. People tend to concentrate on earning enough money to enjoy a relaxed, quality lifestyle. Businesses practically close down during August, when many workers take month-long paid holidays, usually outside the country.

People tend to launch their own businesses when capital is available for new business start-ups and when the cultural stigma of entrepreneurial failure is low. In European countries, start-ups are considered quite risky and capital for entrepreneurial ventures can be scarce. Moreover, if an entrepreneur's venture goes bust, he or she can find it very hard to obtain financing for future projects because of the stigma of failure. This remains true despite some progress recently. The opposite attitude tends to prevail in the United States.

attitudes
Positive or negative evaluations, feelings, and tendencies that individuals harbor toward objects or concepts.

Reference to prior bankruptcy in a business plan is sometimes considered a valuable learning experience (assuming lessons were learned). As long as U.S. bankers or venture capitalists see promising business plans, they are generally willing to loan money. Today, many European nations are working to foster an entrepreneurial spirit similar to that of the United States.

cultural trait

Anything that represents a culture's way of life, including gestures, material objects, traditions, and concepts.

Attitudes Toward Cultural Change   A **cultural trait** is anything that represents a culture's way of life, including gestures, material objects, traditions, and concepts. Such traits include bowing to show respect in Japan (gesture), a Buddhist temple in Thailand (material object), relaxing in a tearoom in Kuwait (tradition), and practicing democracy in the United States (concept). Let's look more closely at the role of cultural traits in causing cultural change over time and the relation between international companies and cultural change.

CULTURAL DIFFUSION   The process whereby cultural traits spread from one culture to another is called **cultural diffusion**. As new traits are accepted and absorbed into a culture, *cultural change* occurs naturally and, as a rule, gradually. Globalization and technological advances are increasing the pace of both cultural diffusion and cultural change. Satellite television, videoconferencing, and videos on the Internet increase the frequency of international contact and expose people of different nations to new ideas and practices.

cultural diffusion

Process whereby cultural traits spread from one culture to another.

WHEN COMPANIES CHANGE CULTURES   International companies are often agents of cultural change. As trade and investment barriers fall, for example, U.S. consumer-goods and entertainment companies are moving into untapped markets. Critics in some of these places charge that in exporting the products of such firms, the United States is practicing **cultural imperialism**—the replacement of one culture's traditions, folk heroes, and artifacts with substitutes from another.

cultural imperialism

Replacement of one culture's traditions, folk heroes, and artifacts with substitutes from another.

Fears of cultural imperialism still drive some French to oppose the products of the Walt Disney Company (www.disney.com) and its Disneyland Paris theme park. They fear "Mickey and Friends" could replace traditional characters rooted in French culture. McDonald's (www.mcdonalds.com) is also sometimes charged with cultural imperialism. It is reported that the average Japanese child thinks McDonald's was invented in Japan and exported to the United States. Chinese children consider "Uncle" McDonald "funny, gentle, kind, and understanding." Meanwhile, politicians in Russia decried the Snickerization of their culture—a snide term that refers to the popularity of the candy bar made by Snickers (www.snickers.com). And when the Miss World Pageant was held in India, conservative groups criticized Western corporate sponsors for spreading the message of consumerism and portraying women as sex objects.

Sensitivity to the cultures in which they operate can help companies avoid charges of cultural imperialism. Firms must focus not only on meeting people's product needs, but also on how their activities and products affect people's traditional ways and habits. Rather than view their influence on culture as the inevitable consequence of doing business, companies can take several steps to soften those effects. For example, policies and practices that are at odds with deeply held beliefs can be introduced gradually. Managers could also seek the advice of highly respected local individuals such as elders, who fulfill key societal roles in many developing countries. And businesses should always make clear to local workers the benefits of any proposed change.

An area in which U.S. companies may be changing other cultures is fairness in the workplace. Just a few years ago, sexual harassment lawsuits were a peculiar phenomenon of U.S. culture. Increased awareness of this issue in other nations coincides with the international outsourcing of jobs. As U.S. companies outsource jobs to other nations, they are being held accountable for how these subcontractors treat their employees. In the process, U.S. companies export values of the U.S. workplace, such as what constitutes harassment.[5]

Here, a customer in Dubai visits an outlet of Sweden-based IKEA. Sweden historically dominated other Scandinavian nations, including Denmark. Now some in Denmark say IKEA is a "cultural imperialist" for portraying Denmark as Sweden's doormat because it assigns Danish names to doormats and rugs, but reserves Swedish names for expensive items such as beds and chairs. IKEA says the product names are simply a coincidence.
Source: © Ed Kashi/CORBIS.
All Rights Reserved.

WHEN CULTURES CHANGE COMPANIES   Culture often forces companies to adjust their business policies and practices. Managers from the United States, for example, often encounter cultural differences that force changes in how they motivate employees in other countries. Although it's a time-consuming practice, managers sometimes use *situational management*—a system in which a supervisor walks an employee through every step of an assignment or task and monitors the results at each stage. This technique helps employees fully understand the scope of their jobs and clarifies the boundaries of their responsibilities.

Other types of changes might also be needed to suit local culture. Vietnam's traditional, agriculture-based economy means people's concept of time revolves around the seasons. The local "timepiece" is the monsoon, not the clock. Western managers, therefore, modify their approach and take a more patient, long-term view of business by modifying employee evaluation and reward systems. For example, individual criticism should be delivered privately to save employees from "losing face" among coworkers. Individual praise for good performance can be delivered either in private or in public, if done carefully. The Vietnamese place great value on group harmony, so an individual can be embarrassed if singled out publicly as being superior to the rest of the work unit.

IS A GLOBAL CULTURE EMERGING?   What does the rapid pace of cultural change worldwide mean for international business? Are we witnessing the emergence of a new, truly global culture in which all people share similar lifestyles, values, and attitudes? The rapid pace of cultural diffusion today is causing cultures to converge to some extent. The successful TV show, *American Idol*, where young people compete for a chance to become a celebrity, is one example of global pop culture. The U.S. show is one of 39 clones around the world based on the original British show, *Pop Idol*. The same company helped develop and market *The Apprentice*, which is seen in 16 countries.[6]

It might be true that people in different cultures are developing similar perspectives on certain issues. But it seems that just as often as we see signs of an emerging global culture, we discover some new habit unique to one culture. When that happens, we are reminded of the roles of history and tradition in defining culture. Though values and attitudes are under continually greater pressure from globalization, their transformation will be gradual rather than abrupt because they are deeply ingrained in culture.

1. What is meant by a culture's *aesthetics*? Give several examples.
2. How can businesses incorporate aesthetics into their Web sites?
3. Compare and contrast *values* and *attitudes*. How do cultures differ in their attitudes toward time, work, and cultural change?
4. Describe the process of *cultural diffusion*. Why should international businesses be sensitive to charges of *cultural imperialism*?

Manners and Customs

When doing business in another culture, it is important to understand a people's manners and customs. At a minimum, understanding manners and customs helps managers avoid making embarrassing mistakes or offending people. In-depth knowledge, meanwhile, improves the ability to negotiate in other cultures, market products effectively, and manage international operations. Let's explore some important differences in manners and customs around the world.

manners
Appropriate ways of behaving, speaking, and dressing in a culture.

Manners   Appropriate ways of behaving, speaking, and dressing in a culture are called **manners**. In Arab cultures that stretch from the Middle East to northwest Africa, for example, one does not extend a hand to greet an older person unless the elder first offers the greeting. In going first, a younger person would be displaying bad manners. Moreover, because Arab culture considers the left hand the one used for personal hygiene, using it to pour tea or serve a meal is considered very bad manners.

Jack Ma founded Alibaba (www.alibaba.com) as a way for suppliers and buyers to increase efficiency by cutting through layers of intermediaries and trading companies. But he realized early that his Chinese clients needed training in business etiquette so they could cross the cultural divide and do business with people from Western cultures. Mr. Chen Xi Guo, who owns a machinery factory in Wenzhou in central China, participated in an Alibaba seminar on business manners. He now promises to spend more time chitchatting with clients. "I will work hard to be nicer," says Mr. Chen. His seminar worksheets instruct him to sprinkle his e-mails with phrases like, "How are you?" "It was great to hear from you," and "Can we work together?"[7]

Conducting business during meals is common practice in the United States. In Mexico, however, it is poor manners to bring up business at mealtime unless the host does so first. Business discussions in Mexico typically begin when coffee and brandy arrive. Likewise, toasts in the United States tend to be casual and sprinkled with lighthearted humor. In Mexico, where a toast should be philosophical and full of passion, a lighthearted toast would be offensive. See the Global Manager's Briefcase titled, "A Globetrotter's Guide to Manners" for additional pointers on appropriate manners when abroad on business.

customs
Habits or ways of behaving in specific circumstances that are passed down through generations in a culture.

folk custom
Behavior, often dating back several generations, that is practiced by a homogeneous group of people.

popular custom
Behavior shared by a heterogeneous group or by several groups.

Customs   When habits or ways of behaving in specific circumstances are passed down through generations, they become **customs**. Customs differ from manners in that they define appropriate habits or behaviors in *specific situations*. Sharing food gifts during the Islamic holy month of Ramadan is a custom, as is the Japanese tradition of throwing special parties for young women and men who turn age 20. Let's examine two types of customs and see how instances of each vary around the world.

FOLK AND POPULAR CUSTOMS   A **folk custom** is behavior, often dating back several generations, that is practiced by a homogeneous group of people. The wearing of turbans by Muslims in southern Asia and the art of belly dancing in Turkey are both folk customs. A **popular custom** is behavior shared by a heterogeneous group or by several groups. Popular customs can exist in just one culture or in two or more cultures at once. Wearing blue jeans and playing golf are both popular customs across the globe. Folk customs that spread by cultural diffusion to other regions develop into popular customs.

GLOBAL MANAGER'S BRIEFCASE
A Globetrotter's Guide to Manners

Large multinationals need top managers who are comfortable living, working, and traveling worldwide. Here are a few guidelines for a manager to follow when meeting colleagues from other cultures:

- **Familiarity.** Avoid the temptation to get too familiar too quickly. Use titles such as "doctor" and "mister." Switch to a first-name basis only when invited to do so and do not shorten people's names from, say, Catherine to Cathy.
- **Personal Space.** Culture dictates what is considered the appropriate distance between two people. Middle Eastern and Latin American nations close the gap significantly. And in Latin America the man-to-man embrace can occur regularly in business.
- **Religious Values.** Be cautious so that your manners do not offend people. Former Secretary of State Madeline Albright acquired the nickname "The Kissing Ambassador" for kissing the Israeli and Palestinian leaders of these two religious peoples.
- **Business Cards.** In Asia, business cards are considered an extension of the individual. Business cards in Japan are typically exchanged after a bow, with two hands extended, and the wording facing the recipient. Leave the card on the table for the entire meeting—don't quickly stuff it in your wallet or toss it into your briefcase.
- **Comedy.** Use humor cautiously because it often does not translate well. Avoid jokes that rely on wordplay and puns or events in your country, of which local people might have little or no knowledge.
- **Body Language.** Do not "spread out" by hanging your arms over the backs of chairs, but don't be too stiff either. Look people in the eye lest they deem you untrustworthy, but don't stare too intently in a challenging manner.

We can also distinguish between folk and popular food. Popular Western-style fast food, for instance, is rapidly replacing folk food around the world. Widespread acceptance of "burgers 'n' fries" (born in the United States) and "fish 'n' chips" (born in Britain) is altering deep-seated dietary traditions in many Asian countries, especially among young people. In Japan and South Korea today, these popular foods are even becoming a part of home-cooked meals. Sadly, many believe this trend is at least partly responsible for a rising proportion of overweight people in those nations.

THE BUSINESS OF GIFT GIVING Although giving token gifts to business and government associates is customary in many countries, the proper type of gift varies. A knife, for example, should not be offered to associates in Russia, France, or Germany, where it signals the severing of a relationship. In Japan, gifts must be wrapped in such a delicate way that it is wise to ask someone trained in the practice to do the honors. It is also Japanese custom for the giver to protest that the gift is small and unworthy of the recipient and for the recipient to not open the gift in front of the giver. This tradition does not endorse trivial gifts but is simply a custom.

Cultures differ in their legal and ethical rules against giving or accepting bribes. Large gifts to business associates are particularly suspicious. The U.S. Foreign Corrupt Practices Act, which prohibits companies from giving large gifts to government officials to win business favors, applies to U.S. firms operating at home *and* abroad. Yet in many cultures bribery is woven into a social fabric that has worn well for centuries. In Germany, bribe payments may even qualify for tax deductions. Though many governments worldwide are adopting stricter measures to control bribery, in some cultures large gifts are still an effective way to obtain contracts, enter markets, and secure protection from competitors.

Social Structure

Social structure embodies a culture's fundamental organization, including its groups and institutions, its system of social positions and their relationships, and the process by which its resources are distributed. Social structure plays a role in many business decisions, including production-site selection, advertising methods, and the costs of doing business in a country. Three important elements of social structure that differ across cultures are social group associations, social status, and social mobility.

Social Group Associations   People in all cultures associate themselves with a variety of **social groups**—collections of two or more people who identify and interact with each other. Social groups contribute to each individual's identity and self-image. Two groups that play especially important roles in affecting business activity everywhere are family and gender.*

FAMILY   There are two different types of family groups:

- The *nuclear family* consists of a person's immediate relatives, including parents, brothers, and sisters. This concept of family prevails in Australia, Canada, the United States, and much of Europe.
- The *extended family* broadens the nuclear family and adds grandparents, aunts and uncles, cousins, and relatives through marriage. It is an important social group in much of Asia, the Middle East, North Africa, and Latin America.

Extended families can present some interesting situations for businesspeople unfamiliar with the concept. In some cultures, owners and managers obtain supplies and materials from another company in which someone from the extended family works. Gaining entry into such family arrangements can be difficult because quality and price are not sufficient motives to ignore family ties.

In extended-family cultures, managers and other employees often try to find jobs for relatives inside their own companies. This practice (called "nepotism") can present a challenge to the human resource operations of a Western company, which typically must establish explicit policies on the practice.

GENDER   *Gender* refers to socially learned traits associated with, and expected of, men or women. It includes behaviors and attitudes such as styles of dress and activity preferences. It is not the same thing as sex, which refers to the biological fact that a person is either male or female.

Though many countries have made great strides toward gender equality in the workplace, others have not. In countries where women are denied equal opportunity in the workplace, their unemployment rate can easily be double that for men and their pay half that for men in the same occupation. Women's salaries can be so low and the cost of child-care so high that it simply makes more sense for mothers to stay home with their children. Caring for children and performing household duties are also likely considered women's work and not the responsibility of the entire family.

Countries operating under Islamic law sometimes segregate women and men in public schools, universities, and social activities, and restrict women to certain professions. Yet women are sometimes allowed teaching careers in all-female classrooms only, or they can become physicians for female patients only.

Social Status   Another important aspect of social structure is the way a culture divides its population according to *status*—that is, according to positions within the structure. Although some cultures have only a few categories, others have many. The process of ranking people into social layers or classes is called **social stratification**.

Three factors that normally determine social status are family heritage, income, and occupation. In most industrialized countries royalty, government officials, and top business leaders occupy the highest social layer. Scientists, medical doctors, and others with a uni-

---

*We put these two "groups" together for the sake of convenience. Strictly speaking, a gender is not a group. Sociologists regard it as a category—people who share some sort of status. A key to group membership is mutual interaction. Individuals in categories know that they are not alone in holding a particular status, but the vast majority remain strangers to one another.

versity education occupy the middle layer. Below are those with vocational training or a secondary-school education, who dominate the manual and clerical occupations. Although rankings are fairly stable, they can and do change over time. For example, because Confucianism (a major Chinese religion) stresses a life of learning, not commerce, Chinese culture frowned on businesspeople for centuries. In modern China, however, people who have obtained wealth and power through business are now considered important role models for younger generations.

Social Mobility   Moving to a higher social class is easy in some cultures but difficult or impossible in others. **Social mobility** is the ease with which individuals can move up or down a culture's "social ladder." For much of the world's population today, one of two systems regulates social mobility: a *caste system* or a *class system*.

CASTE SYSTEM   A **caste system** is a system of social stratification in which people are born into a social ranking, or *caste*, with no opportunity for social mobility. India is the classic example of a caste culture. Although the Indian constitution officially bans discrimination by caste, its influence persists. Little social interaction occurs between castes, and marrying out of one's caste is taboo. Opportunities for work and advancement are defined within the system, and certain occupations are reserved for the members of each caste. For example, a member of a lower caste cannot supervise someone of a higher caste because personal clashes would be inevitable.

The caste system forces Western companies to make some hard ethical decisions when entering the Indian marketplace. They must decide whether to adapt to local human resource policies in India or import their own from the home country. As globalization penetrates deeper into Indian culture, the nation's social system and international companies will face many challenges to overcome.

CLASS SYSTEM   A **class system** is a system of social stratification in which personal ability and actions determine social status and mobility. It is the most common form of social stratification in the world today. But class systems vary in the amount of mobility they allow. Highly class-conscious cultures offer less mobility and, not surprisingly, experience greater class conflict. Across Western Europe, for example, wealthy families have retained power for generations by restricting social mobility. Countries there must sometimes deal with class conflict in the form of labor–management disputes that can increase the cost of doing business.

Conversely, lower levels of class consciousness encourage mobility and lessen conflict. A more cooperative atmosphere in the workplace tends to prevail when people feel that a higher social standing is within their reach. Most U.S. citizens share the belief that hard work can improve their standard of living and social status. People attribute higher status to greater income or wealth, but often with little regard for family background.

social mobility
Ease with which individuals can move up or down a culture's "social ladder."

caste system
System of social stratification in which people are born into a social ranking, or caste, with no opportunity for social mobility.

class system
System of social stratification in which personal ability and actions determine social status and mobility.

Quick Study

1. How do *manners* and *customs* differ? Give examples of each.
2. List several manners that managers should consider when doing business abroad.
3. Define *folk* and *popular* customs. How can a folk custom become a popular custom?
4. Define *social structure*. How do social rank and *social mobility* affect business?

Religion

Human values often originate from religious beliefs. Different religions take different views of work, savings, and material goods. Identifying why they do so may help us understand business practices in other cultures. Knowing how religion affects business is especially important in countries with religious governments.

Map 2.1 shows where the world's major religions are practiced. Religion is not confined to national political boundaries but can exist in different regions of the world

MAP 2.1

World Religions

Christianity

Buddhism

Judaism

Nature religion

Hinduism

Chinese religion

Islam

Other groups

simultaneously. It is also common for several or more religions to be practiced within a single nation. In the following sections, we explore Christianity, Islam, Hinduism, Buddhism, Confucianism, Judaism, and Shinto. We examine their potential effects, both positive and negative, on international business activity.

Christianity   Christianity was born in Palestine around 2,000 years ago among Jews who believed that God sent Jesus of Nazareth to be their savior. Although Christianity boasts more than 300 denominations, most Christians belong to the Roman Catholic, Protestant, or Eastern Orthodox churches. With 2 billion followers, Christianity is the world's single largest religion. The Roman Catholic faith asks its followers to refrain from placing material possessions above God and others. Protestants believe that salvation comes from faith in God and that hard work gives glory to God—a tenet known widely as the "Protestant work ethic." Many historians believe this conviction to be a main factor in the development of capitalism and free enterprise in nineteenth-century Europe.

Christian organizations sometimes get involved in social causes that affect business policy. For example, some conservative Christian groups have boycotted the Walt Disney Company (www.disney.com), charging that in portraying young people as rejecting parental guidance, Disney films impede the moral development of young viewers worldwide.

The Church itself has been involved in some highly publicized controversies. Ireland-based Ryanair (www.ryanair.com), Europe's leading low-fare airline, ruffled the feathers of the Roman Catholic Church with an ad campaign. The ad depicted the pope (the head of the Church) claiming that the fourth secret of Fatima was Ryanair's low fares. The Church sent out a worldwide press release accusing the airline of blaspheming the pope. But much to the Church's dismay, the press release generated an enormous amount of free publicity for Ryanair.[8]

In one classic case, the French Bishops' Conference sued Volkswagen-France (www.volkswagen.fr) for a billboard ad it felt insulted Christians by parodying the famous image of Leonardo Da Vinci's *The Last Supper*. The conference explained that it was reacting to increasing use of sacred things in advertising throughout Europe. The conference said ads aim for the sacred to shock people because using sex no longer worked. Volkswagen halted the $16 million ad campaign in response to the Church's complaint.

Islam   With 1.3 billion adherents, Islam is the world's second-largest religion. The prophet Muhammad founded Islam around A.D. 600 in Mecca, the holy city of Islam located in Saudi Arabia. Islam thrives in northwestern Africa, the Middle East, Central Asia, Pakistan, and some Southeast Asian nations, including Indonesia. Muslim concentrations are also found in most European and U.S. cities. *Islam* means "submission to Allah" and *Muslim* means "one who submits to Allah." Islam revolves around the "five pillars": (1) reciting the *Shahada* (profession of faith), (2) giving to the poor, (3) praying five times daily, (4) fasting during the holy month of *Ramadan*, and (5) making the *Hajj* (pilgrimage) to the Saudi Arabian city of Mecca at least once in one's lifetime.

Religion strongly affects the kinds of goods and services acceptable to Muslim consumers. Islam, for example, prohibits the consumption of alcohol and pork. Popular alcohol substitutes are soda pop, coffee, and tea. Substitutes for pork include lamb, beef, and poultry (all of which must be slaughtered in a prescribed way so as to meet *halal* requirements). Because hot coffee and tea often play ceremonial roles in Muslim nations, the markets for them are quite large. And because usury (charging interest for money lent) violates the laws of Islam, credit card companies collect management fees rather than interest, and each cardholder's credit line is limited to an amount held on deposit.

Nations governed by Islamic law (see Chapter 3) sometimes segregate the sexes at certain activities and in locations such as schools. In Saudi Arabia, women cannot drive cars on public streets. In orthodox Islamic nations, men cannot conduct market research surveys with women at home unless they are family members. Women visiting Islamic cultures need to be especially sensitive to Islamic beliefs and customs. In Iran, for example, the Ministry of Islamic Guidance and Culture posts a reminder to visiting female journalists: "The body is a tool for the spirit and the spirit is a divine song. The holy tool should not be used for sexual intentions." Although the issue of *hejab* (Islamic dress) is hotly debated, both Iranian and non-Iranian women are officially expected to wear body-concealing garments. They are also expected to wear scarves over their hair because hair is considered enticing.

Hinduism   Hinduism formed around 4,000 years ago in present-day India, where over 90 percent of its 900 million adherents live. It is also the majority religion of Nepal and a secondary religion in Bangladesh, Bhutan, and Sri Lanka. Considered by some to be a way of life rather than a religion, Hinduism recalls no founder and recognizes no central authority or spiritual leader. Integral to the Hindu faith is the caste system described earlier.

Hindus believe in reincarnation—the rebirth of the human soul at the time of death. For many Hindus the highest goal of life is *moksha*—escaping from the cycle of reincarnation and entering a state of eternal happiness called *nirvana*. Hindus tend to disdain materialism. Strict Hindus do not eat or willfully harm any living creature because it may be a reincarnated human soul. Because Hindus consider cows sacred animals, they do not eat beef; consuming milk is considered a means of religious purification. Firms such as McDonald's (www.mcdonalds.com) must work closely with government and religious officials in India to respect Hindu beliefs. In many regions, McDonald's has removed all beef products from its menu and prepares vegetable and fish products in separate kitchen areas. And for those Indians who do eat red meat (but not cows because of their sacred status), the company sells the Maharaja Mac, made of lamb, in place of the Big Mac.

In India, there have been attacks on Western consumer-goods companies in the name of preserving Indian culture and Hindu beliefs. Some companies such as Pepsi-Cola (www.pepsi.com) have been vandalized, and local officials even shut down a KFC restaurant (www.kfc.com) for a time. Although it currently operates in India, Coca-Cola (www.cocacola.com) once left the market completely rather than succumb to demands that it reveal its secret formula to authorities. India's investment environment has improved greatly in recent years. Yet labor–management relations sometimes deteriorate to such a degree that strikes cut deeply into productivity.

Buddhism   Buddhism was founded about 2,600 years ago in India by a Hindu prince named Siddhartha Gautama. Today, Buddhism has around 380 million followers, mostly in China, Tibet, Korea, Japan, Vietnam, and Thailand, and there are pockets of Buddhists in Europe and the Americas. Although founded in India, Buddhism has relatively few adherents

Buddhism instructs its followers to live a simple life void of materialistic ambitions. Buddhism also teaches that seeking pleasure for the human senses causes suffering. But as globalization pries open Asia's markets, the products of Western multinationals are streaming in. Here a young Buddhist monk passes in front of an advertisement for Heineken beer. Do you think Asian cultures can modernize while retaining their traditional values and beliefs?
Source: Emmanuel Dunand/AFP. Getty Images, Inc.–Agence France Presse.

there. Unlike Hinduism, Buddhism rejects the caste system of Indian society. But like Hinduism, Buddhism promotes a life centered on spiritual rather than worldly matters. In a formal ceremony, Buddhists take refuge in the "three jewels": the Buddha, the *dharma* (his teachings), and the *sangha* (community of enlightened beings). They seek *nirvana* (escape from reincarnation) through charity, modesty, compassion for others, restraint from violence, and general self-control.

Although monks at many temples are devoted to lives of solitary meditation and discipline, many other Buddhist priests are dedicated to lessening the burden of human suffering. They finance schools and hospitals across Asia and are active in worldwide peace movements. In Tibet, where most people still acknowledge the exiled Dalai Lama as the spiritual and political head of the Buddhist culture, the Chinese communist government suppresses allegiance to any outside authority. In the United States, a coalition of religious groups, human rights advocates, and supporters of the Dalai Lama continue to press the U.S. Congress to apply economic sanctions against countries, such as China, that are seen as practicing religious persecution.

Confucianism   An exiled politician and philosopher named Kung-fu-dz (pronounced *Confucius* in English) began teaching his ideas in China nearly 2,500 years ago. Today, China is home to most of Confucianism's 225 million followers. Confucian thought is also ingrained in the cultures of Japan, South Korea, and nations with large numbers of ethnic Chinese, such as Singapore.

South Korean business practice reflects Confucian thought in its rigid organizational structure and unswerving reverence for authority. Whereas Korean employees do not question strict chains of command, non-Korean managers and workers often feel differently. Efforts to apply Korean-style management in overseas subsidiaries have caused some high-profile disputes with U.S. executives and even physical confrontations with factory workers in Vietnam.

Some observers contend that the Confucian work ethic and educational commitment helped spur East Asia's phenomenal economic growth. But others respond that the link between culture and economic growth is weak. They argue that economic, historical, and international factors are at least as important as culture. They say Chinese leaders distrusted Confucianism for centuries because they believed that it stunted economic growth. Likewise, many Chinese despised merchants and traders because their main objective (earning money) violated Confucian beliefs. As a result, many Chinese businesspeople moved to Indonesia, Malaysia, Singapore, and Thailand, where they launched successful businesses. Today, these countries (along with Taiwan) are financing much of China's economic growth.

Judaism   More than 3,000 years old, Judaism was the first religion to preach belief in a single God. Nowadays, Judaism has roughly 18 million followers worldwide. In Israel, Orthodox ("fully observant") Jews make up 12 percent of the population and constitute an increasingly important economic segment. In Jerusalem, there is even a modeling agency that specializes in casting Orthodox Jews in ads aimed both inside and outside the Orthodox community. Models include scholars and one rabbi. In keeping with Orthodox principles, women model only modest clothing and never appear in ads alongside men.

Employers and human resource managers must be aware of important days in the Jewish faith. Because the Sabbath lasts from sundown on Friday to sundown on Saturday, work schedules might need adjustment. Devout Jews want to be home before sundown on Fridays. On the Sabbath itself, they do not work, travel, or carry money. Several other important observances are Rosh Ha-Shanah (the two-day Jewish New Year, in September or October), Yom Kippur (the Day of Atonement, 10 days after New Year), Passover (which celebrates the Exodus from Egypt, in March or April each year), and Hanukkah (which celebrates an ancient victory over the Syrians, usually in December).

Marketers must take into account foods that are banned among strict Jews. Pork and shellfish (such as lobster and crab) are prohibited. Meat is stored and served separately from milk. Other meats must be slaughtered according to a practice called *shehitah*. Meals prepared according to Jewish dietary traditions are called *kosher*. Most airlines offer *kosher* meals for Jewish passengers on their flights.

Shinto   Shinto (meaning "way of the gods") arose as the native religion of the Japanese. But today Shinto can claim only about four million strict adherents in Japan. Because modern Shinto preaches patriotism, it is sometimes said that Japan's real religion is nationalism. Shinto teaches sincere and ethical behavior, loyalty and respect toward others, and enjoyment of life.

Shinto beliefs are reflected in the workplace through the traditional practice of lifetime employment (although this is waning today) and through the traditional trust extended between firms and customers. Japanese competitiveness in world markets has benefited from loyal workforces, low employee turnover, and good labor–management cooperation. The phenomenal success of many Japanese companies in recent decades gave rise to the concept of a Shinto work ethic, certain aspects of which have been emulated by Western managers.

Quick Study

1. What are the main beliefs of each of the seven religions presented above?
2. In what ways does religion affect international business activities?
3. Identify the dominant religion in each of the following countries: (a) Brazil, (b) China, (c) India, (d) Ireland, (e) Mexico, (f) Russia, and (g) Thailand.

Personal Communication

People in every culture have a **communication** system to convey thoughts, feelings, knowledge, and information through speech, writing, and actions. Understanding a culture's spoken language gives us great insight into why people think and act the way they do. Understanding a culture's body language helps us avoid sending unintended or embarrassing messages. Let's examine each of these forms of communication more closely.

communication
System of conveying thoughts, feelings, knowledge, and information through speech, writing, and actions.

Spoken and Written Language   Spoken and written language is the most obvious difference we notice when traveling in another country. We overhear and engage in a number of conversations and read many signs and documents to find our way. Understanding a people's language is often essential for success in international business because it is the key to understanding their culture.

Linguistically different segments of a population are often culturally, socially, and politically distinct. Malaysia's population is comprised of Malay (60 percent), Chinese (30 percent), and Indian (10 percent). Although Malay is the official national language, each ethnic group speaks its own language and continues its traditions. The United Kingdom includes England, Northern Ireland, Scotland, and Wales. The native languages of Ireland and Scotland are dialects of *Gaelic*, and the speaking of *Welsh* in Wales predates the use of English in Britain. After decades of decline, Gaelic and Welsh are staging comebacks on radio and television and in school curricula.[9] Read the Global Challenges feature titled, "Speaking in Fewer Tongues," to learn about endangered languages around the world.

RELEVANCE FOR MANAGERS   The importance of understanding local languages is becoming increasingly apparent on the Internet. Roughly two-thirds of all Web pages are in English, but around three-fourths of all Internet users are nonnative English speakers. Software solutions providers are assisting companies from English-speaking countries in adapting their Web sites for global e-business. As these software companies are telling their clients, "The 'e' in e-business doesn't stand for English." Web surfers from cultures across the globe bring their own specific tastes, preferences, and buying habits online with them. The company that can provide its customer in Mexico City, Paris, or Tokyo with a quality buying experience in his or her native language will have an edge on the competition.[10]

Speaking in Fewer Tongues

One day this year, somewhere in the world, an old man or woman will die and with them will go their language. Dozens of languages have just one native speaker still living, and some blame globalization. Here are the facts, the consequences, and the challenge.

- **Some Are Losing.** Of the world's roughly 6,000 languages, about 90 percent have fewer than 100,000 speakers. By the end of this century over half of the world's languages may be lost; perhaps fewer than 1,000 will survive. One endangered language is Aramaic, a 2,500-year-old Semitic language that was once the major language in the Middle East.
- **Some Are Gaining.** Even as minority languages die out, three languages continue to grow in popularity: Mandarin, Spanish, and English. English has emerged as the universal language of business, higher education, diplomacy, science, popular music, entertainment, and international travel. Over 70 nations give special status to English and roughly one-quarter of the world's population is fluent or competent in it.

- **The Consequences.** The loss of a language can mean the loss of a people's culture because it is the vehicle for cultural, spiritual, and intellectual life. What is lost includes prayers, myths, humor, poetry, ceremonies, conversational styles, and terms for emotions, behaviors, and habits. When a language dies, all these must be expressed in a new language with different words, sounds, and grammar. The result is that much of a culture can simply vanish.
- **The Challenge.** Linguists are concerned that such a valuable part of human culture could vanish. The impending loss of more languages has linguists creating videotapes, audiotapes, and written records of endangered tongues before they disappear. Communities themselves are also taking action. In New Zealand, Maori communities set up nursery schools called *kohanga reo*, or "language nests," that are staffed by elders and conducted entirely in Maori.
- **Want to Know More?** Visit the Linguistic Society of America (www.lsadc.org), European Union's Eurolang (www.eurolang.net), and Foundation for Endangered Languages (www.ogmios.org).

Language proficiency is crucial in production facilities where nonnative managers are supervising local employees. One U.S. manager in Mexico was confused when his seemingly relaxed and untroubled workers went on strike. The problem lay in different cultural perspectives. Mexican workers generally do not take the initiative in problem solving and workplace complaints. Workers concluded the plant manager knew, but did not care, about their concerns because he did not question employees about working conditions.

American-born Thomas Kwan, who now works for a health products company in Shanghai, China, says similar scenarios occur there. "Whereas Americans are encouraged to challenge their boss to explain things, I have to ask Chinese staff what they think and encourage them to speak up. A lot of [expatriate] managers fail in China because they don't understand that Chinese don't tell you what they think," he says.[11]

Marketers also value insights into the interests, values, attitudes, and habits of teenagers. Habbo (www.habbo.com), the world's largest virtual hangout for teens, surveyed more than 50,000 teenagers in 31 countries to learn how they communicate with each other. The study found that although 72 percent of teens have active e-mail accounts, 76 percent communicate with friends primarily through instant messaging. Teens reserve e-mail for nonpersonal needs such as school, work, and corresponding with family members. Knowledge of these habits help marketers to better target promotions.[12]

LANGUAGE BLUNDERS   Advertising slogans and company documents must be translated carefully so messages are received precisely as intended. There are many stories of companies making terrible language blunders in their international business dealings. General Motors' Chevrolet division (www.chevrolet.com) made perhaps the most well-known blunder when it first launched its Chevrolet Nova in Spanish-speaking markets. The company failed to notice beforehand that "No va" means "No go" in Spanish. Chevrolet had far greater success when it renamed the car *Caribe* (piranha)—the voraciously carnivorous freshwater fish native to South America that attacks and destroys living animals! In Sweden, Kellogg (www.kellogg.com) had to rename its Bran Buds cereal because the Swedish translation came out roughly as "burned farmer." San Francisco-based start-up Evite (www.evite.com) allows visitors to its Web site to send e-mail invitations to special events. But the company's name presents a problem internationally. In the Romance languages, such as French and Spanish, variations of the verb *evite* (*eviter* and *evitar*) mean "to shun or to avoid." Apparently "Avoid My Party" couldn't get European partygoers excited. CEO Josh Silverman concedes, "It's a terrific brand in English, but we're going to have to rebrand for the Romance languages."[13] Several other humorous translation blunders include the following:

- An English-language sign in a Moscow hotel read, "You are welcome to visit the cemetery where famous Russian composers, artists, and writers are buried daily except Thursday."
- A sign for English-speaking guests in a Tokyo hotel read, "You are respectfully requested to take advantage of the chambermaids."
- An airline ticket office in Copenhagen read in English, "We take your bags and send them in all directions."
- A Japanese knife manufacturer labeled its exports to the United States with "Caution: Blade extremely sharp! Keep out of children."
- Braniff Airlines' English-language slogan "Fly in Leather" was translated into "Fly Naked" in Spanish.

Such blunders are not the exclusive domain of humans. The use of machine translation—computer software used to translate one language into another—is booming along with the explosion in the number of nonnative English speakers using the Internet. Nowhere is this technology hotter than in Asia, although its results are often less than perfect. One Singapore-based search engine allows its users to search the Internet in English and Asian languages, translate Web pages, and compose an e-mail in one language and send it in another. The computers attempted a translation of the following: "The Chinese Communist Party is debating whether to drop its ban on private-enterprise owners being allowed to join the party." And it came up with this in Chinese: "The Chinese Communist Party is debating whether to deny its ban in join the Party is allowed soldier enterprise owners on."[14] Various other machine translators turned the French version of "I don't care" ("*Je m'en fou*") into "I myself in crazy," "I of insane," and "Me me in madman."[15]

LINGUA FRANCA   A **lingua franca** is a third or "link" language understood by two parties who speak different native languages. The original *lingua franca* arose to support ancient trading activities and contained a mixture of Italian and French, along with Arabic, Greek, and Turkish. Although only 5 percent of the world's population speaks English as a first language, it is the most common *lingua franca* in international business, followed closely by French and Spanish.

The Cantonese dialect of Chinese spoken in Hong Kong and the Mandarin dialect spoken in Taiwan and on the Chinese mainland are so different that a *lingua franca* is often preferred. And although India's official language is Hindi, its *lingua franca* among the multitude of dialects is English because it was once a British colony. Yet many young people speak what is referred to as "Hinglish"—a combination of Hindi, Tamil, and English words mixed within a single sentence. Finally, even for the single *lingua franca* of English, differences exist. British-accented English is losing out to North American–accented English in certain locales, particularly in China and South Korea, due to their ever-expanding commercial ties with North America.[16] Multinational corporations sometimes choose a *lingua franca* for official internal communications because they operate in many nations, each with its own language. Companies that use English for internal correspondence

lingua franca
Third or "link" language understood by two parties who speak different native languages.

include Philips (www.philips.com) (a Dutch electronics firm), Asea Brown Boveri (www.abb.com) (a Swiss industrial giant), and Alcatel-Lucent (www.alcatel-lucent.com) (a French telecommunications firm).

body language

Language communicated through unspoken cues, including hand gestures, facial expressions, physical greetings, eye contact, and the manipulation of personal space.

Body Language   **Body language** communicates through unspoken cues, including hand gestures, facial expressions, physical greetings, eye contact, and the manipulation of personal space. Similar to spoken language, body language communicates both information and feelings and differs greatly from one culture to another. Italians, French, Arabs, and Venezuelans, for example, animate conversations with lively hand gestures and other body motions. Japanese and Koreans, although more reserved, communicate just as much information through their own body languages; a look of the eye can carry as much or more meaning as two flailing arms.

Most body language is subtle and takes time to recognize and interpret. For example, navigating the all-important handshake in international business can be tricky. In the United States it is a firm grip and can include several pumps of the arm. But in the Middle East and Latin America a softer clasp of the hand with little or no arm pump is the custom. And in some countries, such as Japan, people do not shake hands at all, but bow to one another. Bows of respect carry different meanings, usually depending on the recipient. Associates of equal standing bow about 15 degrees toward one another. But proper respect for an elder requires a bow of about 30 degrees. Bows of remorse or apology should be about 45 degrees.

Proximity is an extremely important element of body language to consider when meeting someone from another culture. If you stand or sit too close to your counterpart (from their perspective), you may invade their personal space and appear aggressive. If you remain too far away, you risk appearing untrustworthy. For North Americans, a distance of about 19 inches is about right between two speakers. For Western Europeans, 14 to 16 inches seems appropriate, but someone from the United Kingdom might prefer about 24 inches. Koreans and Chinese are likely to be comfortable about 36 inches apart; people from the Middle East will close the distance to about 8 to 12 inches.

Physical gestures often cause the most misunderstanding between people of different cultures because they can convey very different meanings. The thumbs-up sign is vulgar in Italy and Greece but means "all right" or even "great" in the United States. Figure 2.1 demonstrates how the meanings of gestures vary across cultures.

FIGURE 2.1

Regional Differences in the Meaning of Gestures

Although Western Europe may be moving toward economic unity, its tapestry of cultures remains diverse. Gestures, for example, continue to reflect centuries of cultural differences. As in the United States, the thumb-and-index circle means "okay" in most of Europe; in Germany, it's an indelicate reference to the receiver's anatomy. In most of Great Britain— England and Scotland—the finger tapping the nose means, "You and I are in on the secret"; in nearby Wales, however, it means, "You're very nosy." If you tap your temple just about anywhere in Western Europe, you're suggesting that someone is "crazy"; in Holland, however, you'll be congratulating someone for being clever.

Quick Study

1. Define *communication*. Why is knowledge of a culture's spoken language important for international business?

2. Describe the threat faced by endangered languages. What is being done to help them survive?

3. What is a *lingua franca*? Describe its implications for conducting international business.

4. Why is *body language* important for international business? Give several examples of how it differs across cultures.

Education

Education is crucial for passing on traditions, customs, and values. Each culture educates its young people through schooling, parenting, religious teachings, and group memberships. Families and other groups provide informal instruction about customs and how to socialize with others. In most cultures, intellectual skills such as reading and mathematics are taught in formal educational settings. Two important topics in education are education level and brain drain.

Education Level   Data that a government provides on its people's education level must be taken with a grain of salt. Comparisons from country to country can be difficult because many nations rely on literacy tests of their own design. Although some countries administer standardized tests, others require only a signature as proof of literacy. Yet searching for untapped markets or new factory locations can force managers to rely on such undependable benchmarks. As you can see from Table 2.1, some countries have further to go than others in increasing national literacy rates. Around 800 million adults remain illiterate globally. And although global illiteracy rates are higher for women, the gap with men is closing.[17]

Countries with poorly educated populations attract the lowest-paying manufacturing jobs. Nations with excellent programs for basic education tend to attract relatively good-paying industries. Those that invest in worker training are usually repaid in productivity increases and rising incomes. Meanwhile, countries with skilled, highly educated workforces attract all sorts of high-paying jobs, often called "brainpower" industries.

TABLE 2.1 Illiteracy Rates of Selected Countries

Country	Adult Illiteracy Rate (Percentage of People Age 15 and Up)
Burkina Faso	76
Niger	71
Pakistan	50
Morocco	48
Nigeria	31
Egypt	29
Cambodia	26
Saudi Arabia	17
Peru	12
Brazil	11
Zimbabwe	10
Jordan	9
Mexico	8
Philippines	7
Colombia	7
Portugal	6

Emerging economies in Asia owe much of their rapid economic development to solid education systems. Hong Kong, South Korea, Singapore, and Taiwan focus on rigorous mathematical training in primary and secondary schooling. University education concentrates on the hard sciences and aims to train engineers, scientists, and managers. On the other hand, some experts say China's rote-learning education system graduates many bright engineers but few managers. This could pose problems for China as quality managers are what the country needs to take its economy to a higher level.[18]

brain drain
Departure of highly educated people from one profession, geographic region, or nation to another.

The "Brain Drain" Phenomenon   The quality of a nation's education system is related to its level of economic development. **Brain drain** is the departure of highly educated people from one profession, geographic region, or nation to another. Over the years, political unrest and economic hardship forced many Indonesians to flee their homeland for other nations, particularly Hong Kong, Singapore, and the United States. Most of Indonesia's brain drain occurred among Western-educated professionals in finance and technology—exactly the people needed for economic development.

Many countries in Eastern Europe experienced high levels of brain drain early in their transition to market economies. Economists, engineers, scientists, and researchers in all fields fled westward to escape poverty. But as these nations continue their long march away from communism, some are luring professionals back to their homelands—a process known as *reverse brain drain*.

Physical and Material Environments

The physical environment and material surroundings of a culture heavily influence its development and pace of change. In this section, we first look at how physical environment and culture are related and then explore the effect of material culture on business.

Physical Environment   Although the physical environment affects a people's culture, it does not directly determine it. Two aspects of the physical environment that heavily influence a people's culture are topography and climate.

topography
All the physical features that characterize the surface of a geographic region.

TOPOGRAPHY   All the physical features that characterize the surface of a geographic region constitute its **topography**. Some surface features such as navigable rivers and flat plains facilitate travel and contact with others. By contrast, treacherous mountain ranges and large bodies of water can discourage contact. Cultures isolated by topographical features can find themselves less exposed to the cultural traits of other peoples, which can mean slower cultural change.

Topography can impact consumers' product needs. For example, there is little market for Honda scooters (www.honda.com) in most mountainous regions because their engines are too small. These are better markets for the company's more rugged, maneuverable motorcycles with larger engines. Thinner air at higher elevations might also entail modifications in carburetor design for gasoline-powered vehicles.

Topography can have a profound impact on personal communication in a culture. For example, mountain ranges and the formidable Gobi Desert consume two-thirds of China's land surface. Groups living in the valleys of these mountain ranges hold on to their own ways of life and speak their own languages. Although the Mandarin dialect was decreed the national language many years ago, the mountains, desert, and vast expanse of China still impair personal communication and, therefore, the proliferation of Mandarin.

CLIMATE   Climate affects where people settle and helps direct systems of distribution. In Australia, for example, intensely hot and dry conditions in two large deserts and jungle conditions in the northeast pushed settlement to coastal areas. These climatic conditions combined with the higher cost of land transport means coastal waters are still used to distribute products between distant cities.

Climate plays a large role in lifestyle and work habits. The heat of the summer sun grows intense in the early afternoon hours in the countries of southern Europe, northern Africa, and the Middle East. For this reason, people often take afternoon breaks of one or two hours in July and August. People use this time to perform errands, such as shopping, or even take short naps before returning to work until about 7 or 8 p.m. Companies doing business in these regions must adapt to this local tradition.

Climate also impacts customs such as the type of clothing people wear. People in many tropical areas wear little clothing and wear it loosely because of the warm, humid climate. In the desert areas of the Middle East and North Africa, people also wear loose clothing, but they wear long robes to protect themselves from intense sunshine and blowing sand.

Material Culture   All the technology used in a culture to manufacture goods and provide services is called its **material culture**. Material culture is often used to measure the technological advancement of a nation's markets or industries. Generally, a firm enters a new market under one of two conditions: demand for its products has developed or the infrastructure is capable of supporting production operations.

> **material culture**
> All the technology used in a culture to manufacture goods and provide services.

Many regions and nations lack the most basic elements of a modern society's material culture. For example, companies are not flocking to the Southeast Asian nation of Myanmar because the nation lacks both sufficient product demand and an adequate infrastructure. Political and social problems under a repressive military government have stalled Myanmar's economic development. Yet technology is helping some nations at the bottom of the global economic pyramid break down barriers that keep their people mired in poverty.

UNEVEN MATERIAL CULTURE   Material culture often displays uneven development across a nation's geography, markets, and industries. For example, much of China's recent economic progress is occurring in coastal cities. Shanghai has long played an important role in China's international trade because of its strategic location and its superb harbor on the East China Sea. Although it is home to only 1 percent of the total population, Shanghai accounts for about 5 percent of China's total output—including about 12 percent of both its industrial production and its financial-services output.

Likewise, Bangkok, the capital city of Thailand, houses only 10 percent of the nation's population but accounts for about 40 percent of its economic output. Meanwhile, the northern parts of the country remain rural, consisting mostly of farms, forests, and mountains.

Quick Study

1. Why is the education level of a country's people important to international companies?
2. What is meant by the terms *brain drain* and *reverse brain drain*?
3. How are a people's culture and physical environment related?
4. What is the significance of *material culture* for international business?

Classifying Cultures

Throughout this chapter, you've seen how cultures can differ greatly from one another. People living in broadly different cultures tend to respond differently in similar business situations. There are two widely accepted ways to classify cultures based on differences in characteristics such as values, attitudes, social structure, and so on. Let's now take a detailed look at each of these tools: the Kluckhohn–Strodtbeck and Hofstede frameworks.

Kluckhohn–Strodtbeck
framework
Framework for studying cultural
differences along six dimensions,
such as focus on past or future
events and belief in individual or
group responsibility for personal
well-being.

Kluckhohn–Strodtbeck Framework

The **Kluckhohn–Strodtbeck framework** compares cultures along six dimensions. It studies a given culture by asking each of the following questions:[19]

- Do people believe that their environment controls them, that they control the environment, or that they are part of nature?
- Do people focus on past events, on the present, or on the future implications of their actions?
- Are people easily controlled and not to be trusted, or can they be trusted to act freely and responsibly?
- Do people desire accomplishments in life, carefree lives, or spiritual and contemplative lives?
- Do people believe that individuals or groups are responsible for each person's welfare?
- Do people prefer to conduct most activities in private or in public?

Case: Dimensions of Japanese Culture   By providing answers to each of these six questions, we can briefly apply the Kluckhohn–Strodtbeck framework to Japanese culture:

1. *Japanese believe in a delicate balance between people and environment that must be maintained.*   Suppose an undetected flaw in a company's product harms customers using it. In many countries, a high-stakes class-action lawsuit would be filed against the manufacturer on behalf of the victims' families. This scenario is rarely played out in Japan. Japanese culture does not feel that individuals can possibly control every situation but that accidents happen. Japanese victims would receive heartfelt apologies, a promise it won't happen again, and a relatively small damage award.

2. *Japanese culture emphasizes the future.*   Because Japanese culture emphasizes strong ties between people and groups, including companies, forming long-term relationships with people is essential when doing business there. Throughout the business relationship, Japanese companies remain in close, continuous contact with buyers to ensure that their needs are being met. This relationship also forms the basis of a communication channel by which suppliers learn about the types of products and services buyers would like to see in the future.

3. *Japanese culture treats people as quite trustworthy.*   Business dealings among Japanese companies are based heavily on trust. After entered into, an agreement to conduct business is difficult to break unless there are extreme uncontrollable factors at work. This is due to the fear of "losing face" if one cannot keep a business commitment. In addition to business applications, society at large reflects the Japanese concern for trustworthiness. Crime rates are quite low, and the streets of Japan's largest cities are very safe to walk at night.

4. *Japanese are accomplishment-oriented—not necessarily for themselves, but for their employers and work units.*   Japanese children learn the importance of groups early by contributing to the upkeep of their schools. They share duties such as mopping floors, washing windows, cleaning chalkboards, and arranging desks and chairs. They carry such habits learned in school into the adult workplace, where management and labor tend to work together toward company goals. Japanese managers make decisions only after considering input from subordinates. Also, materials buyers, engineers, designers, factory floor supervisors, and marketers cooperate closely throughout each stage of a product's development.

5. *Japanese culture emphasizes individual responsibility to the group and group responsibility to the individual.*   This trait has long been a hallmark of Japanese corporations. Traditionally, subordinates promise hard work and loyalty, and top managers provide job security. But to remain competitive internationally, Japanese companies have eliminated jobs and moved production to low-wage nations like China and Vietnam. As the tradition of job security falls by the wayside, more Japanese workers now consider working for non-Japanese companies, whereas others find work as temporary employees. Although this trait of loyalty is

diminishing somewhat in business, it remains a very prominent feature in other aspects of Japanese society, especially family.

6. *The culture of Japan tends to be public.*   You will often find top Japanese managers located in the center of a large, open-space office surrounded by the desks of many employees. By comparison, Western executives are often secluded in walled offices located on the perimeter of workspaces. This characteristic reaches deep into Japanese society—consider, for example, Japan's continued fondness for public baths.

Hofstede Framework

The **Hofstede framework** compares cultures along five dimensions.[20] Dutch psychologist, Geert Hofstede, developed the framework from a study of more than 110,000 people working in IBM subsidiaries (www.ibm.com) in 40 countries and a follow-up study of students in 23 countries. Let's examine each of these dimensions in detail.[21]

1. *Individualism versus collectivism.*   This dimension identifies the extent to which a culture emphasizes the individual versus the group. Individualist cultures (those scoring high on this dimension) value hard work and promote entrepreneurial risk-taking, thereby fostering invention and innovation. Although people are given freedom to focus on personal goals, they are held responsible for their actions. That is why responsibility for poor business decisions is placed squarely on the shoulders of the individual in charge. At the same time, higher individualism may be responsible for higher rates of employee turnover.

   On the contrary, people in collectivist cultures (those scoring low on this dimension) feel a strong association to groups, including family and work units. The goal of maintaining group harmony is probably most evident in the family structure. People in collectivist cultures tend to work toward collective rather than personal goals and are responsible to the group for their actions. In turn, the group shares responsibility for the well-being of each of its members. Thus, in collectivist cultures success or failure tends to be shared among the work unit, rather than any particular individual receiving all the praise or blame. All social, political, economic, and legal institutions reflect the group's critical role.

2. *Power distance.*   This dimension conveys the degree to which a culture accepts social inequality among its people. A culture with large power distance tends to be characterized by much inequality between superiors and subordinates. Organizations tend also to be more hierarchical, with power deriving from prestige, force, and inheritance. This is why executives and upper management in cultures with large power distance often enjoy special recognition and privileges. On the other hand, cultures with small power distance display a greater degree of equality, with prestige and rewards more equally shared between superiors and subordinates. Power in these cultures (relative to cultures with large power distance) is seen to derive more from hard work and entrepreneurial drive and is therefore often considered more legitimate.

   Figure 2.2 shows how various countries rank according to these first two dimensions: power distance and individualism versus collectivism. What is striking about this figure is the tight grouping of nations within the five clusters (plus Costa Rica). You can see the concentration of mostly African, Asian, Central and South American, and Middle Eastern nations in Quadrant 1 (cultures with relatively larger power distance and lower individualism). By contrast, Quadrants 3 and 2 comprise mostly the cultures of Australia and the nations of North America and Western Europe. These nations had the highest individualism scores, and many had relatively smaller power distance scores.

3. *Uncertainty avoidance.*   This dimension identifies the extent to which a culture avoids uncertainty and ambiguity. A culture with large uncertainty avoidance values security and places its faith in strong systems of rules and procedures in society. It is perhaps not surprising then that cultures with large uncertainty avoidance normally have lower employee turnover, more formal rules for regulating employee behavior, and more

Hofstede framework
Framework for studying cultural differences along five dimensions, such as individualism versus collectivism and equality versus inequality.

FIGURE 2.2

Power Distance and Individualism versus Collectivism

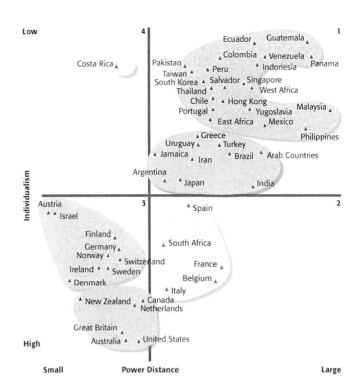

difficulty implementing change. Cultures scoring low on uncertainty avoidance tend to be more open to change and new ideas. This helps explain why individuals in this type of culture tend to be entrepreneurial and organizations tend to welcome the best business practices from other cultures. Because people tend to be less fearful of change, however, these cultures can also suffer from higher levels of employee turnover.

Figure 2.3 plots countries according to the second and third dimensions: power distance and uncertainty avoidance. Although the lines of demarcation are somewhat less obvious in this figure, patterns do emerge among the six clusters (plus Jamaica). Quadrant 4 contains nations characterized by small uncertainty avoidance and small power distance, including Australia, Canada, Jamaica, the United States, and many Western European nations. Meanwhile, Quadrant 2 contains many Asian, Central American, South American, and Middle Eastern nations—nations having large power distance and large uncertainty avoidance indexes.

4. ***Achievement versus nurturing.*** This dimension captures the extent to which a culture emphasizes personal achievement and materialism versus relationships and quality of life. Cultures scoring high on this index tend to be characterized more by personal assertiveness and the accumulation of wealth, typically translating into an entrepreneurial drive. Cultures scoring low on this dimension generally have more relaxed lifestyles, wherein people are more concerned about caring for others as opposed to material gain.

5. ***Long-term orientation.*** This dimension indicates a society's time perspective and an attitude of overcoming obstacles with time, if not with will and strength. It attempts to capture the differences between Eastern and Western cultures. A high-scoring culture (strong long-term orientation) values respect for tradition, thrift, perseverance, and a sense of personal shame. These cultures tend to have a strong work ethic because people expect long-term rewards from today's hard work. A low-scoring culture is characterized by individual stability and reputation, fulfilling social obligations, and reciprocation of greetings and gifts. These cultures can change more rapidly because tradition and commitment are not impediments to change.

Locate your country in Figures 2.2 and 2.3. In your personal experience, do you agree with the placement of your nation in these figures? Do you believe managers in your country display the types of behaviors depicted on each dimension just described?

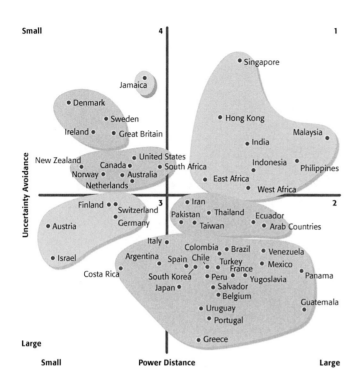

FIGURE 2.3

Power Distance and Uncertainty Avoidance

Quick Study

1. What six dimensions comprise the *Kluckhohn–Strodtbeck framework* for classifying cultures?
2. What are the five dimensions of the *Hofstede framework* for classifying cultures?
3. Briefly explain how each framework can be used to analyze a culture.

Bottom Line FOR BUSINESS

As globalization continues to draw companies into the international arena, understanding local culture can give a company an advantage over rivals. By avoiding ethnocentric thinking, managers can avoid mistakenly disregarding the beneficial aspects of other cultures. By contrast, culturally literate managers who understand local needs and desires bring their companies closer to customers and, therefore, increase their competitiveness. They can become more effective marketers, negotiators, and production managers. Let's explore several areas in which culture has a direct impact on international business activity.

Marketing and Cultural Literacy

Many international companies operating in local markets abroad take advantage of the public relations value of supporting national culture. Some of India's most precious historical monuments and sites are crumbling due to a lack of government funds for upkeep. Companies are helping the

government to maintain key sites and are earning the goodwill of the people.

This chapter introduced the Kluckhohn–Strodtbeck and Hofstede frameworks for classifying cultures. Local culture is important for a company exploring international markets for its products. We see the significance of power distance in the export of luxury items. A nation with large power distance accepts greater inequality among its people and tends to have a wealthy upper class that can afford luxury goods. Thus companies marketing products such as expensive jewelry, high-priced cars, and even yachts could find wealthy market segments within relatively poor nations.

Work Attitudes and Cultural Literacy

National differences in work attitudes are complex and involve other factors in addition to culture. Perceived opportunity for financial reward is no doubt a strong element in attitudes toward work in any culture. Research suggests both U.S. and German employees work longer hours when there is a greater likelihood that good performance will lead to promotion and increased pay. Yet this appears relatively less true in Germany, where wages are less variable and job security and jobless benefits (such as free national health care) are greater. Thus other aspects of German society are at least as important as culture in determining work attitudes. The culturally literate manager understands the complexity of national workplace attitudes and would incorporate this knowledge into reward systems.

Expatriates and Cultural Literacy

As stated in our discussion of classifying cultures, people living in broadly different cultures tend to respond differently in similar business situations. This is why companies that send personnel abroad to unfamiliar cultures are concerned with cultural differences. A Norwegian manager working in Japan for a European car manufacturer, but whose colleagues were mostly Japanese, soon became frustrated with the time needed to make decisions and take action. The main cause for his frustration was that the uncertainty avoidance index for Japan is much larger than that in his native Norway (see Figure 2.3). In Japan, a greater aversion to uncertainty led to the need for a greater number of consultations than would be needed in the home market. The frustrated manager eventually left Japan to return to Europe.

Gender and Cultural Literacy

In Japan, men traditionally hold nearly all positions of responsibility. Women generally serve as office clerks and administrative assistants until their mid to late twenties, when they are expected to marry and then focus on tending to family needs. Although this is still largely true today, progress is being made in expanding the role of women in Japan's business community. Women own nearly a quarter of all businesses in Japan, but many of these businesses are very small and have little economic clout. Greater gender equality prevails in Australia, Canada, Germany, and the United States, but women in these countries still tend to earn less money than men in similar positions.

Chapter Summary

1. Describe culture and explain the significance of both national culture and subcultures.
   - *Culture* is the set of values, beliefs, rules, and institutions held by a specific group of people.
   - Managers should try to avoid *ethnocentricity* (the tendency to view one's own culture as superior to others) and develop *cultural literacy* (detailed knowledge necessary to function effectively in another culture).
   - We are conditioned to think in terms of national culture—that is, to equate a nation-state and its people with a single culture.
   - Governments promote national culture and intervene in business to protect it from the influence of other cultures.
   - Most nations are also home to numerous *subcultures*—groups of people who share a unique way of life within a larger, dominant culture.
   - Subcultures contribute greatly to national culture and must be considered in marketing and production decisions.
2. Identify the components of culture and describe their impact on international business.
   - *Aesthetics* help determine which colors and symbols will be effective in promotions and advertising.
   - *Values* influence a people's *attitudes* toward time, work and achievement, and cultural change.
   - Knowledge of *manners* and *customs* is necessary for negotiating, marketing products, and managing operations in other cultures.
   - *Social structure* affects business decisions including production-site selection, advertising methods, and the costs of doing business in a country.
   - Different *religions* take different views of work, savings, and material goods.
   - Understanding a people's system of *personal communication* provides insight into their values and behavior.
   - A culture's *education* level affects the quality of the workforce and a people's standard of living.
   - *Physical* and *material environments* influence work habits and preferences for products such as clothing and food.
3. Describe cultural change and explain how companies and culture affect each other.
   - *Cultural change* occurs when people integrate into their culture the gestures, material objects, traditions, or concepts of another culture through *cultural diffusion*.
   - Globalization and technology are increasing the pace of cultural change around the world.

- Companies influence culture when they import new products, policies, and business practices into a host country.
- Companies should try to avoid *cultural imperialism*—the replacement of one culture's traditions, folk heroes, and artifacts with substitutes from another.
- Cultures affect management styles, work scheduling, and reward systems.
- Adapting to local cultures around the world means heeding the maxim "Think globally, act locally."

4. Explain how the physical environment and technology influence culture.
- A people's *physical environment* includes *topography* and climate and how people relate to their surroundings.
- Cultures isolated by topographical barriers, such as mountains or seas, normally change relatively slowly, and their languages are often distinct.
- Climate affects a people's work hours, clothing, and food.
- *Material culture* refers to all the technology a culture uses to manufacture goods and provide services, and it can be uneven within a nation.

- Businesspeople measure material culture to determine whether a market has developed adequate demand for a company's products and whether it can support production activities.

5. Describe the two main frameworks used to classify cultures and explain their practical use.
- The *Kluckhohn–Strodtbeck framework* compares cultures along six dimensions by seeking answers to questions on topics including a people's: (1) relation to the environment; (2) focus on past, present, or future; (3) trustworthiness; (4) desire for accomplishment; (5) group-individual responsibility; and (6) public vs. private nature.
- The *Hofstede framework* compares cultures along five dimensions including a people's: (1) individualism versus collectivism; (2) power distance; (3) uncertainty avoidance; (4) achievement vs. nurturing; and (5) long-term orientation.
- Taken together, these frameworks help companies understand many aspects of a culture including risk-taking, innovation, job mobility, team cooperation, pay levels, and hiring practices.

Talk It Over

1. Two students are discussing the various reasons why they are not studying international business. "International business doesn't affect me," declares the first student. "I'm going to stay here, not work in some foreign country." "Yeah, me neither," agrees the second. "Besides, some cultures are real strange. The sooner other countries start doing business our way, the better." What counterarguments can you present to these students' perceptions?

2. In this exercise, two groups of four students each will debate the benefits and drawbacks of individualist versus collectivist cultures. After the first student from each side has spoken, the second student questions the opponent's arguments, looking for holes and inconsistencies. A third student attempts to reply to these counterarguments. Then a fourth student summarizes each side's arguments. Finally, the class votes on which team presented the more compelling case.

Teaming Up

1. Research Project. Select a company in your city or town that does business internationally and make an appointment to interview the owner or a senior manager. Your team's goal is to learn how cultural differences affect the decisions of this business as it pursues international opportunities. How does the company balance the need for global efficiency and local responsiveness in a cultural sense? Has local culture ever required the company to alter its personnel or corporate practices? Be sure to ask your interviewee for specific examples. Present a brief talk or paper on your group's interview findings.

2. Market Entry Strategy Project. This exercise corresponds to the *MESP* online simulation. For the nation you are studying, list several of its people's manners and customs. What values do people hold dear? Describe their attitude toward time, work, and cultural change. What religions are practiced there? What language(s) are spoken? What ethnicities reside in the nation, and do they form distinct subcultures? Describe the nation's social structure and its education system. Turn to Figures 2.2 and 2.3 and either: (a) explain why you think the nation appears where it does, or (b) identify where you think it belongs on the figure and explain why. Integrate your findings into your completed *MESP* report.

Key Terms

aesthetics	cultural trait	material culture
attitudes	culture	popular custom
body language	customs	social group
brain drain	ethnocentricity	social mobility
caste system	folk custom	social stratification
class system	Hofstede framework	social structure
communication	Kluckhohn–Strodtbeck	subculture
cultural diffusion	framework	topography
cultural imperialism	lingua franca	values
cultural literacy	manners	

Take It to the Web

1. **Video Report.** Visit this book's channel on YouTube (YouTube.com/MyIBvideos). Click on "Playlists" near the top of the page and click on the set of videos labeled "Ch 02: Cross-Cultural Business." Watch one video from the list and summarize it in a half-page report. Reflecting on the contents of this chapter, which components of culture can you identify in the video? How might a company engaged in international business act on the information contained in the video?

2. **Web Site Report.** Culture affects the product a company sells in a market or region, how it markets the product, its human resource practices, and so on. It is increasingly important that managers have cultural understanding of their markets in this age of globalization.

Select a well-known multinational company and visit its Web site. Locate the section of the Web site that tells about the company's activities (usually titled "About Us"). Report on the: (1) main products or services the company offers; (2) extent to which the company pursues international business operations (often expressed as percentage of sales or assets); (3) ways that the company has adapted to cultures around the world; and (4) general policies it follows in doing business internationally.

Regarding its Internet presence, does the company offer its Web site in another widely spoken language? Find and click on several of the company's other national Web sites. What kinds of products are advertised on the home page of the different sites? Can you identify how the company adapts its Web site to suit cultural preferences?

Ethical Challenges

1. The Netherlands-based software company you work for has decided to outsource content development to India. You are in charge of the project and have been asked to organize the development team. Do you think it will be possible to uphold the management style that your company currently employs? Should your company be prepared to adjust to local Indian managerial style and human resources practices?

2. You are the owner of an athletic shoe manufacturer, with factories in several countries around the world. Outsourcing work is easy for your company, as developing countries are drawn to your company's ability to create jobs. One of your oldest factories is in Indonesia, victim of a disease epidemic that has slowed production to a standstill. This factory has been your highest producer in the past, and the managers have been loyal to the company. Do you close the factory and relocate due to the drop in production, or do you wait for the epidemic to pass? How strongly do you feel about rewarding the factory's past efforts and loyalty to the company?

3. As the president of a troubled manufacturing company, you are concerned about low production in your foreign facilities. The newest foreign plant, however, allows you to pay the lowest wages thus far and is producing at a much higher rate than the rest. Although you are pleased with this facility's output, rumors have been spreading that the plant is forcing employees to work unreasonable hours. Upon investigating these claims, you find that they are true. Do you allow the plant to continue running as it is because of the high success rate? Or do you make some changes in the way the plant is run and suffer the losses?

PRACTICING INTERNATIONAL MANAGEMENT CASE

A Tale of Two Cultures

Many cultures in Asia are in the midst of an identity crisis. In effect, they are being torn between two worlds. Pulling in one direction is a traditional value system derived from agriculture-based communities and extended families—that is, elements of a culture in which relatives take care of one another and state-run welfare systems are unnecessary. Pulling from the opposite direction is a new set of values emerging from manufacturing- and finance-based economies—elements of a culture in which workers must often move to faraway cities to find work, sometimes leaving family members to fend for themselves.

For decades, Western multinationals set up factories across Southeast Asia to take advantage of relatively low-cost labor. Later, local companies sprang up and became competitive global players in their own right. Spectacular rates of economic growth in a few short decades elevated living standards beyond what was thought possible. Young people in Malaysia and Thailand felt the lure of "Western" brands. Gucci handbags (www.gucci.com), Harley-Davidson motorcycles (www.h-d.com), and other global brands became common symbols of success. Many parents felt brand-consciousness among their teenage children signaled family-wide success.

Despite the growing consumer society, polls of young people show them holding steadfast to traditional values such as respect for family and group harmony. Youth in Hong Kong, for example, overwhelmingly believe that parents should have a say in how hard they study, in how they treat family members and elders, and in their choice of friends.

Now globalization is washing over India. An explosion in outsourcing jobs is causing a social revolution among India's graduates of technical colleges and universities. Unlike India's traditional high-tech service jobs, young call-center staffers are in direct contact with Western consumers, answering inquiries on items such as tummy crunchers and diet pills. For these young, mostly female staffers, the work means money, independence, and freedom—sometimes far away from home in big cities such as Bangalore and Mumbai. But in addition to the training in American accents and geography, they are learning new ideas about family, materialism, and relationships.

Parents are suspicious of call-center work because it must typically be performed nights in India, when consumers are awake in Canada, Europe, or the United States. When her parents objected, Binitha Venugopal quit her call-center job in favor of a "regular" daytime job. Binitha says her former coworkers are materialistic, their values are changing, and that dating and live-in relationships among them are common. Indian tradition dictates that young adults live with their parents at least until they get married (typically to someone their parents choose).

Roopa Murthy works for an Indian company that offers call-center and back-office services. Roopa moved to Bangalore from her native Mysore in 2002 armed with an accounting degree. She now earns $400 per month, which is several times what her father earned before he retired from his government job. Roopa now wears her hair short, and it is styled like that of her idol, Dana Scully from the TV show "X-Files," whose name she also adopted as her "telephone name." She has tossed aside her *salwar kameez*, the traditional loose-fitting clothing she wore back home, in favor of designer-labeled Western attire.

Although she once shunned drinking and her curfew at home was 9 p.m., Roopa now frequents a pub called Geoffrey's, where she enjoys dry martinis and rum, and The Club, a suburban disco. After sending money home to her parents, she has enough left over to spend on imported cosmetics, jeans, a cell phone, and dinner at an American chain restaurant. Roopa confesses that she is "seeing someone" but that her parents would disapprove, adding "it is difficult to talk to Indian parents about things like boyfriends." She said she sometimes envies her callers' lives but that she hopes her job will help her succeed. "I may be a small-town girl, but there is no way I'm going back to Mysore after this," she said.

Arundhati Roy, an Indian novelist and activist, argues that call centers strip young Indian workers of their cultural identities, for example, by making them use American names on the phone. She wrote that call centers show "how easily an ancient civilization can be made to abase itself completely." Many observers wonder whether Asia can embrace modernization and yet retain traditional values.

Thinking Globally

1. If your international firm were doing business in Asia, would you feel partly responsible for these social trends? Is there anything that your company could do to ease the tensions these cultures are experiencing? Be specific.

2. In your opinion, is globalization among the causes of the increasing incidence of divorce, crime, and drug abuse in Asia? Why or why not?

3. Broadly defined, Asia comprises over 60 percent of the world's population—a population that practices Buddhism, Confucianism, Hinduism, Islam, and numerous other religions. Given the fact that there are considerable cultural differences between countries such as China, India, Indonesia, Japan, and Malaysia, is it possible to carry on a valid discussion of "Asian" values? Why or why not?

4. Consider the following statement: "Economic development and capitalism require a certain style of doing business in the twenty-first century. The sooner Asian cultures adapt the better." Do you agree or disagree? Explain.

CHAPTER 3

Understanding the Role of Culture

OBJECTIVES:

1. To understand how culture affects all aspects of international management.

2. To be able to distinguish the major dimensions which define cultural differences among societies or groups.

3. To emphasize the need for international managers to have cultural intelligence in order to interact successfully in host countries.

4. To recognize the critical value differences which frequently affect job behaviors.

5. To be able to develop a working "cultural profile" typical of many people within a certain society, as an aid to expected attitudes toward work, negotiations, etc.

6. To understand the interaction between culture and the use of the internet.

Opening Profile: Adjusting Business to Saudi Arabian Culture

For most outsiders, Saudi Arabia is a land of contrasts and paradoxes. (Map 3-1 shows its location.) It has supermodern cities, but its strict Islamic religious convictions and ancient social customs, on which its laws and customs depend, often clash with modern economic and technical realities. Saudi Arabians sometimes employ latitude in legal formation and enforcement to ease these clashes and sometimes accommodate different behaviors from foreigners. Nevertheless, many foreigners misunderstand Saudi laws and customs or find them contrary to their own value systems. Foreign companies have had mixed success in Saudi Arabia, due in large part to how well they understood and adapted imaginatively to Saudi customs.

Companies from countries with strict separation between state and religion or where few people actively engage in religion find Saudi Arabia's pervasiveness of religion daunting. Religious decrees have sometimes made companies rescind activities. For example, an importer halted sales of the children's game Pokémon because the game might encourage the un-Islamic practice of gambling, and a franchisor was forced to remove the face under the crown in Starbucks' logo because Saudi authorities felt the public display of a woman's face was religiously immoral. However, most companies know the requirements in advance. For instance, Coty Beauty omits models' faces on point-of-purchase displays that it depicts in other countries. Companies know that they must remove the heads and hands from mannequins and must not display them scantily clad. Companies, such as McDonald's, dim their lights, close their doors, and stop attending to customers during the five times per day that men are called to pray. Companies also adjust voluntarily to gain the good will of customers—for example, by converting revenue-generating space to prayer areas. (Saudi Arabian Airlines does this in the rear of its planes, and the U.K.'s Harvey Nichols does this in its department store.) During the holy period of Ramadan, people are less active during the day because they fast, so many stores shift some operating hours to the evenings when people prefer to shop.

In 2000, Saudi Arabia ratified an international agreement designed to eliminate the discrimination of women; however, its prescribed behaviors for women appear paradoxical to outsiders. On the one hand, women now outnumber men in Saudi Arabian universities and own about 20 percent of all Saudi businesses. (There are separate male and female universities, and female-owned businesses can sell only to women.) Women also comprise a large portion of Saudi teachers and doctors. On the other hand, women account for only about 7 percent of the workforce. They cannot have private law or architectural firms, nor can they be engineers. They are not permitted to drive, because this may lead to evil behavior. They must wear *abayas* (robes) and cover their hair completely when in public. They cannot work alongside men except in the medical profession, and they cannot sell directly to male customers. If they are employed where men work, they must have separate work entrances and be separated from males by partitions. They must be accompanied by an adult male relative when dealing with male clerks.

MAP 3-1 Saudi Arabia comprises most of the Arabian peninsula. All of the countries bordering Saudi Arabia are Arab countries (meaning that the first language is Arabic), and all are predominately Islamic.

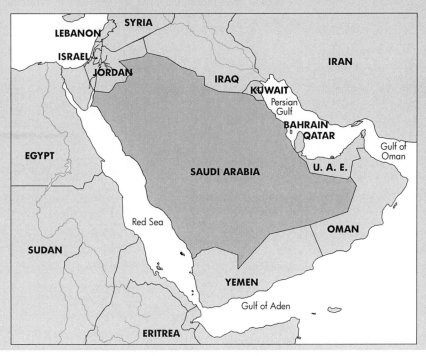

The female prescriptions have implications for business operations. For example, the Saudi American Bank established branches for and staffed only by women. Pizza Hut installed two dining rooms—one for single men and one for families. (Women do not eat there without their families.) Both Harvey Nichols and Saks Fifth Avenue have created women-only floors in their department stores. On lower levels, there is mixed shopping, all male salespeople (even for products like cosmetics and bras), and no changing rooms or places to try cosmetics. On upper floors, women can check their *abayas* and shop in jeans, spandex, or whatever. The stores have also created drivers' lounges for their chauffeurs. A downside is that male store managers can visit upper floors only when the stores are closed, which limits their observations of situations that might improve service and performance. Similarly, market research companies cannot rely on discussions with family-focused groups to determine marketing needs. Because men do much more of the household purchasing, companies target them more in their marketing than in other countries.

Why do high-end department stores and famous designers operate in Saudi Arabia where women cover themselves in *abayas* and men typically wear *thobes* (long robes)? Simply, the many very rich people in Saudi Arabia are said to keep Paris couture alive. Even though Saudi Arabia prohibits fashion magazines and movies, this clientele knows what is in fashion. (The government also prohibits satellite dishes, but some estimates say that two-thirds of Saudi homes have them.) Women buy items from designers' collections, which they wear abroad or in Saudi Arabia only in front of their husbands and other women. Underneath their *abayas*, they often wear very expensive jewelry, makeup, and clothing. Wealthy men also want the latest high-end fashions when traveling abroad.

Another paradox is that about 60 percent of the Saudi private workforce is foreign, even though the unemployment rate is about 30 percent. Changing economic conditions are at least partially responsible for this situation. In the early 1980s, Saudi oil revenues caused per capita income to jump to about $28,000, but this plummeted below $7,000 by the early 2000s. When incomes were high, Saudis brought in foreigners to do most of the work. At the same time, the government liberally supported university training, including study abroad. Saudis developed a mentality of expecting foreigners to do all the work, or at least some of the work, for them. The New Zealand head of National Biscuits & Confectionery said that Saudis now want only to be supervisors and complain if they have to work at the same level as people from Nepal, Bangladesh, and India. Although the government has taken steps to replace foreign workers with Saudis, prevailing work attitudes impede this transition. For example, the acceptance by a Saudi of a bellboy job at the Hyatt Regency hotel in Jidda was so unusual that Saudi newspapers put his picture on their front pages.

Saudi Arabian legal sanctions seem harsh to many outsiders. Religious patrols may hit women if they show any hair in public. The government carries out beheadings and hand-severances in public and expects passers-by to observe the punishments, some of which are for crimes that would not be offenses in other countries. For example, the government publicly beheaded three men in early 2002 for being homosexuals. However, there are inconsistencies. For example, religious patrols are more relaxed about women's dress codes in some Red Sea resorts, and they are more lenient toward the visiting female executives of MNEs than toward Saudi women. Whereas they don't allow Saudi women to be flight attendants on Saudi Arabian Airlines because they would have to work alongside men, they permit women from other Arab countries to do so. Further, in foreign investment compounds where almost everyone is a foreigner, these religious patrols make exceptions to most of the strict religious prescriptions.

Interesting situations concern the charging of interest and the purchase of accident insurance, both of which are disallowed under strict Islamic interpretations of the Koran. In the case of interest, the Saudi government gives interest-free loans for mortgages. This worked well when Saudi Arabia was awash with oil money, but borrowers must now wait about 10 years for a loan. In the case of accident insurance (by strict Islamic doctrine, there are no accidents, only preordained acts of God), the government eliminated prohibitions because businesses needed the insurance.

Personal interactions between cultures are tricky, and those between Saudis and non-Saudis are no exception. For example, Parris-Rogers International (PRI), a British publishing house, sent two salesmen to Saudi Arabia and paid them on a commission basis. They expected that by moving aggressively, the two men could make the same number of calls as they could in the United Kingdom. They were used to working eight-hour days, to having the undivided attention of potential clients, and to restricting conversation to the business transaction. To them, time was money. However, they found that appointments seldom began at the scheduled time and most often took place at cafés where the Saudis would engage in what the salesmen considered idle chitchat. Whether in a café or in the office, drinking coffee or tea and talking to acquaintances seemed to take precedence over business matters. The salesmen began showing so much irritation at "irrelevant" conversations, delays, and interruptions from friends that they caused irrevocable damage to the company's objectives. The Saudi counterparts considered them rude and impatient.

Whereas businesspersons from many countries invite counterparts to social gatherings at their homes to honor them and use personal relationships to cement business arrangements, Saudis view the home as private and even consider questions about their families as rude and an invasion of privacy. In contrast, Saudi businessmen seldom regard business discussions as private; they thus welcome friends to sit in. The opposite is true in many countries.

In spite of contrasts and paradoxes, foreign companies find ways to be highly successful in Saudi Arabia. In some cases, legal barriers to some products, such as alcoholic beverages and pork products, have created boons for other products, such as soft drinks and turkey ham. In addition, some companies have developed specific practices in response to Saudi conditions and have later benefited from them in their home countries. For example, companies, such as Fuji and Kodak, created technology for while-you-wait photo development for Saudi Arabia because customers wanted to retrieve photos without anyone else seeing them. They transferred this technology to the United States several years later.

Source: John D. Daniels, Lee H. Radebaugh, and Daniel P. Sullivan, *International Business: Environments and Operations*, 10th ed. © 2004. Reprinted by permission of Pearson Education, Inc., Upper Saddle River, NJ.

This chapter's opening profile describes how an understanding of the local culture and business environment can give managers an advantage in competitive industries. Foreign companies—no matter how big—can ignore those aspects to their peril. Such differences in culture and the way of life in other countries necessitate that managers develop international expertise to manage on a contingency basis according to the host-country environment. Powerful, interdependent factors in that environment—political, economic, legal, technological, and cultural—influence management strategy, functions, and processes.

A critical skill for managing people and processes in other countries is **cultural savvy**—that is, a working knowledge of the cultural variables affecting management decisions. (More recently, that skill has become known as cultural intelligence, or cultural quotient (CQ)). Managers have often seriously underestimated the significance of cultural factors. According to numerous accounts, many blunders made in international operations can be attributed to a lack of cultural sensitivity.[1] Examples abound. Scott Russell, senior vice president for human resources at Cendant Mobility in Danbury, Connecticut, recounts the following:

An American company in Japan charged its Japanese HR manager with reducing the workforce. The Japanese manager studied the issue but couldn't find a solution within cultural Japanese parameters; so when he came back to the Americans, he reduced the workforce by resigning—which was not what they wanted.[2]

Cultural sensitivity, or **cultural empathy,** is an awareness and an honest caring about another individual's culture. Such sensitivity requires the ability to understand the perspective of those living in other (and very different) societies and the willingness to put oneself in another's shoes.

International managers can benefit greatly from understanding the nature, dimensions, and variables of a specific culture and how these affect work and organizational processes. This cultural awareness enables them to develop appropriate policies and determine how to plan, organize, lead, and control in a specific international setting. Such a process of adaptation to the environment is necessary to successfully implement strategy. It also leads to effective interaction in a workforce of increasing cultural diversity, in both the United States and other countries.

Company reports and management studies make it clear that a lack of cultural sensitivity costs businesses money and opportunities. One study of U.S. multinational corporations found that poor intercultural communication skills still constitute a major management problem. Managers' knowledge of other cultures lags far behind their understanding of other organizational processes.[3] In a synthesis of the research on cross-cultural training, Black and Mendenhall found that up to 40 percent of expatriate managers leave their assignments early because of poor performance or poor adjustment to the local environment. About half of those who remain are considered only marginally effective. Furthermore, they found that cross-cultural differences are the cause of failed negotiations and interactions, resulting in losses to U.S. firms of over $2 billion a year for failed expatriate assignments alone.[4]

Other evidence indicates, however, that cross-cultural training is effective in developing skills and enhancing adjustment and performance. In spite of such evidence, U.S. firms do little to take advantage of such important research and to incorporate it into their ongoing training programs, whose purpose is ostensibly to prepare managers before sending them overseas.

Too often, the importance of such training in developing cultural sensitivity is realized much too late.

This chapter provides a conceptual framework with which companies and managers can assess relevant cultural variables and develop cultural profiles of various countries. This framework is then used to consider the probable effects of cultural differences on an organization and their implications for management. To do this, the powerful environmental factor of cultural context is examined. The nature of culture and its variables and dimensions are first explored, and then specific differences in cultural values and their implications for the on-the-job behavior of individuals and groups are considered. Cultural variables, in general, are discussed in this chapter. The impact of culture on specific management functions and processes is discussed in later chapters as appropriate.

CULTURE AND ITS EFFECTS ON ORGANIZATIONS

Societal Culture

As generally understood, the **culture** of a society comprises the shared values, understandings, assumptions, and goals that are learned from earlier generations, imposed by present members of a society, and passed on to succeeding generations. This shared outlook results, in large part, in common attitudes, codes of conduct, and expectations that subconsciously guide and control certain norms of behavior.[5] One is born into, not with, a given culture, and gradually internalizes its subtle effects through the socialization process. Culture results in a basis for living grounded in shared communication, standards, codes of conduct, and expectations.[6] Over time, cultures evolve as societies adapt to transitions in their external and internal environments and relationships. A manager assigned to a foreign subsidiary, for example, must expect to find large and small differences in the behavior of individuals and groups within that organization. As depicted in Exhibit 3-1, these differences result from the societal, or sociocultural, variables of the culture, such as religion and language, in addition to prevailing national variables, such as economic, legal, and political factors. National and sociocultural variables, thus, provide the context for the development and perpetuation of cultural variables. These cultural variables, in turn, determine basic attitudes toward work, time, materialism, individualism, and change. Such attitudes affect an individual's motivation and expectations regarding work and group relations, and they ultimately affect the outcomes that can be expected from that individual.

EXHIBIT 3-1   Environmental Variables Affecting Management Functions

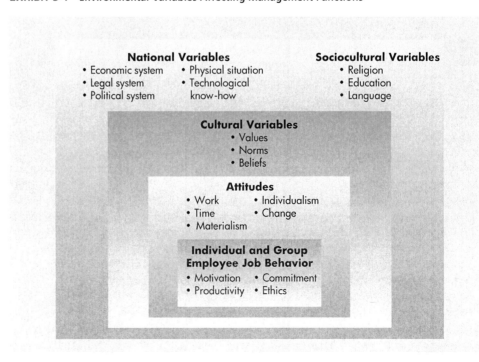

Organizational Culture

Compared to societal culture, which is often widely held within a region or nation, **organizational culture** varies a great deal from one organization, company, institution, or group to another. Organizational culture represents those expectations, norms, and goals held in common by members of that group. For a business example, consider the oft-quoted comparison between IBM, considered traditionally to be very formal, hierarchical, and rules-bound, and with its employees usually in suits, and Apple Computer, whose organizational culture is very organic, or "loose" and informal, with its employees typically wearing casual clothes and interacting informally.

A policy change made by KLM (Royal Dutch Airlines), with which the organizational culture responded to national cultural values and accepted practices, illustrated the way these sets of variables can interact, and how societal culture can influence organizational culture. The culture of social responsiveness in the Netherlands was incorporated into business policy when the airline revised its travel-benefits policy for families of employees. For some time, many KLM stewards had protested the rule that only immediate family members were eligible for low fares on KLM flights. They found it discriminatory that even just-married heterosexual spouses received the benefit, whereas long-term homosexual partners were not eligible. Upon reconsideration, KLM responded that any couple who formally registered as living together, which is a normal legal practice in the Netherlands, would be eligible for the low fares. However, a year had to elapse between partners before a new partner could be registered. By changing its policy, KLM put the emphasis on committed relationships rather than on marital status or sexual preference.

McDonald's provides another example, with its 58 restaurants in Russia. The company's experience with setting up businesses there since the first restaurant opened in Moscow demonstrates the combined effects of national and cultural variables on work. In Russia, local employees require lengthy training to serve up "Bolshoi Maks" in the "McDonald's way." Unfortunately, many Russians are still not familiar with working under the capitalist system; they have been victims of the inertia brought about by the old system of central planning for so long that productivity remains low.

Culture's Effects on Management

Which organizational processes—technical and otherwise—are most affected by cultural differences, and how, is the subject of ongoing cross-cultural management research and debate.[7] Some argue that the effects of culture are more evident at the individual level of personal behavior than at the organizational level, as a result of convergence. **Convergence** describes the phenomenon of the shifting of individual management styles to become more similar to one another. The convergence argument is based on the belief that the demands of industrialization, worldwide coordination, and competition tend to factor out differences in organizational-level processes, such as choice of technology and structure. In a study of Japanese and Korean firms, Lee, Roehl, and Choe found that globalization and firm size were sources of convergence of management styles.[8] These factors are discussed in more detail later in this chapter.

The effects of culture on specific management functions are particularly noticeable when we attempt to impose our own values and systems on another society. Exhibit 3-2 gives some examples of the values typical of U.S. culture, compares some common perspectives held by people in other countries, and shows which management functions might be affected, clearly implying the need for the differential management of organizational processes. For example, American managers plan activities, schedule them, and judge their timely completion based on the belief that people influence and control the future, rather than assuming that events will occur only at the will of Allah, as managers in an Islamic nation might believe.

Many people in the world understand and relate to others only in terms of their own culture. This unconscious reference point of one's own cultural values is called a **self-reference criterion**. The result of such an attitude is illustrated in the following story:

> *Once upon a time there was a great flood, and involved in this flood were two creatures, a monkey and a fish. The monkey, being agile and experienced, was lucky enough to scramble up a tree and escape the raging waters. As he looked down from his safe perch, he saw the poor fish struggling against the swift current. With the very best of intentions, he reached down and lifted the fish from the water. The result was inevitable.*[9]

EXHIBIT 3-2   U.S. Values and Possible Alternatives

Aspects of U.S. Culture*	Alternative Aspect	Examples of Management Function Affected
The individual can influence the future (where there is a will there is a way).	Life follows a preordained course, and human action is determined by the will of God.	Planning and scheduling
The individual can change and improve the environment.	People are intended to adjust to the physical environment rather than to alter it.	Organizational environment, morale, and productivity
An individual should be realistic in his or her aspirations.	Ideals are to be pursued regardless of what is "reasonable."	Goal setting and career development
We must work hard to accomplish our objectives (Puritan ethic).	Hard work is not the only prerequisite for success; wisdom, luck, and time are also required.	Motivation and reward system
Commitments should be honored (people will do what they say they will do).	A commitment may be superseded by a conflicting request, or an agreement may only signify intention and have little or no relationship to the capacity for performance.	Negotiating and bargaining
One should effectively use one's time (time is money that can be saved or wasted).	Schedules are important, but only in relation to other priorities.	Long- and short-range planning
A primary obligation of an employee is to the organization.	The individual employee has a primary obligation to his or her family and friends.	Loyalty, commitment, and motivation
The employer or employee can terminate the relationship.	Employment is for a lifetime.	Motivation and commitment to the company
The best-qualified people should be recruiting selection, given the positions available.	Family, friendship, and other considerations should determine employment practices.	Employment, promotions, and reward

*Aspect here refers to a belief, value, attitude, or assumption that is a part of a culture in that it is shared by a large number of people in that culture.
Source: Excerpted from *Managing Cultural Differences* by Philip R. Harris and Robert T. Moran, 5th ed. Copyright © 2000 by Gulf Publishing Company, Houston, TX. Used with permission. All rights reserved.

The monkey assumed that its frame of reference applied to the fish and acted accordingly. Thus, international managers from all countries must understand and adjust to unfamiliar social and commercial practices—especially the practices of that mysterious and unique nation, the United States. Japanese workers at a U.S. manufacturing plant learned to put courtesy aside and interrupt conversations with Americans when there were problems. Europeans, however, are often confused by Americans' apparent informality, which then backfires when the Europeans do not get work done as the Americans expect.

As a first step toward cultural sensitivity, international managers should understand their own cultures. This awareness helps to guard against adopting either a parochial or an ethnocentric attitude. **Parochialism** occurs, for example, when a Frenchman expects those from or in another country to automatically fall into patterns of behavior common in France. **Ethnocentrism** describes the attitude of those who operate from the assumption that their ways of doing things are best—no matter where or under what conditions they are applied. Companies both large and small have demonstrated this lack of cultural sensitivity in countless subtle (and not so subtle) ways, with varying disastrous effects.

Procter & Gamble (P&G) was one such company. In an early Japanese television commercial for Camay soap, a Japanese woman is bathing when her husband walks into the bathroom. She starts telling him about her new beauty soap. Her husband, stroking her shoulder, hints that he has more on his mind than suds. The commercial, which had been popular in Europe, was a disaster in Japan. For the man to intrude on his wife "was considered bad manners," says Edwin L. Artzt, P&G's vice chairman and international chief. "And the Japanese didn't think it was very funny." P&G has learned from its mistakes and now generates about half of its revenue from foreign sales.[10]

After studying his or her own culture, the manager's next step toward establishing effective cross-cultural relations is to develop cultural sensitivity. Managers not only must be aware of cultural variables and their effects on behavior in the workplace, but also must appreciate cultural diversity and understand how to build constructive working relationships anywhere in the world. The following sections explore cultural variables and dimensions. Later chapters suggest specific ways in which managers can address these variables and dimensions to help build constructive relationships.

Given the great variety of cultures and subcultures around the world, how can a student of cross-cultural management, or a manager wishing to be culturally savvy, develop an understanding of the specific nature of a certain people? With such an understanding, how can a manager anticipate the probable effects of an unfamiliar culture within an organizational setting and thereby manage human resources productively and control outcomes?

One approach is to develop a cultural profile for each country or region with which the company does or is considering doing business. Developing a cultural profile requires some familiarity with the cultural variables universal to most cultures. From these universal variables, managers can identify the specific differences found in each country or people—and hence anticipate their implications for the workplace.

Managers should never assume that they can successfully transplant American, or Japanese, or any other country's styles, practices, expectations, and processes. Instead, they should practice a basic tenet of good management—contingency management. Contingency management requires managers to adapt to the local environment and people and to manage accordingly. That adaptation can be complex because the manager may confront differences not only in culture, but also in business practices.

Influences on National Culture

Managers should recognize, of course, that generalizations in cultural profiles will produce only an approximation, or stereotype, of national character. Many countries comprise diverse **subcultures** whose constituents conform only in varying degrees to the national character. In Canada, distinct subcultures include anglophones and francophones (English-speaking and French-speaking people) and indigenous Canadians.

Above all, good managers treat people as individuals, and they consciously avoid any form of **stereotyping.** However, a cultural profile is a good starting point to help managers develop some tentative expectations—some cultural context—as a backdrop to managing in a specific international setting. It is useful, then, to look at what cultural variables have been studied and what implications can be drawn from the results.

Before we can understand the culture of a society, we need to recognize that there are subsystems in a society which are a function of where people live; these subsystems influence, and are influenced by, people's cultural values and dimensions and so affect their behaviors, both on and off the job. Harris and Moran identified eight categories that form the subsystems in any society.[11] This systems approach to understanding cultural and national variables—and their effects on work behavior—is consistent with the model shown in Exhibit 3-1 that shows those categories as a broad set of influences on societal culture. Those categories are: the *kinship* system of relationships among families; the *education system*; the *economic and political systems*; the associations which make up formal and informal groups; the *health system*; attitudes toward *recreation* and leisure; and—perhaps most importantly—*religion*. Religion underlies both moral and economic norms and influences everyday business transactions and on-the-job behaviors.

CULTURAL VALUE DIMENSIONS

Cultural variables result from unique sets of shared values among different groups of people. Most of the variations between cultures stem from underlying value systems, which cause people to behave differently under similar circumstances. **Values** are a society's ideas about what is good or bad, right or wrong—such as the widespread belief that stealing is immoral and unfair. Values determine how individuals will probably respond in any given circumstance. As a powerful component of a society's culture, values are communicated through the eight subsystems just described and are passed from generation to generation. Interaction and pressure among these subsystems (or more recently from foreign cultures) may provide the impetus for slow change. The dissolution of the Soviet Union and the formation of the Commonwealth of Independent States is an example of extreme political change resulting from internal economic pressures and external encouragement to change.

Project GLOBE Cultural Dimensions

Recent research results on cultural dimensions have been made available by the GLOBE (Global Leadership and Organizational Behavior Effectiveness) Project team. The team comprises 170 researchers who have collected data over seven years on cultural values and practices and leadership attributes from 18,000 managers in 62 countries. Those managers were from a wide variety of industries and sizes of organizations from every corner of the globe. The team identified nine cultural dimensions that distinguish one society from another and have important managerial implications: assertiveness, future orientation, performance orientation, humane orientation, gender differentiation, uncertainty avoidance, power distance, institutional collectivism versus individualism, and in-group collectivism. Only the first four are discussed here; this avoids confusion for readers since the other five dimensions are similar to those researched by Hofstede, which are presented in the next section. (Other research results from the GLOBE Project are presented in subsequent chapters where applicable, such as in the Leadership section in Chapter 11.) The descriptions are as follows and selected results are shown in Exhibit 3-3.[12]

EXHIBIT 3-3   Selected Cultural Dimensions Rankings from the GLOBE Research Project

Country Rankings on Assertiveness

Least Assertive Countries in GLOBE		Medium Assertive Countries in GLOBE		Most Assertive Countries in GLOBE	
Sweden	3.38	Egypt	3.91	Spain	4.42
New Zealand	3.42	Ireland	3.92	United States	4.55
Switzerland	3.47	Philippines	4.01	Greece	4.58
Japan	3.59	Ecuador	4.09	Austria	4.62
Kuwait	3.63	France	4.13	Germany (Former East)	4.73

Country Rankings on Performance Orientation

Least Performance-Oriented Countries in GLOBE		Medium Performance-Oriented Countries in GLOBE		Most Performance-Oriented Countries in GLOBE	
Russia	2.88	Sweden	3.72	United States	4.49
Argentina	3.08	Israel	3.85	Taiwan	4.56
Greece	3.20	Spain	4.01	New Zealand	4.72
Venezuela	3.32	England	4.08	Hong Kong	4.80
Italy	3.58	Japan	4.22	Singapore	4.90

Country Rankings on Future Orientation

Least Future-Oriented Countries in GLOBE		Medium Future-Oriented Countries in GLOBE		Most Future-Oriented Countries in GLOBE	
Russia	2.88	Slovenia	3.59	Denmark	4.44
Argentina	3.08	Egypt	3.86	Canada (English-speaking)	4.44
Poland	3.11	Ireland	3.98	Netherlands	4.61
Italy	3.25	Australia	4.09	Switzerland	4.73
Kuwait	3.26	India	4.10	Singapore	5.07

Country Rankings on Humane Orientation

Least Humane-Oriented Countries in GLOBE		Medium Humane-Oriented Countries in GLOBE		Most Humane-Oriented Countries in GLOBE	
Germany (Former West)	3.18	Hong Kong	3.90	Indonesia	4.69
Spain	3.32	Sweden	4.10	Egypt	4.73
France	3.40	Taiwan	4.11	Malaysia	4.87
Singapore	3.49	United States	4.17	Ireland	4.96
Brazil	3.66	New Zealand	4.32	Philippines	5.12

Source: Adapted from Mansour Javidan and Robert J. House, "Cultural Acumen for the Global Manager: Lessons from Project GLOBE," *Organizational Dynamics* (Spring 2001): 289–305, with permission from Elsevier.

Assertiveness   This dimension refers to how much people in a society are expected to be tough, confrontational, and competitive versus modest and tender. Austria and Germany, for example, are highly assertive societies that value competition and have a "can-do" attitude. This compares with Sweden and Japan, less assertive societies, which tend to prefer warm and co-operative relations and harmony. The GLOBE team concluded that those countries have sympathy for the weak and emphasize loyalty and solidarity.

Future Orientation   This dimension refers to the level of importance a society attaches to future-oriented behaviors such as planning and investing in the future. Switzerland and Singapore, high on this dimension, are inclined to save for the future and have a longer time horizon for decisions. This perspective compares with societies such as Russia and Argentina, which tend to plan more in the shorter term and place more emphasis on instant gratification.

Performance Orientation   This dimension measures the importance of performance improvement and excellence in society and refers to whether or not people are encouraged to strive for continued improvement. Singapore, Hong Kong, and the United States score high on this dimension; typically, this means that people tend to take initiative and have a sense of urgency and the confidence to get things done. Countries like Russia and Italy have low scores on this dimension; they hold other priorities ahead of performance, such as tradition, loyalty, family, and background, and they associate competition with defeat.

Humane Orientation   This dimension measures the extent to which a society encourages and rewards people for being fair, altruistic, generous, caring, and kind. Highest on this dimension are the Philippines, Ireland, Malaysia, and Egypt, indicating a focus on sympathy and support for the weak. In those societies paternalism and patronage are important, and people are usually friendly and tolerant and value harmony. This compares with Spain, France, and the former West Germany, which scored low on this dimension; people in these countries give more importance to power and material possessions, as well as self-enhancement.

Clearly, research results such as these are helpful to managers seeking to be successful in cross-cultural interactions. Anticipating cultural similarities and differences allows managers to develop the behaviors and skills necessary to act and decide in a manner appropriate to the local societal norms and expectations.

Cultural Clusters

Gupta et al., from the GLOBE research team, also analyzed their data on the nine cultural dimensions to determine where similarities cluster geographically. Their results support the existence of ten cultural clusters: South Asia, Anglo, Arab, Germanic Europe, Latin Europe, Eastern Europe, Confucian Asia, Latin America, Sub-Sahara Africa, and Nordic Europe. They point out the usefulness to managers of these clusters:

> *Multinational corporations may find it less risky and more profitable to expand into more similar cultures rather than those which are drastically different.*[13]

These clusters are shown in Exhibit 3-4. To compare two of their cluster findings, for example, Gupta et al. describe the Germanic cluster as masculine, assertive, individualistic, and result-oriented. This compares with the Latin American cluster, which they characterize as practicing high power distance, low performance orientation, uncertainty avoidance, and collective:

> *Latin American societies tend to enact life as it comes, taking its unpredictability as a fact of life, and not overly worrying about results.*[14]

Hofstede's Value Dimensions

Earlier research resulted in a pathbreaking framework for understanding how basic values underlie organizational behavior; this framework was developed by Hofstede, based on his research on over 116,000 people in 50 countries. He proposed four value dimensions: power distance, uncertainty avoidance, individualism, and masculinity.[15] We should be cautious when interpreting these results, however, because his research findings are based on a sample drawn from one

EXHIBIT 3-4   Geographic Culture Clusters

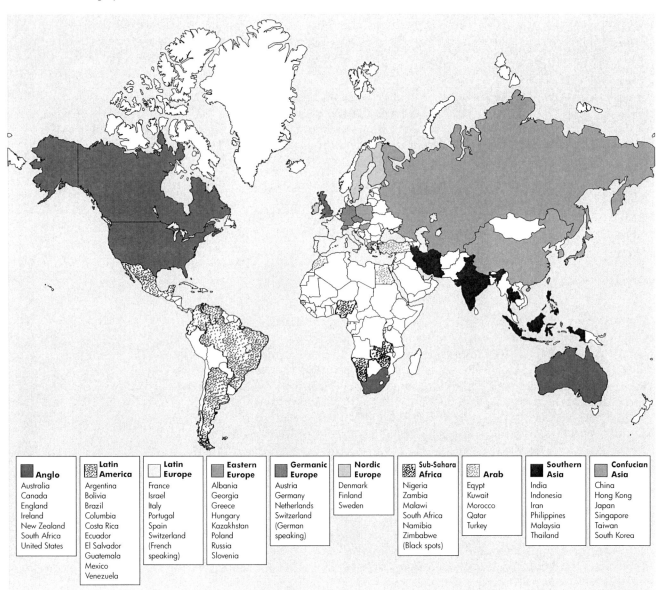

Source: Data from V. Gupta, P. J. Hanes, and P. Dorfman, *Journal of World Business* 37, no. 1 (2002): 13.

multinational firm, IBM, and because he does not account for within-country differences in multicultural countries. Although we introduce these value dimensions here to aid in the understanding of different cultures, their relevance and application to management functions will be discussed in later chapters.

The first of these value dimensions, **power distance,** is the level of acceptance by a society of the unequal distribution of power in institutions. In the workplace, inequalities in power are normal, as evidenced in hierarchical boss–subordinate relationships. However, the extent to which subordinates accept unequal power is societally determined. In countries in which people display high power distance (such as Malaysia, the Philippines, and Mexico), employees acknowledge the boss's authority simply by respecting that individual's formal position in the hierarchy, and they seldom bypass the chain of command. This respectful response results, predictably, in a centralized structure and autocratic leadership. In countries where people display low power distance (such as Austria, Denmark, and Israel), superiors and subordinates are apt to regard one another as equal in power, resulting in more harmony and cooperation. Clearly, an autocratic management style is not likely to be well received in low power distance countries.

The second value dimension, **uncertainty avoidance,** refers to the extent to which people in a society feel threatened by ambiguous situations. Countries with a high level of uncertainty

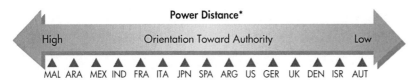

Power Distance*

High   Orientation Toward Authority   Low

MAL ARA MEX IND FRA ITA JPN SPA ARG US GER UK DEN ISR AUT

*Not to scale—indicates relative magnitude.
Note: ARA = Arab Countries
AUT = Austria

Source: Based on G. Hofstede, "National Cultures in Four Dimensions,"
International Studies of Management and Organization (Spring-Summer 1983).

avoidance (such as Japan, Portugal, and Greece) tend to have strict laws and procedures to which their people adhere closely, and a strong sense of nationalism prevails. In a business context, this value results in formal rules and procedures designed to provide more security and greater career stability. Managers have a propensity for low-risk decisions, employees exhibit little aggressiveness, and lifetime employment is common. In countries with lower levels of uncertainty avoidance (such as Denmark, Great Britain, and, to a lesser extent, the United States), nationalism is less pronounced, and protests and other such activities are tolerated. As a consequence, company activities are less structured and less formal, some managers take more risks, and high job mobility is common.

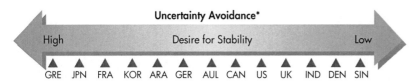

Uncertainty Avoidance*

High   Desire for Stability   Low

GRE JPN FRA KOR ARA GER AUL CAN US UK IND DEN SIN

*Not to scale—indicates relative magnitude.
Note: AUL = Australia

Source: Based on G. Hofstede, 1983.

The third of Hofstede's value dimensions, **individualism,** refers to the tendency of people to look after themselves and their immediate families only and to neglect the needs of society. In countries that prize individualism (such as the United States, Great Britain, and Australia) democracy, individual initiative, and achievement are highly valued; the relationship of the individual to organizations is one of independence on an emotional level, if not on an economic level.

In countries such as Pakistan and Panama, where low individualism prevails—that is, where **collectivism** predominates—one finds tight social frameworks, emotional dependence on belonging to "the organization," and a strong belief in group decisions. People from a collectivist country, like Japan, believe in the will of the group rather than that of the individual, and their pervasive collectivism exerts control over individual members through social pressure and the fear of humiliation. The society valorizes harmony and saving face, whereas individualistic cultures generally emphasize self-respect, autonomy, and independence. Hiring and promotion practices in collectivist societies are based on paternalism rather than achievement or personal capabilities, which are valued in individualistic societies. Other management practices (such as the use of quality circles in Japanese factories) reflect the emphasis on group decision-making processes in collectivist societies.

Hofstede's findings indicate that most countries scoring high on individualism have both a higher gross national product and a freer political system than those countries scoring low on individualism—that is, there is a strong relationship among individualism, wealth, and a political system with balanced power. Other studies have found that the output of individuals working in a group setting differs between individualistic and collectivist societies. In the United States, a highly individualistic culture, social loafing is common—that is, people tend to perform less when working as part of a group than when working alone.[16] In a comparative study of the United States and the People's Republic of China (a highly collectivist society), Earley found that the Chinese did not exhibit as much social loafing as the Americans.[17] This result can be attributed to Chinese cultural values, which subordinate personal interests to the greater goal of helping the group succeed.

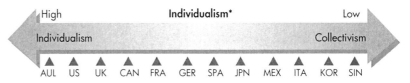

*Not to scale—indicates relative magnitude.

Source: Based on G. Hofstede, 1983.

The fourth value dimension, **masculinity,** refers to the degree of traditionally "masculine" values—assertiveness, materialism, and a lack of concern for others—that prevail in a society. In comparison, femininity emphasizes "feminine" values—a concern for others, for relationships, and for the quality of life. In highly masculine societies (Japan and Austria, for example), women are generally expected to stay home and raise a family. In organizations, one finds considerable job stress, and organizational interests generally encroach on employees' private lives. In countries with low masculinity (such as Switzerland and New Zealand), one finds less conflict and job stress, more women in high-level jobs, and a reduced need for assertiveness. The United States lies somewhat in the middle, according to Hofstede's research. American women typically are encouraged to work, and families often are able to get some support for child care (through day-care centers and maternity leaves).

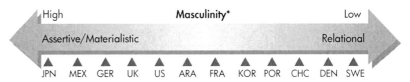

*Not to scale—indicates relative magnitude.

Source: Based on G. Hofstede, 1983.

The four cultural value dimensions proposed by Hofstede do not operate in isolation; rather, they are interdependent and interactive—and thus complex—in their effects on work attitudes and behaviors. For example, in a 2000 study of small to medium-sized firms in Australia, Finland, Greece, Indonesia, Mexico, Norway, and Sweden, based on Hofstede's dimensions, Steensma, Marino, and Weaver found that "entrepreneurs from societies that are masculine and individualistic have a lower appreciation for cooperative strategies as compared to entrepreneurs from societies that are feminine and collectivist. Masculine cultures view cooperation in general as a sign of weakness and individualistic societies place a high value on independence and control."[18] In addition, they found that high levels of uncertainty avoidance prompted more cooperation, such as developing alliances to share risk.

Long-term/Short-term Orientation   Later research in 23 countries, using a survey developed by Bond and colleagues called the Chinese Value Survey, led Hofstede to develop a fifth dimension called the Confucian work dynamism, which he labeled a long-term/short-term dimension. He defined long-term orientation as "the extent to which a culture programs its members to accept delayed gratification of their material, social, and emotional needs."[19] In other words, managers in most Asian countries are more future-oriented and so stride toward long-term goals;

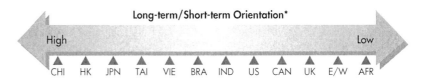

*Not to scale—indicates relative magnitude.

Source: Based on G. Hofstede, 2001.

they value investment in the future and are prepared to sacrifice short-term profits. Those countries such as Great Britain, Canada, and the United States place a higher value on short-term results and profitability, and evaluate their employees accordingly.

Trompenaars's Value Dimensions

Fons Trompenaars also researched value dimensions; his work was spread over a ten-year period, with 15,000 managers from 28 countries representing 47 national cultures. Some of those dimensions, such as individualism, people's attitude toward time, and relative inner-versus outer-directedness, are similar to those discussed elsewhere in this chapter and others, and so are not presented here; other selected findings from Trompenaars's research that affect daily business activities are explained next, along with the placement of some of the countries along those dimensions, in approximate relative order.[20] If we view the placement of these countries along a range from personal to societal, based on each dimension, some interesting patterns emerge.[21] One can see that the same countries tend to be at similar positions on all dimensions, with the exception of the emotional orientation.

Looking at Trompenaars's dimension of **universalism versus particularism,** we find that the universalistic approach applies rules and systems objectively, without consideration for individual circumstances, whereas the particularistic approach—more common in Asia and in Spain, for example—puts the first obligation on relationships and is more subjective. Trompenaars found, for example, that people in particularistic societies are more likely to pass on insider information to a friend than those in universalistic societies.

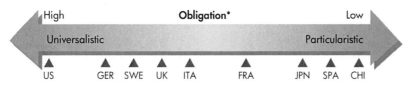

*Not to scale—indicates relative magnitude.

Source: Data based on F. Trompenaars, 1993.

In the **neutral versus affective** dimension, the focus is on the emotional orientation of relationships. The Italians, Mexicans, and Chinese, for example, would openly express emotions even in a business situation, whereas the British and Japanese would consider such displays unprofessional; they, in turn would be regarded as "hard to 'read'."

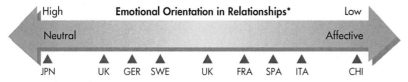

*Not to scale—indicates relative magnitude.

Source: Data based on F. Trompenaars, 1993.

As far as involvement in relationships goes, people tend to be either **specific or diffuse** (or somewhere along that dimension). Managers in specific-oriented cultures—the United States, United Kingdom, France—separate work and personal issues and relationships; they compartmentalize their work and private lives, and they are more open and direct. In diffuse-oriented cultures—Sweden, China—work spills over into personal relationships and vice versa.

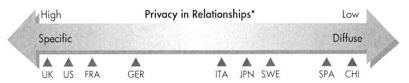

Source: Data based on F. Trompenaars, 1993.

In the **achievement versus ascription** dimension, the question that arises is "What is the source of power and status in society?" In an achievement society, the source of status and influence is based on individual achievement—how well one performs the job and what level of education and experience one has to offer. Therefore, women, minorities, and young people usually have equal opportunity to attain position based on their achievements. In an ascription-oriented society, people ascribe status on the basis of class, age, gender, and so on; one is more likely to be born into a position of influence. Hiring in Indonesia, for example, is more likely to be based on who you are than is the case in Germany or Australia.

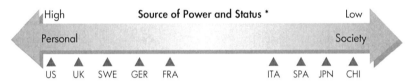

Source: Data based on F. Trompenaars, 1993.

It is clear, then, that a lot of what goes on at work can be explained by differences in people's innate value systems, as described by Hofstede, Trompenaars, and the GLOBE researchers. Awareness of such differences and how they influence work behavior can be very useful to you as a future international manager.

Critical Operational Value Differences

After studying various research results about cultural variables, it helps to identify some specific culturally based variables that cause frequent problems for Americans in international management. Important variables are those involving conflicting orientations toward time, change, material factors, and individualism. We try to understand these operational value differences because they strongly influence a person's attitudes and probable response to work situations.

Time   Americans often experience much conflict and frustration because of differences in the concept of time around the world—that is, differences in temporal values. To Americans, time is a valuable and limited resource; it is to be saved, scheduled, and spent with precision, lest we waste it. The clock is always running—time is money. Therefore, deadlines and schedules have to be met. When others are not on time for meetings, Americans may feel insulted; when meetings digress from their purpose, Americans tend to become impatient. Similar attitudes toward time are found in Western Europe and elsewhere.

In many parts of the world, however, people view time from different and longer perspectives, often based on religious beliefs (such as reincarnation, in which time does not end at death), on a belief in destiny, or on pervasive social attitudes. In Latin America, for example, a common attitude toward time is *mañana,* a word that literally means "tomorrow." A Latin American person using this word, however, usually means an indefinite time in the near future. Similarly, the word *bukra* in Arabic can mean "tomorrow" or "some time in the future." While Americans usually regard a deadline as a firm commitment, Arabs often regard a deadline imposed on them as an insult. They feel that important things take a long time and therefore cannot be rushed. To ask an Arab to rush something, then, is to imply that you have not given him an important task or that he would not treat that task with respect. International managers have to be careful not to offend people—or lose contracts or employee cooperation—because they misunderstand the local language of time.

Change   Based largely on long-standing religious beliefs, values regarding the acceptance of change and the pace of change can vary immensely among cultures. Western people generally believe that an individual can exert some control over the future and can manipulate events, particularly in a business context—that is, individuals feel they have some internal control. In many non-Western societies, however, control is considered external; people generally believe in destiny or the will of their God, and therefore adopt a passive attitude or even feel hostility toward those introducing the "evil" of change. In societies that place great importance on tradition (such as Japan), one small area of change may threaten an entire way of life. However, the younger generations are becoming more exposed to change through globalization, technology, and media exposure. International firms are agents of change throughout the world. Some changes are more popular than others; for example, McDonald's hamburgers are apparently one change the Japanese are willing to accept.

Material Factors   In large part, Americans consume resources at a far greater rate than most of the rest of the world. Their attitude toward nature—that it is there to be used for their benefit—differs from the attitudes of Indians and Koreans, for example, whose worship of nature is part of their religious beliefs. Whereas Americans often value physical goods and status symbols, many non-Westerners find these things unimportant; they value the aesthetic and the spiritual realm. Such differences in attitude have implications for management functions, such as motivation and reward systems, because the proverbial carrot must be appropriate to the employee's value system.

Individualism   In general, Americans tend to work and conduct their private lives independently, valuing individual achievement, accomplishments, promotions, and wealth above any group goals. In many other countries, individualism is not valued (as discussed previously in the context of Hofstede's work). In China, for example, much more of a "we" consciousness prevails, and the group is the basic building block of social life and work. For the Chinese, conformity and cooperation take precedence over individual achievement, and the emphasis is on the strength of the family or community—the predominant attitude being, "We all rise or fall together."

International managers often face conflicts in the workplace as a result of differences in these four basic values of time, change, materialism, and individualism. If these operational value differences and their likely consequences are anticipated, managers can adjust expectations, communications, work organization, schedules, incentive systems, and so forth to provide for more constructive outcomes for the company and its employees. Some of these operational differences are shown in Exhibit 3-5, using Japan and Mexico as examples. Note in particular the factors of time, individualism, change (fatalism), and materialism (attitudes toward work) expressed in the exhibit.

EXHIBIT 3-5   Fundamental Differences Between Japanese and Mexican Culture that Affect Business Organizations[22]

Dimension	Japanese Culture	Mexican Culture
Hierarchical nature	Rigid in rank and most communication; blurred in authority and responsibility	Rigid in all aspects
Individualism vs. collectivism	Highly collective culture; loyalty to work group dominates; group harmony very important	Collective relative to family group; don't transfer loyalty to work group; individualistic outside family
Attitudes toward work	Work is sacred duty; acquiring skills, working hard, thriftiness, patience, and perseverance are virtues	Work is means to support self and family; leisure more important than work
Time orientation	Balanced perspective; future oriented; monochronic in dealings with outside world	Present oriented; time is imprecise; time commitments become desirable objectives
Approach to problem solving	Holistic, reliance on intuition, pragmatic, consensus important	Reliance on intuition and emotion, individual approach
Fatalism	Fatalism leads to preparation	Fatalism makes planning, disciplined routine unnatural
View of human nature	Intrinsically good	Mixture of good and evil

THE INTERNET AND CULTURE

Koreans are an impatient people, and we like technology. So everyone wants the fastest Internet connection.

HWANG KYU-JUNE[23]

We would be remiss if we did not acknowledge the contemporary phenomenon of the increasingly pervasive use of the Internet in society, for it seems to be encroaching on many of the social variables discussed earlier—in particular associations, education, and the economy. In South Korea, for example, where information technology makes up about 30 percent of the gross domestic product (GDP), there is an obsession for anything digital. Over 70 percent of homes are connected to a high-speed Internet service. That compares with 50 percent in Canada—the next highest user—and 23 percent in the United States.[24] This phenomenon seems to be changing the lives of many Koreans. Teenagers, used to hanging out at the mall, now do so at the country's 20,000 personal computer (PC) parlors to watch movies, check email, and surf the Net for as little as US$1. Korean housewives are on a waiting list for ADSL lines when the $35 billion high-speed government telecommunications project is completed. By then 95 percent of Korean households will have Internet access.[25]

At the same time that the Internet is affecting culture, culture is also affecting how the Internet is used. One of the pervasive ways that culture is determining how the Internet may be used in various countries is through the local attitude to **information privacy**—the right to control information about oneself—as observed in the following quote:

You Americans just don't seem to care about privacy, do you?

SWEDISH EXECUTIVE[26]

While Americans collect data about consumers' backgrounds and what they buy, often trading that information with other internal or external contacts, the Swedes, for example, are astounded that this is done, especially without governmental oversight.[27] The Swedes are required to register all databases of personal information with the Data Inspection Board (DIB), their federal regulatory agency for privacy, and to get permission from that board before that data can be used. Indeed, the Swedish system is typical of most countries in Europe in their societal approaches to privacy.[28] One example of a blocked data transfer occurred when Sweden would not allow U.S. airlines to transmit passenger information, such as wheelchair need and meal preferences, to the United States.[29]

Generally in Europe, each person must be informed, and given the chance to object, if the information about that person is going to be used for direct marketing purposes or released to another party. That data cannot be used for secondary purposes if the consumer objects.

In Italy, data cannot be sent outside—even to other EU countries—without the explicit consent of the data subject

In Spain, all direct mail has to include the name and address of the data owner so that the data subject is able to exercise his rights of access, correction, and removal.[30]

The manner in which Europe views information privacy has its roots in culture and history, leading to a different value set regarding privacy. The preservation of privacy is considered a human right, perhaps partially as a result of an internalized fear about how personal records were used in war times in Europe. In addition, research by Smith on the relationship between level of concern about privacy and Hofstede's cultural dimensions revealed that high levels of uncertainty avoidance were associated with the European approach to privacy, whereas higher levels of individualism, masculinity, and power distance were associated with the U.S. approach.[31]

It seems, then, that societal culture and the resultant effects on business models can render the assumptions about the "global" nature of information technology incorrect. U.S. businesspeople, brought up on a strong diet of the market economy, need to realize that they will often need to "localize" their use of IT to different value sets about its use. This advice applies in particular to the many e-commerce companies doing business overseas. With 75 percent of the world's Internet market living outside the United States, multinational e-businesses are learning the hard way that their Web sites must reflect local markets, customs, languages, and currencies to be successful in foreign markets. Different legal systems, financial structures, tastes, and experiences necessitate attention to every detail to achieve global appeal. In other words, e-businesses must localize to globalize, which means much more than translating online content to local languages. Lycos Europe, for example, based its privacy policies upon German law since it is the most stringent.

One problem area often beyond the control of e-business is the costs of connecting to the Internet for people in other countries. In Asia, for example, such costs are considerably higher than in the United States. Other practical problems in Asia, as well as in Germany, the Netherlands, and Sweden, include the method of payment, which in most of these places still involves cash or letters of credit and written receipts. Dell tackled this problem by offering debit payments from consumers' checking accounts. Some companies have learned the hard way that they need to do their homework before launching sites aimed at overseas consumers. Dell, for example, committed a faux pas when it launched an e-commerce site in Japan with black borders on the site; black is considered negative in the Japanese culture, so many consumers took one look and didn't want anything else to do with it. Dell executives learned that the complexity of language translation into Japanese was only one area in which they needed to localize.

As much as cultural and societal factors can affect the use of the internet for business, it is also clear that IT can have dramatic changes on culture and society, as illustrated by the accompanying Management Focus about the changes occurring as a result of India's burgeoning IT industry.

MANAGEMENT FOCUS

India's IT Industry Brings Cultural Changes[32]

Many longtime residents of Bangalore, India, seem locked in a cultural struggle with Infosys Technologies (INFY), Wipro Technologies (WIT), and others in the software industry, even though they have made Bangalore famous and increased its wealth. They complain that Bangalore used to be one of India's most pleasant cities. But with the addition of 500,000 IT workers living alongside nearly 7 million other residents, the city has become very crowded and expensive. The locals ask:

> Does the city belong to the IT industry, with all its riches? Or does it belong to those who arrived first, whose children must now work for outsiders who don't speak the local language, Kannada?[33]

Apart from the early curfew on nightlife, the old-timers contend, in a city where few locals can afford cars, the government is spending too much of the city's resources on building wider roads to speed tech workers around. In its defense, the software industry claims that it has benefited everyone by improving the city and bringing new wealth and services such as a new subway system. Although the global credit crunch has slowed its growth, over the past decade the tech sector has created tens of thousands of jobs, not only in the software and back-office support industries, but also for all the people who support those companies. While most of India's IT companies still get at least half of their revenue from the United States alone, now they are finding more business domestically. As a result the digital divide between urban and rural areas is narrowing and helping support industries to grow in a domestic economy expanding 9 percent a year—this all thanks to India's IT talent.

It is these kinds of opportunities, amid the benefits of increasing economic openness in India, that have attracted Anand Giridharad, and others whose families had earlier emigrated to the United States, to return to India. The idea of returning to India is spreading virally in émigré

A Typical Call Center in India for Business Process Outsourcing (BPO) for Foreign Companies.

Source: Getty Images Inc.

homes as the U.S. economy declines and the job market tightens. This phenomenon led Anand to ask:

> *If our parents left India and trudged westward for us, if they manufactured from scratch a new life there for us, if they slogged, saved, sacrificed to make our lives lighter than theirs, then what does it mean when we choose to migrate to the place they forsook?*[34]

He noted that his father, in the 1970s, felt frustrated in companies that awarded roles based on age, not achievement, and that doctors and engineers were revered and others neglected and mistreated. Since then, India has liberalized, privatized, globalized with the economy growing rapidly, bringing with it much optimism for its people. At the same time, America has declined and many jobs have moved to India, particularly in IT and back-office services.

In a sign of the times, India offered an Overseas Citizen of India card in 2006, offering foreign citizens of Indian origin visa-free entry for life and making it easier to work in the country. By July 2008 more than 280,000 émigrés had signed up, including 120,000 from the United States.

Those émigrés are now re-learning those many aspects of Indian culture that remain, for example the formalities and hierarchies left from British rule; that making friends entails befriending the whole family; and the very relaxed attitude toward time. Those second-generation returnees to their motherland are now mixing western and Indian cultures:

> *They have built boutiques that fuse Indian fabrics with Western cuts, founded companies that train a generation to work in Western companies, become dealmakers in investment firms that speak equally to Wall Street and Dalal Street, mixed albums that combine throbbing tabla with Western melodies.*[35]

Much of the traditional cultural underpinnings remain, of course. Narayana Murthy, founder and now chairman of the board of Infosys, the Indian IT giant, was asked recently to comment on what explains the success of great Indian businesses such as Infosys, Wipro, and the Tata group. Mr. Murthy said that there are some culturally specific qualities, but also some universal ones, that lie behind the achievements. He commented that, of course honesty, decency, integrity and a strong work ethic all matter. But these are not unique to India. Rather, he said:

It is the concept of the family which perhaps sets India apart. Family bonds are strong and intense in India. People inevitably bring that ethos to work with them.[36]

Of course, much of India has not been directly touched by the IT industry, and so in those areas the Indian culture remains untouched by the IT industry and globalization. Management is often paternalist and autocratic, based on formal authority and charisma, with decision making mostly centralized, an emphasis on rules and a low propensity for risk. Nepotism prevails in job hiring and placement, and for the most part:

Relationship orientation seems to be a more important characteristic of effective leaders in India than performance or task orientation.[37]

DEVELOPING CULTURAL PROFILES

Managers can gather considerable information on cultural variables from current research, personal observation, and discussions with people. From these sources, managers can develop cultural profiles of various countries—composite pictures of working environments, people's attitudes, and norms of behavior. As we have previously discussed, these profiles are often highly generalized; many subcultures, of course, may exist within a country. However, managers can use these profiles to anticipate drastic differences in the level of motivation, communication, ethics, loyalty, and individual and group productivity that may be encountered in a given country. More such homework may have helped Wal-Mart's expansion efforts into Germany and South Korea, from which it withdrew in 2006. Wal-Mart's executives simply did not do enough research about the culture and shopping habits of people there; for example:

In Germany, Wal-Mart stopped requiring sales clerks to smile at customers—a practice that some male shoppers interpreted as flirting—and scrapped the morning Wal-Mart chant by staff members. "People found these things strange; Germans just don't behave that way," said Hans-Martin Poschmann, the secretary of the Verdi union, which represents 5,000 Wal-Mart employees here.

NEW YORK TIMES,
July 31, 2006[38]

It is relatively simple for Americans to pull together a descriptive profile of U.S. culture, even though regional and individual differences exist, because Americans know themselves and because researchers have thoroughly studied U.S. culture. The results of one such study by Harris and Moran are shown in Exhibit 3-6, which provides a basis of comparison with other cultures and, thus, suggests the likely differences in workplace behaviors.

It is not so easy, however, to pull together descriptive cultural profiles of peoples in other countries unless one has lived there and been intricately involved with those people. Still, managers can make a start by using what comparative research and literature are available. The following Comparative Management in Focus provides brief, generalized country profiles based on a synthesis of research, primarily from Hofstede[39] and England,[40] as well as numerous other sources.[41] These profiles illustrate how to synthesize information and gain a sense of the character of a society—from which implications may be drawn about how to manage more effectively in that society. More extensive implications and applications related to managerial functions are drawn in later chapters.

EXHIBIT 3-6 Americans at a Glance

1. *Goal and achievement oriented*—Americans think they can accomplish just about anything, given enough time, money, and technology.

2. *Highly organized and institutionally minded*—Americans prefer a society that is institutionally strong, secure, and tidy or well kept.

3. *Freedom-loving and self-reliant*—Americans fought a revolution and subsequent wars to preserve their concept of democracy, so they resent too much control or interference, especially by government or external forces. They believe in an ideal that all persons are created equal; though they sometimes fail to fully live that ideal, they strive through law to promote equal opportunity and to confront their own racism or prejudice.

   They also idealize the self-made person who rises form poverty and adversity, and think they can influence and create their own futures. Control of one's destiny is popularly expressed as "doing your own thing." Americans think, for the most part, that with determination and initiative, one can achieve whatever one sets out to do and thus, fulfill one's individual human potential.

4. *Work-oriented and efficient*—Americans possess a strong work ethic, though they are learning in the present generation to constructively enjoy leisure time. They are conscious of time and efficient in doing things. They tinker with gadgets and technological systems, always searching for easier, better, more efficient ways to accomplish tasks.

5. *Friendly and informal*—Americans reject the traditional privileges of royalty and class but defer to those with affluence and power. Although informal in greeting and dress, they are a noncontact culture (e.g., usually avoid embracing in public) and maintain a certain physical/psychological distance with others (e.g., about 2 feet).

6. *Competitive and aggressive*—Americans in play or business generally are so oriented because of their drives to achieve and succeed. This is partially traced to their heritage of having to overcome a wilderness and hostile elements in their environment.

7. *Values in transition*—Traditional American values of family loyalty, respect and care of the aged, marriage and the nuclear family, patriotism, material acquisition, forthrightness, and the like are undergoing profound reevaluation as people search for new meanings.

8. *Generosity*—Although Americans seemingly emphasize material values, they are a sharing people, as has been demonstrated in the Marshall Plan, foreign aid programs, refugee assistance, and their willingness at home and abroad to espouse a good cause and to help neighbors in need. They tend to be altruistic and some would say naive as a people.

Source: From *Managing Cultural Differences* by Philip R. Harris and Robert T. Moran, 5th ed. Copyright © 2000 by Gulf Publishing Company, Houston, TX. Used with permission. All rights reserved.

Recent evidence points to some convergence with Western business culture resulting from Japan's economic contraction and subsequent bankruptcies. Focus on the group, lifetime employment, and a pension has given way to a more competitive business environment with job security no longer guaranteed and an emphasis on performance-based pay. This has led Japan's "salarymen" to recognize the need for personal responsibility on the job and in their lives. Although only a few years ago emphasis was on the group, Japan's long economic slump seems to have caused some cultural restructuring of the individual. Corporate Japan is changing from a culture of consensus and groupthink to one touting the need for an "era of personal responsibility" as a solution to revitalize its competitive position in the global marketplace.[42]

To tell you the truth, it's hard to think for yourself, says Mr. Kuzuoka . . . [but, if you don't] . . . in this age of cutthroat competition, you'll just end up drowning.[43]

COMPARATIVE MANAGEMENT IN FOCUS
Profiles in Culture—Japan, Germany, Latin America, and South Korea

Japan

The traditional Japanese business characteristics of politeness and deference have left companies without the thrusting culture needed to succeed internationally.

FINANCIAL TIMES,
October 10, 2005[44]

With intense global competition many Japanese companies are recognizing the need for more assertiveness and clarity in their business culture in order to expand abroad. As a result, many Japanese employees are recognizing the need to manage their own careers as companies move away from lifetime employment to be more competitive. Only a handful of large businesses, such as Toyota, Komatsu, and Canon, have managed to become indisputable global leaders by maintaining relationships and a foundation for their operations around the world.[45] For the majority of Japanese, the underlying cultural values still predominate—for now anyway.

Much of Japanese culture—and the basis of working relationships—can be explained by the principle of *wa*, "peace and harmony." This principle, embedded in the value the Japanese attribute to *amae* ("indulgent love"), probably originated in the Shinto religion, which focuses on spiritual and physical harmony. *Amae* results in *shinyo*, which refers to the mutual confidence, faith, and honor necessary for successful business relationships. Japan ranks high on pragmatism, masculinity, and uncertainty avoidance, and fairly high on power distance. At the same time, much importance is attached to loyalty, empathy, and the guidance of subordinates. The result is a mix of authoritarianism

MAP 3-2   Japan and South Korea

and humanism in the workplace, similar to a family system. These cultural roots are evident in a homogeneous managerial value system, with strong middle management, strong working relationships, strong seniority systems that stress rank, and an emphasis on looking after employees. The principle of *wa* carries forth into the work group—the building block of Japanese business. The Japanese strongly identify and thus seek to cooperate with their work groups. The emphasis is on participative management, consensus problem solving, and decision making with a patient, long-term perspective. Open expression and conflict are discouraged, and it is of paramount importance to avoid the shame of not fulfilling one's duty. These elements of work culture result in a devotion to work, collective responsibility, and a high degree of employee productivity.

Professor Nonaka, a specialist in how companies tap the collective intelligence of their workers discusses a similar Japanese concept of *ba*: an interaction among colleagues on the job that leads to knowledge-sharing. He says that

> Ba *can occur in a work group, a project team, an ad hoc meeting, a virtual e-mail list, or at the frontline point of contact with customers. It serves as a petri dish in which shared insights are cultivated and grown. Companies can foster ba by designing processes that encourage people to think together.*[46]

The message is clear that, in Japan, companies that give their employees freedom to interact informally are likely to benefit from new ideas and collaboration.

If we extend this cultural profile to its implications for specific behaviors in the workplace, we can draw a comparison with common American behaviors. Most of those behaviors seem to be opposite to those of their counterparts; it is no wonder that many misunderstandings and conflicts in the workplace arise between Americans and Japanese (see Exhibit 3-7). For example, a majority of the

EXHIBIT 3-7   The American–Japanese Cultural Divide

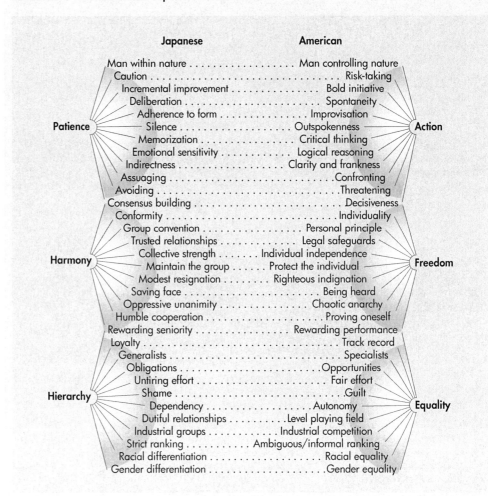

Source: R. G. Linowes, "The Japanese Manager's Traumatic Entry into the United States: Understanding the American–Japanese Cultural Divide," *The Academy of Management Executive* 7, no. 4 (1993): 24.

attitudes and behaviors of many Japanese stems from a high level of collectivism, compared with a high level of individualism common to Americans. This contrast is highlighted in the center of Exhibit 3-7—"Maintain the group"—compared with "Protect the individual." In addition, the strict social order of the Japanese permeates the workplace in adherence to organizational hierarchy and seniority and in loyalty to the firm. This contrasts markedly with the typical American responses to organizational relationships and duties based on equality. In addition, the often blunt, outspoken American businessperson offends the indirectness and sensitivity of the Japanese for whom the virtue of patience is paramount, causing the silence and avoidance that so frustrates Americans. As a result, Japanese businesspeople tend to think of American organizations as having no spiritual quality and little employee loyalty, and of Americans as assertive, frank, and egotistic. Their American counterparts, in turn, respond with the impression that Japanese businesspeople have little experience and are secretive, arrogant, and cautious.[47]

GERMANY The reunited Germany is somewhat culturally diverse inasmuch as the country borders several nations. Generally, Germans rank quite high on Hofstede's dimension of individualism, although their behaviors seem less individualistic than those of Americans. They score fairly high on uncertainty avoidance and masculinity and have a relatively small need for power distance. These cultural norms show up in the Germans' preference for being around familiar people and situations; they are also reflected in their propensity to do a detailed evaluation of business deals before committing themselves.

Christianity underlies much of German culture—more than 96 percent of Germans are Catholics or Protestants. This may be why Germans tend to like rule and order in their lives, and why there is a clear public expectation of acceptable and the unacceptable ways to act. Public signs everywhere in Germany dictate what is allowed or *verboten* (forbidden). Germans are very strict with their use of time, whether for business or pleasure, frowning on inefficiency or on tardiness.

In business, Germans tend to be assertive, but they downplay aggression. Decisions are typically centralized, although hierarchical processes sometimes give way to consensus decision making. However, strict departmentalization is present in organizations, with centralized and final authority at the departmental manager level. Employees do not question the authority of their managers. German companies typically have a vertical hierarchical structure with detailed planning and standardized rules and procedures; the emphasis is on order and control to avoid risk.

> In the business setting, Germans look for security, well-defined work procedures, rules, established approaches, and clearly defined individual assignments. In short, the German business environment is highly structured. "Ordnung" (order) is the backbone of company life.[48]

What the Germans call *Ordnung* (the usual translation is "order," but it is a much broader concept) is the unwritten road map of how to live one's life. "A group of Germans lined up on an empty street corner, even in the middle of the night, waiting for a light to change before crossing, is one of the favorite first impressions taken away by visiting Americans, who are usually jaywalking past as they observe it."[49] For self-reliant Americans, the German adherence to precise rules and regulations is impressive but often stifling.

Hall and Hall describe the German preference for closed doors and private space as evidence of the affinity for compartmentalization in organizations and in their own lives. They also prefer more physical space around them in conversation than do most other Europeans, and they seek privacy so as not to be overheard. German law prohibits loud noises in public areas on weekend afternoons. Germans are conservative, valuing privacy, politeness, and formality; they usually use last names and titles for all except those close to them. Business interactions are specifically task-focused, not for relationship-building.

Most Germans prefer to focus on one task or issue at a time, that task taking precedence over other demands; strict schedules are important, as is punctuality, both showing respect for all concerned. Overall, Germany is what Walker et al call a "doing-oriented" culture—that is, a task and achievement orientation of "work first, pleasure second."[50] Such cultures include Switzerland, Germany, Austria, the Netherlands, and the Scandinavian countries. (This compares with "being-oriented" cultures—such as those of Belgium, France Greece, Ireland, and most Latin American countries—where the general predisposition is more towards "work to live," rather than "live to work." Priority is given to affiliation and personal qualities in "being-oriented" cultures.)

In negotiations, Germans want detailed information before and during discussions, which can become lengthy. They give factors such as voice and speech control much weight. However, since Germany is a low-context society, communication is explicit, and Americans find negotiations easy to understand.[51] On the other hand, Germans communicating with businesspeople from a high-context culture such as those in Japan will be perceived as abrupt, insensitive, and indifferent. Whereas most

Asians, for example, will be implicit and indirect, always aware of the need to "save face" for everyone concerned, most Germans are very direct and straightforward; tact and diplomacy takes second place to voicing their opinions.

LATIN AMERICA   Latin America is not one homogenous area, of course; rather, it comprises many diverse, independent nations (most commonly referred to as those territories in the Americas where the Spanish or Portuguese languages prevail: Mexico, most of Central and South America, plus Cuba, the Dominican Republic, and Puerto Rico in the Caribbean). Business people are most likely to go to the rapidly developing economies of Chile and Brazil, and, of course, to Mexico. (Portuguese is the language in Brazil.) Christianity—predominantly Roman Catholicism—prevails throughout Latin America. (The reader is referred to www.wikipedia.org for further information on demographics, geography, economies, lifestyles, etc.)

While we acknowledge the many cultural differences, for our purposes here we can draw upon the similarities of culture and business practices as a starting point in developing a helpful profile. Some of these generalities are discussed here.

Using Hofstede's dimensions, we can generalize that most people are high on Power Distance and Uncertainty Avoidance, fairly high on Masculinity, low on Individualism, and tend to have a comparatively short-term orientation towards plans.

Latin Americans are typically "being-oriented"—with a primary focus on relationships and enjoying life in the present—as compared with the "doing-oriented" German (and mostly Western) culture discussed earlier. For Latin Americans, work lives and private lives are much more closely integrated than that of Westerners and so they emphasize enjoying life and have a more relaxed attitude towards work; because of that, Westerners often stereotype them as "lazy," rather than realizing that it is simply a different attitude to the role of work in life. Connected with that attitude is the tendency to be rather fatalistic—that is that events will be determined by God—rather than a feeling of their own control or responsibility for the future.

Most people in those countries have a fluid orientation towards time and tend to be multi-focused, as discussed earlier in this chapter. Planning, negotiations, and scheduling take place in a more relaxed and loose time framework; those processes take second place to building a trusting relationship and reaching a satisfactory agreement.[52] Communication is based on their high-context culture (this concept is discussed further in Chapter 4). This means that communication tends to be indirect and implicit, based largely on non-verbal interactions and the expectation that the listener draws inference from understanding the people and the circumstances, without the need to be blunt or critical. Westerners need to take time, to be subtle and tactful, and to be incremental at discussing business to avoid being viewed as being pushy and so cutting off the relationship. Maintaining harmony and saving face is very important, as is the need to avoid embarrassing the other people involved. Managers must avoid any public criticism of employees and any reprimand should be by way of suggestion.

Communication is also very expressive and demonstrative; courtesy, formality, and good manners are respected and lead to very complimentary and hospitable expressions to guests. They tend to stand closer and touch more often than most Westerners, exuding the warmth and hospitality that is typical in the region.

Hierarchy prevails in all areas of life, from family to institutions such as government and the workplace. Each level and relationship is expected to show deference, honor, and respect to the next person or level. Status is conveyed by one's position and title and the formality of dress and etiquette. Traditional managers have the respect of their position and are typically autocratic and paternal. Loyalty is to the superior as a person. Employees expect to be assigned tasks with little participation involved, although younger managers who have been educated in Europe or the United States are starting to delegate. However, while most Latin Americans can show some flexibility in structure, Chile is probably the most order-oriented country; managers there are very high on uncertainty and try hard to minimize risk and strictly adhere to social and business norms.[53]

Relationships have priority whether family, friends, or business contacts. Loyalty among family and friends leads to obligations, and, often, nepotism, which can lead to varying levels of quality in the work performance and less initiative than a Western business person might expect. Business is conducted through social contacts and referrals—that is, success depends not on what you know as much as whom you know. Latin Americans do business with people with whom they develop a trusting relationship, so it behooves business people, as in much of the world, to take time to develop a friendly, trusting relationship before getting down to business.

Western managers need to develop a warm attitude towards employees and business contacts and cultivate a sense of family at work; they should communicate individually with employees and colleagues and develop a trusting relationship.

Further discussion about the Mexican culture in particular is in the Comparative Management in Focus section in Chapter 11.

SOUTH KOREA   Koreans rank high on collectivism and pragmatism, fairly low on masculinity, moderate on power distance, and quite high on uncertainty avoidance. Although greatly influenced by U.S. culture, Koreans are still very much bound to the traditional Confucian teachings of spiritualism and collectivism. Korea and its people have undergone great changes, but the respect for family, authority, formality, class, and rank remain strong. Koreans are demonstrative, friendly, quite aggressive and hard-working, and very hospitable. For the most part, they do not subscribe to participative management. Family and personal relationships are important, and connections are vital for business introductions and transactions. Business is based on honor and trust; most contracts are oral. Although achievement and competence are important to Koreans, the priority of guarding both parties' social and professional reputations is a driving force in relationships. Thus, praise predominates, and honest criticism is rare.

Further insight into the differences between U.S. and Korean culture can be derived from the following excerpted letter from Professor Jin K. Kim in Plattsburgh, New York, to his high school friend, MK, in South Korea, who just returned from a visit to the United States. MK, whom Dr. Kim had not seen for 20 years, planned to emigrate to the United States, and Dr. Kim wanted to help ward off his friend's culture shock by telling him about U.S. culture from a Korean perspective.

Dear MK,

I sincerely hope the last leg of your trip home from the five-week fact-finding visit to the United States was pleasant and informative. Although I may not have expressed my sense of exhilaration about your visit through the meager lodging accommodations and "barbaric" foods we provided, it was sheer joy to spend four weeks with you and Kyung-Ok. (Please refrain from hitting the ceiling. My use of your charming wife's name, rather than the usual Korean expression "your wife" or "your house person," is not an indication of my amorous intentions toward her as any red-blooded Korean man would suspect. Since you are planning to immigrate to this country soon, I thought you might as well begin to get used to the idea of your wife exerting her individuality. Better yet, I thought you should be warned that the moment the plane touches U.S. soil, you will lose your status as the center of your familial universe.) At any rate, please be assured that during your stay here my heart was filled with memories of our three years together in high school when we were young in Pusan.

During your visit, you called me, on several occasions, an American. What prompted you to invoke such a reference is beyond my comprehension. Was it my rusty Korean expressions? Was it my calculating mind? Was it my pitifully subservient (at least when viewed through your cultural lens) role that I was playing in my family life? Or, was it my familiarity with some facets of the cultural landscape? This may sound bewildering to you, but it is absolutely true that through all the years I have lived in this country, I never truly felt like an American. Sure, on the surface, our family followed closely many ritualistic routines of the American culture: shopping malls, dining out, PTA, Little League, picnics, camping trips, credit card shopping sprees, hot dogs, and so on. But mentally I remained stubbornly in the periphery. Naturally, then, my subjective cultural attitudes stayed staunchly Korean. Never did the inner layers of my Korean psyche yield to the invading American cultural vagaries, I thought. So, when you labeled me an American for the first time, I felt a twinge of guilt.

Several years ago, an old Korean friend of mine, who settled in the United States about the same time I did, paid a visit to Korea for the first time in some fifteen years. When he went to see his best high school friend, who was now married and had two sons, his friend's wife made a bed for him and her husband in the master bedroom, declaring that she would spend the night with the children. It was not necessarily the sexual connotation of the episode that made my friend blush; he was greatly embarrassed by the circumstance in which he imposed himself to the extent that the couple's privacy had to be violated. For his high school friend and his wife, it was clearly their age-old friendship to which the couple's privacy had to yield. MK, you might empathize rather easily with this Korean couple's state of mind, but it would be a gross mistake even to imagine there may be occasions in your adopted culture when a gesture of friendship breaks the barrier of privacy. Zealously guarding their privacy above all, Americans are marvelously adept at drawing the line where friendship—that elusive "we" feeling—stops and privacy begins. . . .

Indeed, one of the hardest tasks you will face as an "alien" is how to find that delicate balance between your individuality (for example, privacy) and your collective identity (for example, friendship or membership in social groups).

Privacy is not the only issue that stems from this individuality—collectivity continuum. Honesty in interpersonal relationships is another point that may keep you puzzled. Americans are almost brutally honest and frank about issues that belong to public domains; they are not afraid of discussing an embarrassing topic in most graphic details as long as the topic is a matter of public concern. Equally frank and honest gestures are adopted when they discuss their own personal lives once the presumed benefits from such gestures are determined to outweigh the risks involved. Accordingly, it is not uncommon to encounter friends who volunteer personally embarrassing and even shameful information lest you find it out from other sources. Are Americans equally straightforward and forthcoming in laying out heartfelt personal criticisms directed at their friends? Not likely. Their otherwise acute sense of honesty becomes significantly muted when they face the unpleasant task of being negative toward their personal friends. The fear of an emotion-draining confrontation and the virtue of being polite force them to put on a facade or mask.

The perfectly accepted social behavior of telling "white lies" is a good example. The social and personal virtues of accepting such lies are grounded in the belief that the potential damage that can be inflicted by directly telling a friend the hurtful truth far outweighs the potential benefit that the friend could gain from it. Instead of telling a hurtful truth directly, Americans use various indirect communication channels to which their friend is likely to be tuned. In other words, they publicize the information in the form of gossip or behind-the-back recriminations until it is transformed into a sort of collective criticism against the target individual. Thus objectified and collectivized, the "truth" ultimately reaches the target individual with a minimal cost of social discomfort on the part of the teller. There is nothing vile or insidious about this communication tactic, since it is deeply rooted in the concern for sustaining social pleasantry for both parties.

This innocuous practice, however, is bound to be perceived as an act of outrageous dishonesty by a person deeply immersed in the Korean culture. In the Korean cultural context, a trusted personal relationship precludes such publicizing prior to direct," criticism to the individual concerned, no matter what the cost in social and personal unpleasantry. Indeed, as you are well aware, MK, such direct reproach and even recrimination in Korea is in most cases appreciated as a sign of one's utmost love and concern for the target individual. Stressful and emotionally draining as it is, such a frank expression of criticism is done out of "we" feeling. Straight-talking friends did not want me to repeat undesirable acts in front of others, as it would either damage "our reputation" or go against the common interest of "our collective identity." In Korea, the focus is on the self-discipline that forms a basis for the integrity of "our group." In America, on the other hand, the focus is on the feelings of two individuals. From the potential teller's viewpoint, the primary concern is how to maintain social politeness, whereas from the target person's viewpoint, the primary concern is how to maintain self-esteem. Indeed, these two diametrically opposed frames of reference—self-discipline and self-esteem—make one culture collective and the other individualistic.

MK, the last facet of the individualism-collectivism continuum likely to cause a great amount of cognitive dissonance in the process of your assimilation to American life is the extent to which you have to assert your individuality to other people. You probably have no difficulty remembering our high school principal, K. W. Park, for whom we had a respect–contempt complex. He used to lecture, almost daily at morning assemblies, on the virtue of being modest. As he preached it, it was a form of the Confucian virtue of self-denial. Our existence or presence among other people, he told us, should not be overly felt through communicated messages (regardless of whether they are done with a tongue or pen). . . . One's existence, we were told, should be noticed by others in the form of our acts and conduct. One is obligated to provide opportunities for others to experience one's existence through what he or she does. Self-initiated effort for public recognition or self-aggrandizement was the most shameful conduct for a person of virtue.

This idea is interesting and noble as a philosophical posture, but when it is practiced in America, it will not get you anywhere in most circumstances. The lack of self-assertion is translated directly into timidity and lack of self-confidence. This is a culture where you must exert your individuality to the extent that it would make our high school principal turn in his grave out of shame and disgust. Blame the size of the territory or the population of this country. You may even blame the fast-paced cadence of life or the social mobility that moves people around at a dizzying speed. Whatever the specific reason might be,

Americans are not waiting to experience you or your behaviors as they exist. They want a "documented" version of you that is eloquently summarized, decorated, and certified. What they are looking for is not your raw, unprocessed being with rich texture; rather, it is a slickly processed self, neatly packaged, and, most important, conveniently delivered to them. Self-advertising is encouraged almost to the point of pretentiousness.

The curious journey toward the American end of the individualism–collectivism continuum will be inevitable, I assure you. The real question is whether it will be in your generation, your children's, or their children's. Whenever it happens, it will be a bittersweet revenge for me, since only then will you realize how it feels to be called an American by your best high school chum.

Source: Excerpted from a letter by Dr. Jin K. Kim, State University of New York—Plattsburgh. Copyright © 2001 by Dr. Jin K. Kim. Used with permission of Dr. Kim.

CULTURE AND MANAGEMENT STYLES AROUND THE WORLD

As an international manager, once you have researched the culture of a country in which you may be going to work or with which to do business, and after you have developed a cultural profile, it is useful then to apply that information to develop an understanding of the expected management styles and ways of doing business that predominate in that region, or with that type of business setting. Two examples follow: Saudi Arabia and Chinese Small Family Businesses.

Saudi Arabia

Understanding how business is conducted in the modern Middle East requires an understanding of the Arab culture, since the Arab peoples are the majority there and most of them are Muslim. As discussed in the opening profile, the Arab culture is intertwined with the pervasive influence of Islam. Even though not all Middle Easterners are Arab, Arab culture and management style predominate in the Arabian Gulf region. Shared culture, religion, and language underlie behavioral similarities throughout the Arab world. Islam permeates Saudi life—Allah is always present, controls everything, and is frequently referred to in conversation. Employees may spend more than two hours a day in prayer as part of the life pattern that intertwines work with religion, politics, and social life.

Arab history and culture are based on tribalism, with its norms of reciprocity of favors, support, obligation, and identity passed on to the family unit, which is the primary structural model. Family life is based on closer personal ties than in the West. Arabs value personal relationships, honor, and saving face for all concerned; these values take precedence over the work at hand or verbal accuracy. "Outsiders" must realize that establishing a trusting relationship and respect for Arab social norms has to precede any attempts at business discussions. Honor, pride, and dignity are at the core of "shame" societies, such as the Arabs. As such, shame and honor provide the basis for social control and motivation. Circumstances dictate what is right or wrong and what constitutes acceptable behavior.

Arabs avoid open admission of error at all costs because weakness (*muruwwa*) is a failure to be manly. It is sometimes difficult for westerners to get at the truth because of the Arab need to avoid showing weakness; instead, Arabs present a desired or idealized situation. Shame is also brought on someone who declines to fulfill a request or a favor; therefore, a business arrangement is left open if something has yet to be completed.

The communication style of Middle Eastern societies is high context (that is, implicit and indirect), and their use of time is polychronic: Many activities can be taking place at the same time, with constant interruptions commonplace. The imposition of deadlines is considered rude, and business schedules take a backseat to the perspective that events will occur "sometime" when Allah wills (*bukra insha Allah*). Arabs give primary importance to hospitality; they are cordial to business associates and lavish in their entertainment, constantly offering strong black coffee (which you should not refuse) and banquets before considering business transactions. Westerners must realize the importance of personal contacts and networking, socializing and building close relationships and trust, practicing patience regarding schedules, and doing

EXHIBIT 3-8   Behavior that Will Likely Cause Offense in Saudi Arabia

- Bringing up business subjects until you get to know your host, or you will be considered rude.
- Commenting on a man's wife or female children over 12 years of age.
- Raising colloquial questions that may be common in your country but possibly misunderstood in Saudi Arabia as an invasion of privacy.
- Using disparaging or swear words and off-color or obscene attempts at humor.
- Engaging in conversations about religion, politics, or Israel.
- Bringing gifts of alcohol or using alcohol, which is prohibited in Saudi Arabia.
- Requesting favors from those in authority or esteem, for it is considered impolite for Arabs to say no.
- Shaking hands too firmly or pumping—gentle or limp handshakes are preferred.
- Pointing your finger at someone or showing the soles of your feet when seated.

Source: P. R. Harris and R. T. Moran, *Managing Cultural Differences*, 5th ed. (Houston: Gulf Publishing, 2000).

business in person. Exhibit 3-8 gives some selected actions and nonverbal behaviors that may offend Arabs. The relationship between cultural values and norms in Saudi Arabia and managerial behaviors is illustrated in Exhibit 3-9.

EXHIBIT 3-9   The Relationship Between Culture and Managerial Behaviors in Saudi Arabia

Cultural Values	Managerial Behaviors
Tribal and family loyalty	Work group loyalty
	Paternal sociability
	Stable employment and a sense of belonging
	A pleasant workplace
	Careful selection of employees
	Nepotism
Arabic language	Business as an intellectual activity
	Access to employees and peers
	Management by walking around
	Conversation as recreation
Close and warm friendships	A person rather than task and money orientation
	Theory Y management
	Avoidance of judgment
Islam	Sensitivity to Islamic virtues
	Observance of the Qur'an and Sharia
	Work as personal or spiritual growth
	Consultative management
	A full and fair hearing
	Adherence to norms
Honor and shame	Clear guidelines and conflict avoidance
	Positive reinforcement
	Training and defined job duties
	Private correction of mistakes
	Avoidance of competition
An idealized self	Centralized decision making
	Assumption of responsibility appropriate to position
	Empathy and respect for the self-image of others
Polychronic use of time	Right- and left-brain facility
	A bias for action
	Patience and flexibility
Independence	Sensitivity to control
	Interest in the individual
Male domination	Separation of sexes
	Open work life; closed family life

Source: R. R. Harris and R. T. Moran, *Managing Cultural Differences* 5th ed. (Houston: Gulf Publishing, 2000).

Chinese Small Family Businesses

The predominance of small businesses in China and the region highlights the need for managers from around the world to gain an understanding of how such businesses operate. Many small businesses—most of which are family or extended-family businesses—become part of the value chain (suppliers, buyers, retailers, etc.) within industries in which "foreign" firms may compete.

Some specifics of Chinese management style and practices in particular are presented here as they apply to small businesses. (Further discussion of the Chinese culture continues in Chapter 5 in the context of negotiation.) It is important to note that no matter the size of a company, but especially in small businesses, it is the all-pervasive presence and use of *guanxi* that provides the little red engine of business transactions in China. *Guanxi* means "connections"— the network of relationships the Chinese cultivate through friendship and affection; it entails the exchange of favors and gifts to provide an obligation to reciprocate favors. Those who share a *guanxi* network share an unwritten code.[54] The philosophy and structure of Chinese businesses comprise paternalism, mutual obligation, responsibility, hierarchy, familialism, personalism, and connections. Autocratic leadership is the norm, with the owner using his or her power—but with a caring about other people that may predominate over efficiency.

According to Lee, the major differences between Chinese management styles and those of their Western counterparts are human-centeredness, family-centeredness, centralization of power, and small size.[55] Their human-centered management style puts people ahead of a business relationship and focuses on friendship, loyalty, and trustworthiness.[56] The family is extremely important in Chinese culture, and any small business tends to be run like a family.

Globalization has resulted in the ethnic Chinese businesses (in China or other Asian countries) to adapt to more competitive management styles. They are moving away from the traditional centralized power structure in Chinese organizations which comprised the boss and a few family members at the top and the employees at the bottom, with no ranking among the workers. In fact, many are no longer managed by family members. Frequently, the managers are those sons and daughters who have studied and worked overseas before returning to the family company; or even foreign expatriates. Examples of Chinese capitalism responding to change and working to globalize through growth are Eu Yan Sang Holdings Ltd., the Hiap Moh Printing businesses, and the Pacific International Line.[57]

As Chinese firms in many modern regions in the Pacific Rim seek to modernize and compete locally and globally, a tug of war has begun between the old and the new: the traditional Chinese management practices and the increasingly "imported" Western management styles. As discussed by Lee, this struggle is encapsulated in the different management perspectives of the old and young generations. A two-generational study of Chinese managers by Ralston et al. also found generational shifts in work values in China. They concluded that the new generation manager is more individualistic, more independent, and takes more risks in the pursuit of profits. However, they also found the new generation holding on to their Confucian values, concluding that the new generation may be viewed as "crossverging their Eastern and Western influences, while on the road of modernization."[58]

CONCLUSION

This chapter has explored various cultural values and how managers can understand them with the help of cultural profiles. The following chapters focus on application of this cultural knowledge to management in an international environment (or, alternatively in a domestic multi-cultural environment)—especially as relevant to cross-cultural communication (Chapter 4), negotiation and decision making (Chapter 5), and motivating and leading (Chapter 11). Culture and communication are essentially synonymous; what happens when people from different cultures communicate, and how can international managers understand the underlying process and adapt their styles and expectations accordingly? For the answers, read the next chapter.

Summary of Key Points

1. The culture of a society comprises the shared values, understandings, assumptions, and goals that are passed down through generations and imposed by members of the society. These unique sets of cultural and national differences strongly influence the attitudes and expectations and therefore the on-the-job behavior of individuals and groups.

2. Managers must develop cultural sensitivity to anticipate and accommodate behavioral differences in various societies. As part of that sensitivity, they must avoid parochialism—an attitude that assumes one's own management techniques are best in any situation or location and that other people should follow one's patterns of behavior.

3. From his research in 50 countries, Hofstede proposes four underlying value dimensions that help to identify and describe the cultural profile of a country and affect organizational processes: power distance, uncertainty avoidance, individualism, and masculinity.

4. Through his research, Fons Trompenaars confirmed some similar dimensions, and found other unique dimensions: obligation, emotional orientation, privacy, and source of power and status.

5. The GLOBE project team of 170 researchers in 62 countries concluded the presence of a number of other dimensions, and ranked countries on those dimensions, including assertiveness, performance orientation, future orientation, and humane orientation. Gupta et al. from that team found geographical clusters on nine of the GLOBE project cultural dimensions.

6. On-the-job conflicts in international management frequently arise out of conflicting values and orientations regarding time, change, material factors, and individualism.

7. Managers can use research results and personal observations to develop a character sketch, or cultural profile, of a country. This profile can help managers anticipate how to motivate people and coordinate work processes in a particular international context.

Discussion Questions

1. What is meant by the culture of a society, and why is it important that international managers understand it? Do you notice cultural differences among your classmates? How do those differences affect the class environment? How do they affect your group projects?

2. Describe the four dimensions of culture proposed by Hofstede. What are the managerial implications of these dimensions? Compare the findings with those of Trompenaars and the GLOBE project team.

3. Discuss the types of operational conflicts that could occur in an international context because of different attitudes toward time, change, material factors, and individualism. Give examples relative to specific countries.

4. Discuss how the internet and culture interact. Which most affects the other, and how? Give some examples.

5. Discuss collectivism as it applies to the Japanese workplace. What managerial functions does it affect?

6. Discuss the role of Islam in cross-cultural relations and business operations.

Application Exercises

1. Develop a cultural profile for one of the countries in the following list. Form small groups of students and compare your findings in class with those of another group preparing a profile for another country. Be sure to compare specific findings regarding religion, kinship, recreation, and other subsystems. What are the prevailing attitudes toward time, change, material factors, and individualism?

   Any African country
   People's Republic of China
   Saudi Arabia
   Mexico
   France
   India

2. In small groups of students, research Hofstede's findings regarding the four dimensions of power distance, uncertainty avoidance, masculinity, and individualism for one of the following countries in comparison to the United States. (Your instructor can assign the countries to avoid duplication.) Present your findings to the class. Assume you are a U.S. manager of a subsidiary in the foreign country and explain how differences on these dimensions are likely to affect your management tasks. What suggestions do you have for dealing with these differences in the workplace?

   Brazil
   Italy
   People's Republic of China
   Russia

Experiential Exercises

1. A large Baltimore manufacturer of cabinet hardware had been working for months to locate a suitable distributor for its products in Europe. Finally invited to present a demonstration to a reputable distributing company in Frankfurt, it sent one of its most promising young executives, Fred Wagner, to make the presentation. Fred not only spoke fluent German but also felt a special interest in this assignment because his paternal grandparents had immigrated to the United States from the Frankfurt area during the

1920s. When Fred arrived at the conference room where he would be making his presentation, he shook hands firmly, greeted everyone with a friendly *guten tag,* and even remembered to bow the head slightly as is the German custom. Fred, an effective speaker and past president of the Baltimore Toastmasters Club, prefaced his presentation with a few humorous anecdotes to set a relaxed and receptive atmosphere. However, he felt that his presentation was not well received by the company executives. In fact, his instincts were correct, for the German company chose not to distribute Fred's hardware products.

What went wrong?

2. Bill Nugent, an international real estate developer from Dallas, had made a 2:30 P.M. appointment with Mr. Abdullah, a high-ranking government official in Riyadh, Saudi Arabia. From the beginning things did not go well for Bill. First, he was kept waiting until nearly 3:45 P.M. before he was ushered into Mr. Abdullah's office. When he finally did get in, several other men were also in the room. Even though Bill felt that he wanted to get down to business with Mr. Abdullah, he was reluctant to get too specific because he considered much of what they needed to discuss sensitive and private. To add to Bill's sense of frustration, Mr. Abdullah seemed more interested in engaging in meaningless small talk than in dealing with the substantive issues concerning their business.

How might you help Bill deal with his frustration?

3. Tom Forrest, an up-and-coming executive for a U.S. electronics company, was sent to Japan to work out the details of a joint venture with a Japanese electronics firm. During the first several weeks, Tom felt that the negotiations were proceeding better than he had expected. He found that he had very cordial working relationships with the team of Japanese executives, and in fact, they had agreed on the major policies and strategies governing the new joint venture. During the third week of negotiations, Tom was present at a meeting held to review their progress. The meeting was chaired by the president of the Japanese firm, Mr. Hayakawa, a man in his mid-forties, who had recently taken over the presidency from his 82-year-old grandfather. The new president, who had been involved in most of the negotiations during the preceding weeks, seemed to Tom to be one of the strongest advocates of the plan that had been developed to date. Hayakawa's grandfather, the recently retired president, also was present at the meeting. After the plans had been discussed in some detail, the octogenarian past president proceeded to give a long soliloquy about how some of the features of this plan violated the traditional practices on which the company had been founded. Much to Tom's amazement, Mr. Hayakawa did nothing to explain or defend the policies and strategies that they had taken weeks to develop. Feeling extremely frustrated, Tom then gave a fairly strong argued defense of the plan. To Tom's further amazement, no one else in the meeting spoke up in defense of the plan. The tension in the air was quite heavy, and the meeting adjourned shortly thereafter. Within days the Japanese firm completely terminated the negotiations on the joint venture.

How could you help Tom better understand this bewildering situation?

Source: Gary P. Ferraro, *The Cultural Dimensions of International Business,* 2nd ed. (Upper Saddle River, NJ: Prentice Hall, 1994).

Internet Resources

Visit the Deresky Companion Website at www.pearsonhighered.com/deresky for this chapter's Internet resources.

CASE STUDY

Australia and New Zealand: Doing business with Indonesia

There are thousands of Australians, both individually and as members of organizations, who share trade and education with Indonesia and provide support—as do New Zealanders. Yet, though geographically part of Asia, citizens of Australia and New Zealand are members of cultures very different from any other in Asia.

As increasingly they seek to trade in Asia, so also do they need to learn to manage such differences; and doing business in Indonesia is a good example. Travelling time by air from Perth, Western Australia, is slightly less than four hours, yet the cultural distance is immeasurable.

In January 2007 the Jakarta Post reported GDP growth had risen to over 5%. Consumer consumption drives the economy but exports are thriving and therein lies opportunities for Australia and New Zealand.

Indonesia is a country of more than 17,000 islands and the world's largest Muslim nation. In her lecture, Dr Joan Hardjono[59] of Monash University, discussed the historical and geographic contexts of modern Indonesia. She spoke of the many clusters of islands worldwide that have come together as nation states—for example, the Philippines and some island groups in the Pacific—but described the Indonesian archipelago as in a class of its own.

It is unique in terms of extent and diversity. For example, Java and Bali have fertile volcanic soils, while elsewhere the land is rich in mineral resources such as oil, natural gas and coal. Climatic conditions vary from island to island. Some regions experience annual heavy rains and floods, while others suffer regularly from droughts that often lead to famines.

With a population of more than 230 million people, Indonesia is the fourth most populous country in the world but there is a great imbalance in population distribution within the archipelago. Settlement has always been greatest on the island of Java, and today about 60% of the Indonesian population lives there.

National ties are strong, as revealed by the great response from within Indonesia to the recent natural disasters in Aceh and Nias. Unfortunately, there are still very obvious socio-economic disparities in all regions of the country. At the top of the social structure are wealthy elites, below them an increasingly demanding middle class, and at the bottom an impoverished majority.

As Indonesia has become more integrated with ASEAN, North Asian trading partners have become more important: but well-to-do Indonesians now travel the world. Globalization has been the buzzword of international business for many years. International markets have split up into unified trade zones; individual marketplaces, particularly in the developing countries, are exposed to transnational pressures.

Some Asian countries are pulling back from perceived threats of international contagion, but Indonesia continues to open up its markets to world enterprise. However Australians and New Zealanders cannot expect to do business with Indonesians just because they are neighbours. They have to learn the moves.

Business opportunities in Indonesia include agribusiness, the automotive industry, business and financial services, construction and infrastructure, information and communication technology, e-commerce, education and training; environmental products and services, food and beverages, fresh produce, health and medical provisions, mining and mineral services, oil and petroleum drilling, transport and storage, science and technology.

Taking advantage of these opportunities requires skilful negotiation. One of the biggest challenges of working in a foreign country is learning how to operate in a different cultural setting. International managers tell endless stories of cross-cultural breakdowns, missed appointments, problems over differences in management style, lost orders or down time on production lines, labour problems between foreign management and local staff and many other examples of miscommunication. Many could have been avoided or at least mitigated had the expatriate managers and their local counterparts been better prepared for differences in work patterns.

Some cross cultural behaviour such as patience and courtesy is no more than good manners, it applies to all interpersonal communication: but in Indonesia, as in the rest of Asia, there is more need to develop a long-term relationship to produce a profit than there is in Australia or New Zealand. Relationships rely on shared expectations—for example, about how first contacts should be made, how appointments should be set and kept, how deals should be closed, how time should be managed (including the Indonesian concept of 'jam karet', or 'rubber time,' that infuriates punctuality-conscious Westerners).

Sensible but inexperienced international managers seek information that more seasoned veterans can provide. They might be colleagues, business associates, friends, or paid consultants, but in any case most people are eager to give advice. On the other hand, even managers with a highly developed global outlook may have too generalist a viewpoint on international business. They may overlook the need for a local perspective in each host country.

Indonesia is one of those countries in which a foreign manager's home office priorities of task over relationship, of corporate rather than human priorities, may not be the most effective ways to achieve productivity and effectiveness. Indonesian managers usually place more value on harmony, understanding, and mutual respect. It may be sometimes that this emphasis outweighs the importance of job performance and productivity.

On the other hand there are a number of concerns for Indonesian managers working with their Western counterparts. For example, they believe Westerners should make an effort to adjust to the culture, taboos, and language of their Indonesian colleagues. Foreign managers should avoid bad language that might set a bad example for the workers. They should give instructions slowly and clearly in Standard English and should ask for paraphrase to ensure understanding. They should be willing to consider individual cases and cultural needs (e.g., prayer times or other religious obligations, time off for cemetery visits before Ramadan, weddings, funerals).

On the other hand, Indonesian managers should be willing to make many adjustments to working in an international company. Important areas where Western management techniques are most successful include strategic planning and timetable deadlines, efficiency and punctuality, handling conflict and taking responsibility.

Sensitivity to the needs of employees is a management area that is seldom stressed in most Western business cultures where efficiency, productivity, and effectiveness take priority. For example, when somebody loses their self-control through anger, distress, or confusion, Javanese will usually advise the need to 'eling' (in translation, not to allow oneself to be overwhelmed by feelings and mixed-up thoughts but to regain self-control). Self-control is of high value to Javanese, maybe of the highest. This value is not unique to Indonesia. It is shared by the indigenous peoples of South Asia, the Himalayan Range and Central Asia, East Asia, South-east Asia, Africa; Oceania, the Caribbean and South America; and Northern America and the Arctic: hence a common cultural emphasis on the art of making and wearing masks to represent hidden emotions. Regardless of the cultures they come from, masks convey the essential emotions.[60]

Thus situations can arise in business contexts where hiding true feelings and keeping up appearances may take precedence over solving a problem.

Maintaining the harmony of the office by giving the outward appearance that there is nothing wrong is a fairly common situation in traditional Indonesian offices. Bad news may not be communicated to the boss and situations that seem insurmountable to an employee may simply be ignored.[61] Since this behaviour is not generally accepted to be part of Western culture—though certainly it exists there—Western managers need to spend more time observing and listening to their Indonesian employees than they would back home.

Another reason why such attentiveness is important is that Indonesian business relationships are paternal or maternal. Workers expect their supervisors to look after their interests rather as parents do for their children; and their supervisors understand and accept this responsibility. Furthermore, the tension involved in being the bearer of bad news to one's boss is felt very keenly by Indonesian employees, and this needs to be taken into account by supervisors and managers. The English language injunction is "Don't shoot the messenger" but some Indonesian workers seem to expect a firing squad when they have to report failure. Therefore, Western managers should make clear that they want and expect subordinates to come to them with questions or problems and that the response will be non-judgmental and self-controlled. Faces should be without masks; they should not portray negative emotions of anger, confrontation, or aggression. Managers in Indonesia are expected always be polite and to keep smiling, no matter how angry they may be inside.

Nevertheless, cross-cultural sensitivity works—or should work—both ways. Foreign managers should understand Indonesian culture and business customs, and Indonesian managers should be given clearly to understand what foreign managers will expect from them.

Case Questions

1. Using this case and the cultural dimensions explored in this chapter, discuss some of the ways in which citizens of Australia and New Zealand are members of cultures very different from any other in Asia.
2. In what respects is the Indonesian archipelago unique in Asia?
3. What characteristics of Indonesian workplaces are referred to in this profile?
4. How does the population appear to be socially stratified?
5. What are some business opportunities in Indonesia for foreign direct investment?

Sources:

Joan Hardjono, 05/08/2005, Herb Feith Lecture, "Can Indonesia Hold?" Centre of Southeast Asian Studies and Faculty of Arts, Monash University, in association with ABC Radio Australia and the Melbourne Institute of Asian Languages & Societies, University of Melbourne: http://www.abc.net.au/ra/news/ infocus/s1429967.htm;

Javanese mystical movements, January 2007, http://www.xs4all.nl/~wichm/javmys1.html

Phil King, December 2006, "Facing disaster: The 27 May earthquake shook a kingdom, not just a city," Inside Indonesia: http://www.insideindonesia.org/

Rupa-Pratirupa - Man & Mask 20th Feb.1998 - 12th Apr.1998, Matighar, IGNCA, http://ignca.nic.in/ ex_0032.htm.

Stephen Schwartz, January 2007, "Maintain momentum to overcome challenges" in Jakarta Post: http://www.thejakartapost.com/Outlook2006/eco11b.asp

Patrick Underwood, 23/11/2006, "Asia Update", Meat & Livestock Australia Limited (MLA) http://www.mla.com.au/; Inside indonesia, http://www.insideindonesia.org/edit80/p11-12mahony.html

Western Australia Dept of Industry and resources: export and trade, http://www.doir.wa.gov.au/exportandtrade/F3130D5AECA54ACF8ABBBBA831766203.asp

George B. Whitfield, 2006, Executive Orientation Services of Jakarta (EOS) www.indo.net.id/EOS/.

World Bank, http://0-siteresources.worldbank.org.library.vu.edu.au/INTINDONESIA/Resources/htm

Source: Adapted from Helen Deresky and Elizabeth Christopher, "Australia and New Zealand as part of Asia: Doing Business with Indonesia," *International Management: Managing across borders and Cultures,* Pearson Education Australia, 2008.

Communicating Across Cultures

OBJECTIVES:

1. To recognize the cultural variables in the communication process and what factors can cause "noise" in that process.

2. To develop an awareness of differences in non-verbal behaviors, context, and attitudes and how they affect cross-cultural communication.

3. To understand the complexities of Western-Arab communications.

4. To be aware of the impact of IT on cross-border communications.

5. To learn how to successfully manage cross-cultural business communications.

Opening Profile: Google's Internet Communications Clash with European Culture[1]

Google has been expanding into European markets for five years and now has a headquarters in Dublin, large offices in Zurich and London, and smaller centers in countries like Denmark, Russia and Poland. However, Google is now getting caught in a cultural web of privacy laws that threaten its growth and the positive image it has cultivated.

The latest clash is over Google's plan to introduce "Street View," a mapping service that provides a vivid, 360-degree, ground-level photographic panorama from any address. However, data protection officials in Switzerland are pressing Google to cancel those plans, since "Street View" would violate strict Swiss privacy laws that prohibit the unauthorized use of personal images or property. In Germany, where Street View is also not available, simply taking photographs for the service violates privacy laws. At the same time, the EU Article 29 Data Protection Working Group, which is a collaboration among all the information and data protection watchdogs within the European Union, is also contesting Google's practices. The EU Justice Commissioner, Franco Frattini, was backing the investigation. Google, the world's largest search engine, provoked a debate about internet privacy in May 2008, when it announced it would institute changes to its policies on holding personal information about its customers. The policy change related to Google's server logs (the information a browser sends back to Google when somebody visits a site). At present, the search engine retains a log of every search indefinitely, including information—such as the unique computer address, browser type and language—which could be traced back to a particular computer. The policy change was to reduce how long that information was retained to 18–24 months.

Peter Schaar, chair of Article 29, who is also Germany's federal commissioner for freedom of information, developed a report on the relationship between search-engine business models and European privacy laws. The draft report concluded that IP addresses are personal information because they can help identify a person. Europeans fiercely protect their privacy and trust that the government enforces it in law. Mr. Schaar has challenged Peter Fleischer of Google's global privacy law team to explain why such a long storage period was chosen and to give a legal justification for the storage of server logs in general. Google's response so far, from founders Sergei Brin and Larry Page, was to identify others as the bigger threat to internet users' privacy. They stated that information posted on social networking sites, such as photographs of young people at drunken parties, are a greater privacy concern. They defended the value of users' information for refining search results, and blamed the way some companies have used that information for privacy problems in the industry. The outcome of this cross-cultural internet communication clash remains to be seen. One thing that is clear is that the European Union (EU) has fired a warning shot across the bows of the search-engine companies.

> *Cultural communications are deeper and more complex than spoken or written messages. The essence of effective cross-cultural communication has more to do with releasing the right responses than with sending the "right" messages.*
>
> HALL AND HALL[2]

> *Multi-local online strategy . . . is about meeting global business objectives by tuning in to the cultural dynamics of their local markets.*
>
> "THINK GLOBALLY, INTERACT LOCALLY,"
> *New Media Age*[3]

As the opening profile suggests, communication is a critical factor in the cross-cultural management issues discussed in this book, particularly those of an interpersonal nature, involving motivation, leadership, group interactions, and negotiation. Culture is conveyed and perpetuated through communication in one form or another. Culture and communication are so intricately intertwined that they are, essentially, synonymous.[4] By understanding this relationship, managers can move toward constructive intercultural management.

Communication, whether in the form of writing, talking, listening, or via the Internet, is an inherent part of a manager's role and takes up the majority of a manager's time on the job. Studies by Mintzberg demonstrate the importance of oral communication; he found that most managers spend between 50 and 90 percent of their time talking to people.[5] The ability of a manager to effectively communicate across cultural boundaries will largely determine the success of international business transactions or the output of a culturally diverse workforce. It is useful, then, to break down the elements involved in the communication process, both to understand the cross-cultural issues at stake and to maximize the process.

THE COMMUNICATION PROCESS

The term **communication** describes the process of sharing meaning by transmitting messages through media such as words, behavior, or material artifacts. Managers communicate to co-ordinate activities, to disseminate information, to motivate people, and to negotiate future plans. It is of vital importance, then, for a receiver to interpret the meaning of a particular communication in the way the sender intended. Unfortunately, the communication process (see Exhibit 4-1) involves stages during which meaning can be distorted. Anything that serves to undermine the communication of the intended meaning is typically referred to as **noise.**

The primary cause of noise stems from the fact that the sender and the receiver each exist in a unique, private world thought of as her or his life space. The context of that private world, largely based on culture, experience, relations, values, and so forth, determines the interpretation of meaning in communication. People filter, or selectively understand, messages consistent with their own expectations and perceptions of reality and their values and norms of behavior. The more dissimilar the cultures of those involved, the more the likelihood of misinterpretation. In this way, as Samovar, Porter, and Jain state, cultural factors pervade the communication process:

> *Culture not only dictates who talks with whom, about what, and how the communication proceeds, it also helps to determine how people encode messages, the meanings they have for messages, and the conditions and circumstances under which various messages may or may not be sent, noticed, or interpreted. In fact, our entire repertory of communicative behaviors is dependent largely on the culture in which we have been raised. Culture, consequently, is the foundation of communication. And, when cultures vary, communication practices also vary.*[6]

Communication, therefore, is a complex process of linking up or sharing the perceptual fields of sender and receiver; the perceptive sender builds a bridge to the life space of the receiver.[7] After the receiver interprets the message and draws a conclusion about what the sender meant, he or she will, in most cases, encode and send back a response, making communication a circular process.

The communication process is rapidly changing, however, as a result of technological developments, therefore propelling global business forward at a phenomenal growth rate. These changes are discussed later in this chapter.

Cultural Noise in the Communication Process

> *In Japanese there are several words for "I" and several words for "you" but their use depends on the relationship between the speaker and the other person. In short, there is no "I" by itself; the "I" depends on the relationship.*[8]

EXHIBIT 4-1   The Communication Process

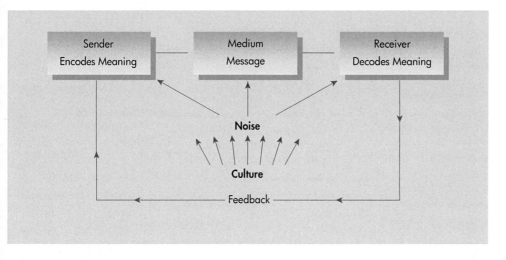

Because the focus in this text is on effective cross-cultural communication, it is important to understand what cultural variables cause noise in the communication process. This knowledge of **cultural noise**—the cultural variables that undermine the communications of intended meaning—will enable us to take steps to minimize that noise and so to improve communication.

When a member of one culture sends a message to a member of another culture, **intercultural communication** takes place. The message contains the meaning intended by the encoder. When it reaches the receiver, however, it undergoes a transformation in which the influence of the decoder's culture becomes part of the meaning.[9] Exhibit 4-2 provides an example of intercultural communication in which the meaning got all mixed up. Note how the attribution of behavior differs for each participant. **Attribution** is the process in which people look for an explanation of another person's behavior. When they realize that they do not understand another, they tend, say Hall and Hall, to blame their confusion on the other's "stupidity, deceit, or craziness."[10]

In the situation depicted in Exhibit 4-2, the Greek employee becomes frustrated and resigns after experiencing communication problems with his American boss. How could this outcome have been avoided? We do not have much information about the people or the context of the situation, but we can look at some of the variables that might have been involved and use them as a basis for analysis.

EXHIBIT 4-2   Cultural Noise in International Communication[11]

Behavior		Attribution	
American:	"How long will it take you to finish this report?"	*American*:	I asked him to participate.
		Greek:	His behavior makes no sense. He is the boss. Why doesn't he tell me?
Greek:	"I don't know. How long should it take?"	*American*:	He refuses to take responsibility.
		Greek:	I asked him for an order.
American:	"You are in the best position to analyze time requirements."	*American*:	I press him to take responsibility for his actions.
		Greek:	What nonsense: I'd better give him an answer.
Greek:	"10 days."	*American*:	He lacks the ability to estimate time; this time estimate is totally inadequate.
American:	"Take 15. Is it agreed? You will do it in 15 days?"	*American*:	I offer a contract.
		Greek:	These are my orders: 15 days.
In fact, the report needed 30 days of regular work. So the Greek worked day and night, but at the end of the 15th day, he still needed to do one more day's work.			
American:	"Where is the report?"	*American*:	I am making sure he fulfills his contract.
		Greek:	He is asking for the report.
Greek:	"It will be ready tomorrow."	(Both attribute that it is not ready.)	
American:	"But we agreed it would be ready today."	*American*:	I must teach him to fulfill a contract.
		Greek:	The stupid, incompetent boss! Not only did he give me the wrong orders, but he doesn't even appreciate that I did a 30-day job in 16 days.
The Greek hands in his resignation.		The American is surprised.	
		Greek:	I can't work for such a man.

THE CULTURE–COMMUNICATION LINK

The following sections examine underlying elements of culture that affect communication. The degree to which one is able to effectively communicate largely depends on how similar the other person's cultural expectations are to our own. However, cultural gaps can be overcome by prior learning and understanding of those variables and how to adjust to them.

Trust in Communication

The key ingredient in a successful alliance is trust.

JAMES R. HOUGHTON,
Former Chairman, Corning, Inc.[12]

Effective communication, and therefore collaboration in alliances across national boundaries, depends on the informal understandings among the parties that are based on the trust that has developed between them. However, the meaning of trust and how it is developed and communicated vary across societies. In China and Japan, for example, business transactions are based on networks of long-standing relationships based on trust rather than on the formal contracts and arm's-length relationships typical of the United States. When there is trust between parties, implicit understanding arises within communications. This understanding has numerous benefits in business, including encouraging communicators to overlook cultural differences and minimize problems. It allows communicators to adjust to unforeseen circumstances with less conflict than would be the case with formal contracts, and it facilitates open communication in exchanging ideas and information.[13] From his research on trust in global collaboration, John Child suggests the following guidelines for cultivating trust:

- Create a clear and calculated basis for mutual benefit. There must be realistic commitments and good intentions to honor them.
- Improve predictability: Strive to resolve conflicts and keep communication open.
- Develop mutual bonding through regular socializing and friendly contact.[14]

What can managers anticipate with regard to the level of trust in communications with people in other countries? If trust is based on how trustworthy we consider a person to be, then it must vary according to that society's expectations about whether that culture supports the norms and values that predispose people to behave credibly and benevolently. Are there differences across societies in those expectations of trust? Research by the World Values Study Group of 90,000 people in 45 societies provides some insight on cultural values regarding predisposition to trust. When we examine the percentage of respondents in each society who responded that "most people can be trusted," we can see that the Nordic countries and China had the highest predisposition to trust, followed by Canada, the United States, and Britain, while Brazil, Turkey, Romania, Slovenia, and Latvia had the lowest level of trust in people.[15]

The GLOBE Project

Results from the GLOBE research on culture, discussed in Chapter 3, provide some insight into culturally appropriate communication styles and expectations for the manager to use abroad. GLOBE researchers Javidan and House make the following observations:[16] For people in societies that ranked high on performance orientation—for example, the United States—presenting objective information in a direct and explicit way is an important and expected manner of communication; this compares with people in Russia or Greece—which ranked low on performance orientation—for whom hard facts and figures are not readily available or taken seriously. In those cases, a more indirect approach is preferred. People from countries ranking low on assertiveness, such as Sweden, also recoil from explicitness; their preference is for much two-way discourse and friendly relationships.

People ranking high on the "humane" dimension, such as those from Ireland and the Philippines, make avoiding conflict a priority and tend to communicate with the goal of being supportive of people rather than of achieving objective end results. This compares to people from France and Spain whose agenda is achievement of goals.

The foregoing provides examples of how to draw implications for appropriate communication styles from the research findings on cultural differences across societies. Astute global managers have learned that culture and communication are inextricably linked and that they should prepare themselves accordingly. Most will also suggest that you carefully watch and listen to how your hosts are communicating and to follow their lead.

Cultural Variables in the Communication Process

On a different level, it is also useful to be aware of cultural variables that can affect the communication process by influencing a person's perceptions; some of these variables have been identified by Samovar and Porter and discussed by Harris and Moran, and others.[17] These variables are as follows: attitudes, social organization, thought patterns, roles, language (spoken or written), nonverbal communication (including kinesic behavior, proxemics, paralanguage, and object language), and time. Although these variables are discussed separately in this text, their effects are interdependent and inseparable—or, as Hecht, Andersen, and Ribeau put it, "Encoders and decoders process nonverbal cues as a conceptual, multichanneled gestalt."[18]

Attitudes   We all know that our attitudes underlie the way we behave and communicate and the way we interpret messages from others. Ethnocentric attitudes are a particular source of noise in cross-cultural communication. In the incident described in Exhibit 4-2, both the American and the Greek are clearly attempting to interpret and convey meaning based on their own experiences of that kind of transaction. The American is probably guilty of stereotyping the Greek employee by quickly jumping to the conclusion that he is unwilling to take responsibility for the task and the scheduling.

This problem, **stereotyping,** occurs when a person assumes that every member of a society or subculture has the same characteristics or traits. Stereotyping is a common cause of misunderstanding in intercultural communication. It is an arbitrary, lazy, and often destructive way to find out about people. Astute managers are aware of the dangers of cultural stereotyping and deal with each person as an individual with whom they may form a unique relationship.

Social Organization   Our perceptions can be influenced by differences in values, approach, or priorities relative to the kind of social organizations to which we belong. These organizations may be based on one's nation, tribe, or religious sect, or they may consist of the members of a certain profession. Examples of such organizations include the Academy of Management or the United Auto Workers (UAW).[19]

Thought Patterns   The logical progression of reasoning varies widely around the world and greatly affects the communication process. Managers cannot assume that others use the same reasoning processes, as illustrated by the experience of a Canadian expatriate in Thailand:

> *While in Thailand a Canadian expatriate's car was hit by a Thai motorist who had crossed over the double line while passing another vehicle. After failing to establish that the fault lay with the Thai driver, the Canadian flagged down a policeman. After several minutes of seemingly futile discussion, the Canadian pointed out the double line in the middle of the road and asked the policeman directly, "What do these lines signify?" The policeman replied, "They indicate the center of the road and are there so I can establish just how far the accident is from that point." The Canadian was silent. It had never occurred to him that the double line might not mean "no passing allowed.*[20]

In the Exhibit 4-2 scenario, perhaps the American did not realize that the Greek employee had a different rationale for his time estimate for the job. Because the Greek was not used to having to estimate schedules, he just took a guess, which he felt he had been forced to do.

Roles   Societies differ considerably in their perceptions of a manager's role. Much of the difference is attributable to their perceptions of who should make the decisions and who has responsibility for what. In the Exhibit 4-2 example, the American assumes that his role as manager is to delegate responsibility, to foster autonomy, and to practice participative management. He prescribes the role of the employee without any consideration of whether the employee will understand that role. The Greek's frame of reference leads him to think that the manager is the boss and should give the order about when to have the job completed. He interprets the

American's behavior as breaking that frame of reference, and therefore he feels that the boss is "stupid and incompetent" for giving him the wrong order and for not recognizing and appreciating his accomplishment. The manager should have considered what behaviors Greek workers would expect of him and then either should have played that role or discussed the situation carefully, in a training mode.

Language   Spoken or written language, of course, is a frequent cause of miscommunication, stemming from a person's inability to speak the local language, a poor or too-literal translation, a speaker's failure to explain idioms, or a person missing the meaning conveyed through body language or certain symbols. Even among countries that share the same language, problems can arise from the subtleties and nuances inherent in the use of the language, as noted by George Bernard Shaw: "Britain and America are two nations separated by a common language." This problem can exist even within the same country among subcultures or subgroups.[21]

Many international executives tell stories about lost business deals or lost sales because of communication blunders:

> When Pepsi Cola's slogan "Come Alive with Pepsi" was introduced in Germany, the company learned that the literal German translation of "come alive" is "come out of the grave."
>
> A U.S. airline found a lack of demand for its "rendezvous lounges" on its Boeing 747s. They later learned that "rendezvous" in Portuguese refers to a room that is rented for prostitution.[22]

More than just conveying objective information, language also conveys cultural and social understandings from one generation to the next. Examples of how language reflects what is important in a society include the 6,000 different Arabic words used to describe camels and their parts and the 50 or more classifications of snow used by the Inuit, the Eskimo people of Canada.

Inasmuch as language conveys culture, technology, and priorities, it also serves to separate and perpetuate subcultures. In India, 14 official and many unofficial languages are used, and over 800 languages are spoken on the African continent.

Because of increasing workforce diversity around the world, the international business manager will have to deal with a medley of languages. For example, assembly-line workers at the Ford plant in Cologne, Germany, speak Turkish and Spanish as well as German. In Malaysia, Indonesia, and Thailand, many of the buyers and traders are Chinese. Not all Arabs speak Arabic; in Tunisia and Lebanon, for example, French is the language of commerce.

In North Africa—Morocco, Tunisia, Algeria, Libya, Egypt—people are used to doing business with Europe and the United States. People in Morocco, Algeria, and Tunisia, with their history of French rule, are familiar with the business practices in Europe—they speak French and use the metric system, for example. Egypt has a similar history with the British and so its citizens commonly speak English as their second language. Egypt also has a close political relationship and business ties with the United States.[23]

International managers need either a good command of the local language or competent interpreters. The task of accurate translation to bridge cultural gaps is fraught with difficulties, as Joe Romano, a partner of High Ground, an emerging technology-marketing company in Boston, found out on a business trip to Taiwan, how close a one-syllable slip of the tongue can come to torpedoing a deal. He noted that one is supposed to say 'au-ban,' meaning 'Hello, No.1. Boss.' But instead he said 'Lau-ban ya," which means 'Hello, wife of the boss." Essentially Mr. Romano called him a woman in front of twenty senior Taiwanese executives, who all laughed; but the boss was very embarrassed, because men in Asia have a very macho attitude.[24]

Even the direct translation of specific words does not guarantee the congruence of their meaning, as with the word "yes" used by Asians, which usually means only that they have heard you, and, often, that they are too polite to disagree. The Chinese, for example, through years of political control, have built into their communication culture a cautionary stance to avoid persecution by professing agreement with whatever opinion was held by the person questioning them.[25]

Sometimes even a direct statement can be misinterpreted instead as an indirect expression, as when a German businessman said to his Algerian counterpart, "My wife would love something like that beautiful necklace your wife was wearing last night. It was beautiful." The next day the Algerian gave him a box with the necklace in it as a gift to his wife. The Algerian had interpreted the compliment as an indirect way of expressing a wish to possess a similar necklace. The German was embarrassed, but had to accept the necklace. He realize he needed to be careful how he expressed such things in the future—such as asking where that kind of jewelry is sold.[26]

Politeness and a desire to say only what the listener wants to hear creates noise in the communication process in much of the world. Often, even a clear translation does not help a person to understand what is meant because the encoding process has obscured the true message. With the poetic Arab language—replete with exaggeration, elaboration, and repetition—meaning is attributed more to how something is said rather than what is said.

Businesspeople need to consider another dimension of communication style that can cause noise whether in verbal or non-verbal language—that of *instrumental versus expressive communicators.* Expressive communicators—such as those from Russia, Hungary, Poland—are those who make their communications personal by showing their emotions openly or using emotional appeals to persuade others. This compares with instrumental communicators—whom we find as one moves west and north, such as in the Czech Republic, Slovenia; emphasis is on the content of the communication, not personal expressions.[27]

For the American supervisor and Greek employee cited in Exhibit 4-2, it is highly likely that the American could have picked up some cues from the employee's body language, which probably implied problems with the interpretation of meaning. How might body language have created noise in this case?

Nonverbal Communication   Behavior that communicates without words (although it often is accompanied by words) is called **nonverbal communication.** People will usually believe what they see over what they hear—hence the expression, "A picture is worth a thousand words." Studies show that these subtle messages account for between 65 and 93 percent of interpreted communication.[28] Even minor variations in body language, speech rhythms, and punctuality, for example, often cause mistrust and misperception of the situation among cross-national parties.[29] The media for such nonverbal communication can be categorized into four types: (1) kinesic behavior, (2) proxemics, (3) paralanguage, and (4) object language.

The term **kinesic behavior** refers to communication through body movements— posture, gestures, facial expressions, and eye contact. Although such actions may be universal, often their meaning is not. Because kinesic systems of meaning are culturally specific and learned, they cannot be generalized across cultures. Most people in the West would not correctly interpret many Chinese facial expressions; sticking out the tongue expresses surprise, a widening of the eyes shows anger, and scratching the ears and cheeks indicates happiness.[30] Research has shown for some time, however, that most people worldwide can recognize displays of the basic emotions of anger, disgust, fear, happiness, sadness, surprise, and contempt.[31]

Visitors to other countries must be careful about their gestures and how they might be interpreted. In the United States, for example, a common gesture is that for "O.K."—making a circle with the index finger and the thumb. That is an obscene gesture to the Brazilians, Greeks and Turks. On the other hand people in Japan may point with their middle finger, considered an obscene gesture to others. To Arabs, showing the soles of one's feet is an insult; recall the reporter who threw his shoe at President Bush in late 2008 during his visit to Iraq. This was, to Arabs, the ultimate insult.

Many businesspeople and visitors react negatively to what they feel are inappropriate facial expressions, without understanding the cultural meaning behind them. In his studies of cross-cultural negotiations, Graham observed that the Japanese feel uncomfortable when faced with the Americans' eye-to-eye posture. They are taught since childhood to bow their heads out of humility, whereas the automatic response of Americans is "look at me when I'm talking to you!"[32]

Subtle differences in eye behavior (called *oculesics*) can throw off a communication badly if they are not understood. Eye behavior includes differences not only in eye contact but also in the use of eyes to convey other messages, whether or not that involves mutual gaze. Edward T. Hall, author of the classic *The Silent Language*, explains the differences in eye contact between the British and the Americans. During speech, Americans will look straight at you, but the British keep your attention by looking away. The British will look at you when they have finished speaking, which signals that it is your turn to talk. The implicit rationale for this is that you can't interrupt people when they are not looking at you.[33]

It is helpful for U.S. managers to be aware of the many cultural expectations regarding posture and how they may be interpreted. In Europe or Asia, a relaxed posture in business meetings may be taken as bad manners or the result of poor upbringing. In Korea, you are expected to sit upright, with feet squarely on the floor, and to speak slowly, showing a blending of body and spirit.

Managers can also familiarize themselves with the many different interpretations of hand and finger signals around the world, some of which may represent obscene gestures. Of course, we cannot expect to change all of our ingrained, natural kinesic behavior, but we can be aware of what it means to others. We also can learn to understand the kinesic behavior of others and the role it plays in their society, as well as how it can affect business transactions. Misunderstanding the meanings of body movements—or an ethnocentric attitude toward the "proper" behavior—can have negative repercussions.

Proxemics deals with the influence of proximity and space on communication—both personal space and office space or layout. Americans expect office layout to provide private space for each person, and usually a larger and more private space as one goes up the hierarchy. In much of Asia, the custom is open office space, with people at all levels working and talking in close proximity to one another. Space communicates power in both Germany and the United States, evidenced by the desire for a corner office or one on the top floor. The importance of French officials, however, is made clear by a position in the middle of subordinates, communicating that they have a central position in an information network, where they can stay informed and in control.[34]

Do you ever feel vaguely uncomfortable and start moving backward slowly when someone is speaking to you? This is because that person is invading your "bubble"—your personal space. Personal space is culturally patterned, and foreign spatial cues are a common source of misinterpretation. When someone seems aloof or pushy, it often means that she or he is operating under subtly different spatial rules.

Hall and Hall suggest that cultural differences affect the programming of the senses and that space, perceived by all the senses, is regarded as a form of territory to be protected.[35] South Americans, Southern and Eastern Europeans, Indonesians, and Arabs are **high-contact cultures,** preferring to stand close, touch a great deal, and experience a "close" sensory involvement. Latin Americans, for example, have a highly physical greeting such as putting their arms around a colleague's back and grabbing him by the arm. On the other hand, North Americans, Asians, and Northern Europeans are **low-contact cultures** and prefer much less sensory involvement, standing farther apart and touching far less. They have a "distant" style of body language. In France, a relationship-oriented culture, good friends greet members of the opposite sex with a peck on each cheek; a handshake is a way to make a personal connection.

Interestingly, high-contact cultures are mostly located in warmer climates, and low-contact cultures in cooler climates. Americans are relatively nontouching, automatically standing at a distance so that an outstretched arm will touch the other person's ear. Standing any closer than that is regarded as invading intimate space. However, Americans and Canadians certainly expect a warm handshake and maybe a pat on the back from closer friends, though not the very warm double handshake of the Spaniards (clasping the forearm with the left hand). The Japanese, considerably less **haptic (touching),** do not shake hands; an initial greeting between a Japanese and a Spanish businessperson would be uncomfortable for both parties if they were untrained in cultural haptics. The Japanese bow to one another—the depth of the bow revealing their relative social standing.

When considering high- and low-contact cultures, we can trace a correlation between Hofstede's cultural variables of individualism and collectivism and the types of kinesic and proxemic behaviors people display. Generally, people from individualistic cultures are more remote and distant, whereas those from collectivist cultures are interdependent: They tend to work, play, live, and sleep in close proximity.[36]

The term **paralanguage** refers to how something is said rather than the content—the rate of speech, the tone and inflection of voice, other noises, laughing, or yawning. The culturally aware manager learns how to interpret subtle differences in paralanguage, including silence. Silence is a powerful communicator. It may be a way of saying no, of being offended, or of waiting for more information to make a decision. There is considerable variation in the use of silence in meetings. While Americans get uncomfortable after 10 or 15 seconds of silence, Chinese prefer to think the situation over for 30 seconds before speaking. The typical scenario between Americans and Chinese, then, is that the American gets impatient, says something to break the silence, and offends the Chinese by interrupting his or her chain of thought and comfort level with the subject.[37] Graham, a researcher on international negotiations, taped a bargaining session held at Toyota's U.S. headquarters in California. The U.S. executive had made a proposal to open a new production facility in Brazil and was waiting for a response from the three Japanese executives, who sat with lowered eyes and hands folded on the table. After about 30 seconds—an eternity to Americans, accustomed to a conversational response time of a few tenths of a second—the American blurted out that they were getting nowhere—and the meeting ended in a stalemate. More sensitivity to cultural differences in communication might have led him to wait longer or perhaps to prompt some further response through another polite question.[38]

The term **object language, or material culture,** refers to how we communicate through material artifacts, whether architecture, office design and furniture, clothing, cars, or cosmetics. Material culture communicates what people hold as important. In the United States, for example, someone wishing to convey his important status and wealth would show guests his penthouse office or expensive car. In Japan, a businessman presents his business card to a new contact and expects the receiver to study it and appreciate his position. In Mexico, a visiting international executive or salesperson is advised to take time out, before negotiating business, to show appreciation for the surrounding architecture, which is prized by Mexicans. The importance of family to people in Spain and much of Latin America, would be conveyed by family photographs around the office and therefore an expectation that the visitor would enquire about the family.

Time   Another variable that communicates culture is the way people regard and use time (see also Chapter 3). To Brazilians, relative punctuality communicates the level of importance of those involved. To Middle Easterners, time is something controlled by the will of Allah.

To initiate effective cross-cultural business interactions, managers should know the difference between *monochronic time systems* and *polychronic time systems* and how they affect communications. Hall and Hall explain that in **monochronic cultures** (Switzerland, Germany, and the United States), time is experienced in a linear way, with a past, a present, and a future, and time is treated as something to be spent, saved, made up, or wasted. Classified and compartmentalized, time serves to order life. This attitude is a learned part of Western culture, probably starting with the Industrial Revolution. Monochronic people, found in individualistic cultures, generally concentrate on one thing at a time, adhere to time commitments, and are accustomed to short-term relationships.

In contrast, **polychronic cultures** tolerate many things occurring simultaneously and emphasize involvement with people. Two Latin friends, for example, will put an important conversation ahead of being on time for a business meeting, thus communicating the priority of relationships over material systems. Polychronic people—Latin Americans, Arabs, and those from other collectivist cultures—may focus on several things at once, be highly distractible, and change plans often.[39]

The relationship between time and space also affects communication. Polychronic people, for example, are likely to hold open meetings, moving around and conducting transactions with one party and then another, rather than compartmentalizing meeting topics, as do monochronic people.

The nuances and distinctions regarding cultural differences in nonverbal communication are endless. The various forms are listed in Exhibit 4-3; wise intercultural managers will take careful account of the role that such differences might play.

What aspects of nonverbal communication might have created noise in the interactions between the American supervisor and the Greek employee in Exhibit 4-2? Undoubtedly, some cues could have been picked up from the kinesic behavior of each person. It was the responsibility of the manager, in particular, to notice any indications from the Greek that could have prompted him to change his communication pattern or assumptions. Face-to-face communication permits the sender of the message to get immediate feedback, verbal and nonverbal, and thus to have some idea as to how that message is being received and whether additional information is needed. What aspects of the Greek employee's kinesic behavior or paralanguage might have been evident to a more culturally sensitive manager? Did both parties' sense of time affect the communication process?

EXHIBIT 4-3   Forms of Nonverbal Communication

- Facial expressions
- Body posture
- Gestures with hands, arms, head, etc.
- Interpersonal distance (proxemics)
- Touching, body contact
- Eye contact
- Clothing, cosmetics, hairstyles, jewelry
- Paralanguage (voice pitch and inflections, rate of speech, and silence)
- Color symbolism
- Attitude toward time and the use of time in business and social interactions
- Food symbolism and social use of meals

Context

East Asians live in relatively complex social networks with prescribed role relations; attention to context is, therefore, important for their effective functioning. In contrast, westerners live in less constraining social worlds that stress independence and allow them to pay less attention to context.

RICHARD E. NISBETT,
September 2005[40]

A major differentiating factor that is a primary cause of noise in the communication process is that of context—which actually incorporates many of the variables discussed earlier. The **context** in which the communication takes place affects the meaning and interpretation of the interaction. Cultures are known to be high- or low-context cultures, with a relative range in between.[41] In **high-context cultures** (Asia, the Middle East, Africa, and the Mediterranean), feelings and thoughts are not explicitly expressed; instead, one has to read between the lines and interpret meaning from one's general understanding. Two such high-context cultures are those of South Korea and Arab cultures. In such cultures, key information is embedded in the context rather than made explicit. People make assumptions about what the message means through their knowledge of the person or the surroundings. In these cultures, most communication takes place within a context of extensive information networks resulting from close personal relationships. See the following Management Focus for further explanation of the Asian communication style.

In **low-context cultures** (Germany, Switzerland, Scandinavia, and North America), where personal and business relationships are more compartmentalized, communication media have to be more explicit. Feelings and thoughts are expressed in words, and information is more readily available. Westerners focus more on the individual, and therefore tend to view events as the result of specific agents, while easterners view events in a broader and longer-term context.[42]

In cross-cultural communication between high- and low-context people, a lack of understanding may preclude reaching a solution, and conflict may arise. Germans, for example, will expect considerable detailed information before making a business decision, whereas Arabs will base their decisions more on knowledge of the people involved—the information is present, but it is implicit. People in low-context cultures, such as those in Germany, Switzerland Austria, and the United States, convey their thoughts and plans in a direct, straightforward communication style, saying something like "we have to make a decision on this today." People in high-context cultures, such as in Asia, and, to a lesser extent, in England, convey their thoughts in a more indirect, implicit manner; this means that someone from Germany needs to have more patience and tact and be willing to listen for clues—verbal and nonverbal—as to their colleagues' wishes.

People in high-context cultures expect others to understand unarticulated moods, subtle gestures, and environmental clues that people from low-context cultures simply do not process. Misinterpretation and misunderstanding often result.[43] People from high-context cultures

MANAGEMENT FOCUS

Oriental Poker Face: Eastern Deception or Western Inscrutability?

Among many English expressions that are likely to offend those of us whose ancestry may be traced to the Far East, two stand out quite menacingly for me: "Oriental poker face" and "idiotic Asian smile." The former refers to the supposedly inscrutable nature of a facial expression that apparently reflects no particular state of mind, while the latter pokes fun at a face fixed with a perpetually friendly smile. Westerners' perplexity, when faced with either, arises from the impression that these two diametrically opposed masquerading strategies prevent them from extracting useful information—at least the type of information that at least they could process with a reasonable measure of confidence—about the feelings of the person before them. An Asian face that projects no signs of emotion, then, seems to most Westerners nothing but a facade. It does not matter whether that face wears an unsightly scowl or a shining ray; a facial expression they cannot interpret poses a genuine threat.

Compassionate and sympathetic to their perplexity as I may be, I am also insulted by the Western insensitivity to the significant roles that subtle signs play in Asian cultures. Every culture has its unique modus operandi for communication. Western culture, for example, apparently emphasizes the importance of direct communication. Not only are the communicators taught to look directly at each other when they convey a message, but they also are encouraged to come right to the point of the message. Making bold statements or asking frank questions in a less than diplomatic manner (i.e., "That was really a very stupid thing to do!" or "Are you interested in me?") is rarely construed as rude or indiscreet. Even embarrassingly blunt questions such as "President Clinton, did you have sexual intercourse with Monica Lewinsky?" are tolerated most of the time. Asians, on the other hand, find this direct communicative communication style quite unnerving. In many social interactions, they avoid direct eye contact. They "see" each other without necessarily looking directly at each other, and they gather information about inner states of mind without asking even the most discreet or understated questions. Many times they talk around the main topic, and, yet, they succeed remarkably well in understanding one another's position. (At least they believe they have developed a reasonably clear understanding.)

To a great extent, Asian communication is listening-centered; the ability to listen (and a special talent for detecting various communicative cues) is treated as equally important as, if not more important than, the ability to speak. This contrasts clearly with the American style of communication that puts the utmost emphasis on verbal expression; the speaker carries most of the burden for ensuring that everyone understands his or her message. An Asian listener, however, is prone to blame himself or herself for failing to reach a comprehensive understanding from the few words and gestures performed by the speaker. With this heavier burden placed on the listener, an Asian speaker does not feel obliged to send clearly discernible message cues (at least not nearly so much as he or she is obliged to do in American cultural contexts). Not obligated to express themselves without interruption, Asians use silence as a tool in communication. Silence, by most Western conventions, represents discontinuity of communication and creates a feeling of discomfort and anxiety. In the Orient, however, silence is not only comfortably tolerated but is considered a desirable form of expression. Far from being a sign of displeasure or animosity, it serves as an integral part of the communication process, used for reflecting on messages previously exchanged and for carefully crafting thoughts before uttering them.

It is not outlandish at all, then, for Asians to view Americans as unnecessarily talkative and lacking in the ability to listen. For the Asian, it is the American who projects a mask of confidence by being overly expressive both verbally and nonverbally. Since the American style of communication places less emphasis on the act of listening than on speaking, Asians suspect that their American counterparts fail to pick up subtle and astute communicative signs in conversation. To one with a cultural outlook untrained in reading those signs, an inscrutable face represents no more than a menacing or amusing mask.

Source: Dr. Jin Kim, State University of New York–Plattsburgh. Copyright © 2003 by Dr. Jin Kim. Used with permission of Dr. Kim.

EXHIBIT 4-4 Cultural Context and Its Effects on Communication[45]

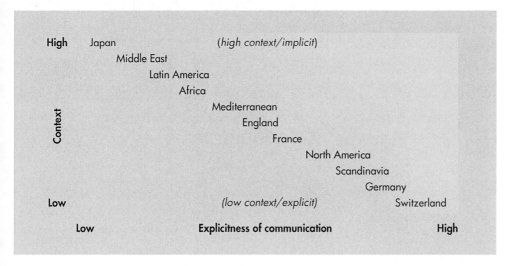

perceive those from low-context cultures as too talkative, too obvious, and redundant. Those from low-context cultures perceive high-context people as nondisclosing, sneaky, and mysterious. Research indicates, for example, that Americans find talkative people more attractive, whereas Koreans, high-context people, perceive less verbal people as more attractive. Finding the right balance between low- and high-context communications can be tricky, as Hall and Hall point out: "Too much information leads people to feel they are being talked down to; too little information can mystify them or make them feel left out."[44] Exhibit 4-4 shows the relative level of context in various countries.

The importance of understanding the role of context and nonverbal language to avoid misinterpretation is illustrated in the Comparative Management in Focus: Communicating with Arabs.

COMPARATIVE MANAGEMENT IN FOCUS
Communicating with Arabs

In the Middle East, the meaning of a communication is implicit and interwoven, and consequently much harder for Americans, accustomed to explicit and specific meanings, to understand.

Arabs are warm, emotional, and quick to explode: "sounding off" is regarded as a safety valve. In fact, the Arabic language aptly communicates the Arabic culture, one of emotional extremes. The language contains the means for overexpression, many adjectives, words that allow for exaggeration, and metaphors to emphasize a position. What is said is often not as important as *how* it is said. Eloquence and flowery speech are admired for their own sake, regardless of the content. Loud speech is used for dramatic effect.

At the core of Middle Eastern culture are friendship, honor, religion, and traditional hospitality. Family, friends, and connections are very important on all levels in the Middle East and will take precedence over business transactions. Arabs do business with people, not companies, and they make commitments to people, not contracts. A phone call to the right person can help to get around seemingly insurmountable obstacles. An Arab expects loyalty from friends, and it is understood that giving and receiving favors is an inherent part of the relationship; no one says no to a request for a favor. A lack of follow-through is assumed to be beyond the friend's control.[46]

Because hospitality is a way of life and highly symbolic, a visitor must be careful not to reject it by declining refreshment or rushing into business discussions. Part of that hospitality is the elaborate system of greetings and the long period of getting acquainted, perhaps taking up the entire first meeting. While the handshake may seem limp, the rest of the greeting is not. Kissing on the cheeks is common among men, as is hand-holding between male friends. However, any public display of intimacy between men and women is strictly forbidden by the Arab social code.

Women play little or no role in business or entertainment; the Middle East is a male-dominated society, and it is impolite to inquire about women. Other nonverbal taboos include showing the soles of one's feet and using the left (unclean) hand to eat or pass something. In discussions, slouching in a seat or leaning against a wall communicates a lack of respect.

Westerner Meeting with Arab Businessmen.

Source: Getty Images/Digital Vision

The Arab society also values honor. Harris and Moran explain: "Honor, social prestige, and a secure place in society are brought about when conformity is achieved. When one fails to conform, this is considered to be damning and leads to a degree of shame."[47] Shame results not just from doing something wrong but from having others find out about that wrongdoing. Establishing a climate of honesty and trust is part of the sense of honor. Therefore, considerable tact is needed to avoid conveying any concern or doubt. Arabs tend to be quite introverted until a mutual trust is built, which takes a long time.[48]

In their nonverbal communication, most Arab countries are high-contact cultures. Arabs stand and sit closer and touch people of the same sex more than Westerners. They do not have the same concept of "public" and "private" space, or as Hall puts it, "Not only is the sheer noise level much higher, but the piercing look of the eyes, the touch of the hands, and the mutual bathing in the warm moist breath during conversation represent stepped-up sensory inputs to a level which many Europeans find unbearably intense. On the other hand, the distance preferred by North Americans may leave an Arab suspicious of intentions because of the lack of olfactory contact."[49]

The Muslim expression *Bukra insha Allah*—"Tomorrow if Allah wills"—explains much about the Arab culture and its approach to business transactions. A cultural clash typically occurs when an American tries to give an Arab a deadline. "I am going to Damascus tomorrow morning and will have to have my car tonight," is a sure way to get the mechanic to stop work," explains Hall, "because to give another person a deadline in this part of the world is to be rude, pushy, and demanding."[50] In such instances, the attitude toward time communicates as loudly as words.

In verbal interactions, managers must be aware of different patterns of Arab thought and communication. Compared to the direct, linear fashion of American communication, Arabs tend to meander: They start with social talk, discuss business for a while, loop round to social and general issues, then back to business, and so on.[51] American impatience and insistence on sticking to the subject will "cut off their loops," triggering confusion and dysfunction. Instead, westerners should accept that there will be considerable time spent on "small talk" and socializing, with frequent interruptions, before getting down to business.

Exhibit 4-5 illustrates some of the sources of noise that are likely to interfere in the communication process between Americans and Arabs.

For people doing business in the Middle East, the following are some useful guidelines for effective communication:

- Be patient. Recognize the Arab attitude toward time and hospitality—take time to develop friendship and trust, for these are prerequisites for any social or business transactions.
- Recognize that people and relationships matter more to Arabs than the job, company, or contract—conduct business personally, not by correspondence or telephone.
- Avoid expressing doubts or criticism when others are present—recognize the importance of honor and dignity to Arabs.
- Adapt to the norms of body language, flowery speech, and circuitous verbal patterns in the Middle East, and don't be impatient to "get to the point."
- Expect many interruptions in meetings, delays in schedules, and changes in plans.[52]

EXHIBIT 4-5   Miscommunication Between Americans and Arabs Caused by Cross-cultural Noise

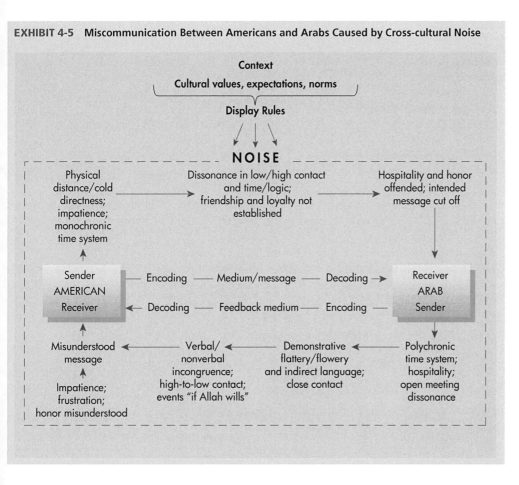

Communication Channels

In addition to the variables related to the sender and receiver of a message, the variables linked to the channel itself and the context of the message must be taken into consideration. These variables include fast or slow messages and information flows, as well as different types of media.

Information Systems   Communication in organizations varies according to where and how it originates, the channels, and the speed at which it flows, whether it is formal or informal, and so forth. The type of organizational structure, the staffing policies, and the leadership style will affect the nature of an organization's information system.

As an international manager, it is useful to know where and how information originates and the speed at which it flows, both internally and externally. In centralized organizational structures, as in South America, most information originates from top managers. Workers take less responsibility to keep managers informed than in a typical company in the United States, where delegation results in information flowing from the staff to the managers. In a decision-making system in which many people are involved, such as the **ringi system** of consensus decision making in Japan, the expatriate needs to understand that there is a systematic pattern for information flow.

Context also affects information flow. In high-context cultures (such as in the Middle East), information spreads rapidly and freely because of the constant close contact and the implicit ties among people and organizations. Information flow is often informal. In low-context cultures (such as Germany or the United States), information is controlled and focused, and thus it does not flow so freely.[53] Compartmentalized roles and office layouts stifle information channels; information sources tend to be more formal.

It is crucial for an expatriate manager to find out how to tap into a firm's informal sources of information. In Japan, employees usually have a drink together on the way home from work, and this becomes an essential source of information. However, such communication networks are based on long-term relationships in Japan (and in other high-context cultures). The same information may not be readily available to "outsiders." A considerable barrier in Japan separates strangers from familiar friends, a situation that discourages communication.

Americans are more open and talk freely about almost anything, whereas Japanese will disclose little about their inner thoughts or private issues. Americans are willing to have a wide "public self," disclosing their inner reactions verbally and physically. In contrast, the Japanese prefer to keep their responses largely to their "private self." The Japanese expose only a small portion of their thoughts; they reduce, according to Barnlund, "the unpredictability and emotional intensity of personal encounters."[54] Cultural clashes between the public and private selves in intercultural communication between Americans and Japanese result when each party forces its cultural norms of communication on the other. In the American style, the American's cultural norms of explicit communication impose on the Japanese by invading the person's private self. The Japanese style of implicit communication causes a negative reaction from the American because of what is perceived as too much formality and ambiguity, which wastes time.[55]

Cultural variables in information systems and context underlie the many differences in communication style between Japanese and Americans. Exhibit 4-6 shows some specific differences. The Japanese *ningensei* ("human beingness") style of communication refers to the preference for humanity, reciprocity, a receiver orientation, and an underlying distrust of words and analytic logic.[56] The Japanese believe that true intentions are not readily revealed in words or contracts but are, in fact, masked by them. In contrast to the typical American's verbal agility and explicitness, Japanese behaviors and communications are directed to defend and give face for everyone concerned; to do so, they avoid public disagreements at all costs. In cross-cultural negotiations, this last point is essential.

EXHIBIT 4-6   (*Continued*)

Japanese Ningensei Style of Communication	U.S. Adversarial Style of Communication
1. Indirect verbal and nonverbal communication	1. More direct verbal and nonverbal communication
2. Relationship communication	2. More task communication
3. Discourages confrontational strategies acceptable	3. Confrontational strategies more
4. Strategically ambiguous communication communication	4. Prefers more to-the-point communication
5. Delayed feedback	5. More immediate feedback
6. Patient, longer-term negotiators	6. Shorter-term negotiators
7. Uses fewer words	7. Favors verbosity
8. Distrustful of skillful verbal communicators	8. Exalts verbal eloquence
9. Group orientation	9. More individualistic orientation
10. Cautious, tentative	10. More assertive, self-assured
11. Complementary communicators	11. More publicly critical communication
12. Softer, heart like logic	12. Harder, analytic logic preferred
13. Sympathetic, empathetic, complex use of pathos	13. Favors logos, reason
14. Expresses and decodes complex relational strategies and nuances	14. Expresses and decodes complex logos, cognitive nuances
15. Avoids decision making in public	15. Frequent decision making in public
16. Makes decisions in private venues, away from public eye	16. Frequent decision in public at negotiating tables
17. Decisions via *ringi* and *nemawashi* (complete consensus process)	17. Decisions by majority rule and public compromise is more commonplace
18. Uses go-betweens for decision making	18. More extensive use of direct person-to-person, player-to-player interaction for decisions
19. Understatement and hesitation in verbal and nonverbal communication	19. May publicly speak in superlatives, exaggerations, nonverbal projection

EXHIBIT 4-6   Difference Between Japanese and American Communication Styles

20. Uses qualifiers, tentativeness, humility as communicator	20. Favors fewer qualifiers, more ego-centered
21. Receiver/listening-centered	21. More speaker- and message-centered
22. Inferred meanings, looks beyond words to nuances, nonverbal communication	22. More face-value meaning, more denotative
23. Shy, reserved communicators	23. More publicly self-assertive
24. Distaste for purely business transactions	24. Prefers to "get down to business" or "nitty gritty"
25. Mixes business and social communication	25. Tends to keep business negotiating more separated from social communication
26. Utilizes *matomari* or "hints" for achieving group adjustment and saving face in negotiating	26. More directly verbalizes management's preference at negotiating tables
27. Practices *haragei* or "belly logic" and communication	27. Practices more linear, discursive, analytical logic; greater reverence for cognitive than for affective

Source: Reprinted from A. Goldman, "The Centrality of 'Ningensei' to Japanese Negotiating and Interpersonal Relationships: Implications for U.S. Japanese Communication," *International Journal of Intercultural Relations* 18, no. 1 (1994), with permission from Elsevier.

The speed with which we try to use information systems is another key variable that needs attention to avoid misinterpretation and conflict. Americans expect to give and receive information very quickly and clearly, moving through details and stages in a linear fashion to the conclusion. They usually use various media for fast messages—letters or emails giving all the facts and plans up front, faxes, and familiar relationships. In contrast, the French use the slower message channels of deep relationships, culture, and sometimes mediators to exchange information. A French written communication will be tentative, with subsequent letters slowly building up to a new proposal. The French preference for written communication, even for informal interactions, echoes the formality of their relationships—and results in a slowing down of message transmission that often seems unnecessary to Americans. Jean-Louis Reynal, a plant manager at Citröen, explains that "it wouldn't be too much of an exaggeration to say that, until they are written, until they are entrusted to the blackboard, the notepad, or the flip chart, ideas have no reality for the French manager. You could even say that writing is an indispensable aid to 'being' for us."[57]

In short, it behooves Americans to realize that, because most of the world exchanges information through slower message media, it is wise to schedule more time for transactions, develop patience, and learn to get at needed information in more subtle ways—after building rapport and taking time to observe the local system for exchanging information.

We have seen that cross-cultural misinterpretation can result from noise in the actual transmission of the message—the choice or speed of media. Interpreting the meaning of a message can thus be as much a function of the transmission channel (or medium) as it is of examining the message itself.

INFORMATION TECHNOLOGY: GOING GLOBAL AND ACTING LOCAL

All information is local; IT systems can connect every corner of the globe, but IT managers are learning they have to pay attention to regional differences.

COMPUTERWORLD[58]

Deploying B2B e-commerce technology [globally] . . . becomes exponentially more difficult because systems must address concerns not germane to domestic networks, such as language translation, currency conversion and even cultural differences.

INTERNETWEEK[59]

Using the Internet as a global medium for communication has enabled companies of all sizes to quickly develop a presence in many markets around the world—and, in fact, has enabled them to "go global." However, their global reach cannot alone translate into global business. Those companies are learning that they have to adapt their e-commerce and their enterprise resource planning (ERP) applications to regional idiosyncrasies beyond translation or content management issues; even asking for a name or an email address can incur resistance in many countries where people do not like to give out personal information.[60] While communication over the Internet is clearly not as personal as face-to-face cross-cultural communication, those transactions must still be regionalized and personalized to adjust to differences in language, culture, local laws, and business models, as well as differences in the level of development in the local telecommunications infrastructure. Yet, if the Internet is a global medium for communication, why do so many U.S. companies treat the Web as a U.S.-centric phenomenon? Giving preference to some geographic regions, languages, and cultures is "a short-sighted business decision that will result in diminished brand equity, market share, profits and global leadership."[61] With an annual predicted growth rate of 70 percent in non–English-language sites and usage, this soon puts English-language sites in the minority.[62]

It seems essential, then, that a global online strategy must also be multilocal. The impersonal nature of the Web must somehow be adapted to local cultures to establish relationships and create customer loyalty. Effective technological communication requires even more cultural sensitivity than face-to-face communication because of the inability to assess reactions and get feedback, or even to retain contact in many cases. It is still people, after all, who respond to and interact with other people through the medium of the Internet, and those people interpret and respond according to their own languages and cultures, as well as their local business practices and expectations. In Europe, for example, significant differences in business cultures and e-business technology have slowed e-business progress there. However, some companies are making progress in pan-European integration services, such as *leEurope*, which aims to cross language, currency, and cultural barriers. Specifically, *leEurope* is building a set of services "to help companies tie their back-end e-business systems together across European boundaries through a series of mergers involving regional e-business integrators in more than a dozen countries."[63]

MANAGING CROSS-CULTURAL COMMUNICATION

Steps toward effective intercultural communication include the development of cultural sensitivity, careful encoding, selective transmission, careful decoding, and appropriate follow-up actions.

Developing Cultural Sensitivity

When acting as a sender, a manager must make it a point to know the receiver and to encode the message in a form that will most likely be understood as intended. On the manager's part, this requires an awareness of his or her own cultural baggage and how it affects the communication process. In other words, what kinds of behaviors does the message imply, and how will they be perceived by the receiver? The way to anticipate the most likely meaning that the receiver will attach to the message is to internalize honest cultural empathy with that person. What is the cultural background—the societal, economic, and organizational context—in which this communication is taking place? What are this person's expectations regarding the situation, what are the two parties' relative positions, and what might develop from this communication? What kinds of transactions and behaviors is this person used to? Cultural sensitivity (discussed in Chapter 3) is really just a matter of understanding the other person, the context, and how the person will respond to the context. Americans, unfortunately, have a rather negative reputation overseas of not being culturally sensitive. One not-for-profit group, called Business for Diplomatic Action, has the following advice for Americans when doing business abroad, in its attempts to counteract the stereotypical American traits such as boastfulness, loudness, and speed:

- **Read a map:** Familiarize yourself with the local geography to avoid making insulting mistakes.
- **Dress up:** In some countries, casual dress is a sign of disrespect
- **Talk small:** Talking about wealth, power, or status—corporate or personal—can create resentment.
- **No slang:** Even casual profanity is unacceptable.

- **Slow down:** Americans talk fast, eat fast, move fast, live fast. Many cultures do not.
- **Listen as much as you talk:** Ask people you're visiting about themselves and their way of life.
- **Speak lower and slower:** A loud voice is often perceived as bragging.
- **Religious restraint:** In many countries, religion is not a subject for public discussion.
- **Political restraint:** Steer clear of this subject. If someone is attacking U.S. politicians or policies, agree to disagree.[64]

Careful Encoding

In translating his or her intended meaning into symbols for cross-cultural communication, the sender must use words, pictures, or gestures that are appropriate to the receiver's frame of reference. Of course, language training is invaluable, but senders should also avoid idioms and regional sayings (such as "Go fly a kite" or "Foot the bill") in a translation, or even in English when speaking to a non-American who knows little English.

Literal translation, then, is a limited answer to language differences. Even for people in English-speaking countries, words may have different meanings. Ways to avoid problems are to speak slowly and clearly, avoid long sentences and colloquial expressions, and explain things in several different ways and through several media, if possible. However, even though English is in common use around the world for business transactions, the manager's efforts to speak the local language will greatly improve the climate. Sometimes people from other cultures resent the assumption by English-speaking executives that everyone else will speak English.

Language translation is only part of the encoding process; the message also is expressed in nonverbal language. In the encoding process, the sender must ensure congruence between the nonverbal and the verbal message. In encoding a message, therefore, it is useful to be as objective as possible and not to rely on personal interpretations. To further clarify their messages, managers can hand out written summaries of verbal presentations and use visual aids, such as graphs or pictures. A good general guide is to move slowly, wait, and take cues from the receivers.

Selective Transmission

The type of medium chosen for the message depends on the nature of the message, its level of importance, the context and expectations of the receiver, the timing involved, and the need for personal interaction, among other factors. Typical media include email, letters or memos, reports, meetings, telephone calls, teleconferences, videoconferences, or face-to-face conversations. The secret is to find out how communication is transmitted in the local organization—how much is downward versus upward or vertical versus horizontal, how the grapevine works, and so on. In addition, the cultural variables discussed earlier need to be considered: whether the receiver is from a high- or low-context culture, whether he or she is used to explicit or implicit communication, and what speed and routing of messages will be most effective.

For the most part, it is best to use face-to-face interaction for relationship building or for other important transactions, particularly in intercultural communications, because of the lack of familiarity between parties. Personal interactions give the manager the opportunity to get immediate verbal and visual feedback and to make rapid adjustments in the communication process.

International dealings are often long-distance, of course, limiting the opportunity for face-to-face communication. However, personal rapport can be established or enhanced through telephone calls or videoconferencing and through trusted contacts. Modern electronic media can be used to break down communication barriers by reducing waiting periods for information, clarifying issues, and allowing instant consultation. Global telecommunications and computer networks are changing the face of cross-cultural communication through the faster dissemination of information within the receiving organization. Ford Europe uses videoconferencing for engineers in Britain and Germany to consult about quality problems. Through the video monitors, they examine one another's engineering diagrams and usually find a solution that gets the factory moving again in a short time.

Careful Decoding of Feedback

Timely and effective feedback channels can also be set up to assess a firm's general communication about the progression of its business and its general management principles. The best means for getting accurate feedback is through face-to-face interaction because this allows the manager to hear, see, and immediately sense how a message is being interpreted. When visual feedback on important issues is not possible or appropriate, it is a good idea to use several means of attaining feedback, in particular, employing third parties.

Decoding is the process of translating the received symbols into the interpreted message. The main causes of incongruence are (1) the receiver misinterprets the message, (2) the receiver encodes his or her return message incorrectly, or (3) the sender misinterprets the feedback. Two-way communication is thus essential for important issues so that successive efforts can be made until an understanding has been achieved. Asking other colleagues to help interpret what is going on is often a good way to break a cycle of miscommunication.

Perhaps the most important means for avoiding miscommunication is to practice careful decoding by improving one's listening and observation skills. A good listener practices projective listening, or empathetic listening—listening without interruption or evaluation to the full message of the speaker, attempting to recognize the feelings behind the words and nonverbal cues, and understanding the speaker's perspective.

At the multinational corporation (MNC) level, avenues of communication and feedback among parent companies and subsidiaries can be kept open through telephone calls, regular meetings and visits, reports, and plans, all of which facilitate cooperation, performance control, and the smooth running of the company. Communication among far-flung operations can be best managed by setting up feedback systems and liaison people. The headquarters people should maintain considerable flexibility in cooperating with local managers and allowing them to deal with the local context as they see fit.

Follow-up Actions

Managers communicate through both action and inaction. Therefore, to keep open the lines of communication, feedback, and trust, managers must follow through with action on what has been discussed and then agreed upon—typically a contract, which is probably the most important formal business communication. Unfortunately, the issue of contract follow-through is a particularly sensitive one across cultures because of the different interpretations regarding what constitutes a contract (perhaps a handshake, perhaps a full legal document) and what actions should result. Trust, future communications, and future business are based on such interpretations, and it is up to managers to understand them and to follow through on them.

The management of cross-cultural communication depends largely on a manager's personal abilities and behavior. Those behaviors that researchers indicate to be most important to intercultural communication effectiveness (ICE) are listed here, as reviewed by Ruben:

1. Respect (conveyed through eye contact, body posture, voice tone, and pitch)
2. Interaction posture (the ability to respond to others in a descriptive, nonevaluative, and nonjudgmental way)
3. Orientation to knowledge (recognizing that one's knowledge, perception, and beliefs are valid only for oneself and not for everyone else)
4. Empathy
5. Interaction management
6. Tolerance for ambiguity
7. Other-oriented role behavior (one's capacity to be flexible and to adopt different roles for the sake of greater group cohesion and group communication)[65]

Whether at home or abroad, certain personal capabilities facilitate effective intercultural communication; these abilities can help the expatriate to adapt to the host country and enable productive working relations to develop in the long term. Researchers have established a relationship between personality traits and behaviors and the ability to adapt to the host-country's cultural environment.[66] What is seldom pointed out, however, is that communication is the mediating factor between those behaviors and the relative level of adaptation the expatriate achieves. The communication process facilitates cross-cultural adaptation, and, through this process, expatriates learn the dominant communication patterns of the host society. Therefore, we can link those personality factors shown by research to ease adaptation with those necessary for effective intercultural communication.

Kim has consolidated the research findings of these characteristics into two categories: (1) **openness**—traits such as open-mindedness, tolerance for ambiguity, and extrovertedness; and (2) **resilience**—traits such as having an internal locus of control, persistence, a tolerance of ambiguity, and resourcefulness.[67] These personality factors, along with the expatriate's cultural and racial identity and the level of preparedness for change, comprise that person's potential for adaptation. The level of preparedness can be improved by the manager before his or her assignment by gathering information about the host country's verbal and nonverbal communication patterns and norms of behavior. Kim explains that the major variables that affect the level of communication competence achieved between the host and the expatriate are the adaptive predisposition of the expatriate and the conditions of receptivity and conformity to pressure in the host environment. These factors affect the process of personal and social communication, and, ultimately, the adaptation outcome. Explains Kim, "Three aspects of strangers' adaptive change—increased functional fitness, psychological health, and intercultural identity—have been identified as direct consequences of prolonged communication-adaptation experiences in the host society."[68] Chapter 10 explores areas where the firm has responsibility to improve the employee/managerial ability to adapt.

In identifying personal and behavioral specifics that facilitate ICE, however, we cannot lose sight of the whole picture. We must remember the basic principle of contingency management, which is that managers operate in a system of many interacting variables in a dynamic context. Studies show that situational factors—such as the physical environment, time constraints, degree of structure, feelings of boredom or overwork, and anonymity—are strong influences on intercultural communication competence.[69]

It is this interdependence of many variables that makes it difficult for intercultural researchers to isolate and identify factors for success. Although managers try to understand and control up front as many factors as possible that will lead to management effectiveness, often they only find out what works from the results of their decisions.

CONCLUSION

Effective intercultural communication is a vital skill for international managers and domestic managers of multicultural workforces. Because miscommunication is much more likely to occur among people from different countries or racial backgrounds than among those from similar backgrounds, it is important to be alert to how culture is reflected in communication—in particular through the development of cultural sensitivity and an awareness of potential sources of cultural noise in the communication process. A successful international manager is thus attuned to these variables and is flexible enough to adjust his or her communication style to best address the intended receivers—that is, to do it "their way."

Cultural variables and the manner in which culture is communicated underlie the processes of negotiation and decision making. How do people around the world negotiate: What are their expectations and their approach to negotiations? What is the importance of understanding negotiation and decision-making processes in other countries? Chapter 5 addresses these questions and makes suggestions for the international manager to handle these important tasks.

Summary of Key Points

1. Communication is an inherent part of a manager's role, taking up the majority of the manager's time on the job. Effective intercultural communication largely determines the success of international transactions or the output of a culturally diverse workforce.

2. Culture is the foundation of communication, and communication transmits culture. Cultural variables that can affect the communication process by influencing a person's perceptions include attitudes, social organizations, thought patterns, roles, language, nonverbal language, and time.

3. Language conveys cultural understandings and social norms from one generation to the next. Body language, or nonverbal communication, is behavior that communicates without words. It accounts for 65 to 93 percent of interpreted communication.

4. Types of nonverbal communication around the world are kinesic behavior, proxemics, paralanguage, and object language.

5. Effective cross-cultural communication must take account of whether the receiver is from a country with a monochronic or a polychronic time system.

6. Variables related to channels of communication include high- and low-context cultures, fast or slow messages and information flows, and various types of media.

7. In high-context cultures, feelings and messages are implicit and must be accessed through an understanding of the person and the system. In low-context cultures, feelings and thoughts are expressed, and information is more readily available.

8. The effective management of intercultural communication necessitates the development of cultural sensitivity, careful encoding, selective transmission, careful decoding, and follow-up actions.

9. Certain personal abilities and behaviors facilitate adaptation to the host country through skilled intercultural communication.

10. Communication via the Internet must still be localized to adjust to differences in language, culture, local laws, and business models.

Discussion Questions

1. How does culture affect the process of attribution in communication? Can you relate this to some experiences you have had with your classmates?

2. What is stereotyping? Give some examples. How might people stereotype you? How does a sociotype differ from a stereotype?

3. What is the relationship between language and culture? How is it that people from different countries who speak the same language may still miscommunicate?

4. Give some examples of cultural differences in the interpretation of body language. What is the role of such nonverbal communication in business relationships?

5. Explain the differences between monochronic and polychronic time systems. Use some examples to illustrate their differences and the role of time in intercultural communication.

6. Explain the differences between high- and low-context cultures, giving some examples. What are the differential effects on the communication process?

7. Discuss the role of information systems in a company, how and why they vary from country to country, and the effects of these variations.

Application Exercises

1. Form groups in your class—multicultural groups, if possible. Have each person make notes about his or her perceptions of (1) Mexican-Americans, (2) Native Americans, (3) African-Americans, and (4) Americans of European descent. Discuss your notes and draw conclusions about common stereotypes. Discuss any differences and why stereotyping occurs.

2. Invite some foreign students to your class. Ask them to bring photographs, slides, and so forth of people and events in their native countries. Have them explain the meanings of various nonverbal cues, such as gestures, dress, voice inflections, architecture, and events. Discuss with them any differences between their explanations and the attributions you assigned to those cues.

3. Interview a faculty member or a businessperson who has worked abroad. Ask him or her to identify factors that facilitated or inhibited adaptation to the host environment. Ask whether more preparation could have eased the transition and what, if anything, that person would do differently before another trip.

Experiential Exercise: Script for Juan Perillo and Jean Moore

Scene I: February 15, San Juan, Puerto Rico

JUAN: Welcome back to Puerto Rico, Jean. It is good to have you here in San Juan again. I hope that your trip from Dayton was a smooth one.

JEAN: Thank you, Juan. It's nice to be back here where the sun shines. Fred sends his regards and also asked me to tell you how important it is that we work out a firm production schedule for the next three months. But first, how is your family? All doing well, I hope.

JUAN: My wife is doing very well, but my daughter, Marianna, broke her arm and has to have surgery to repair the bone. We are very worried about that because the surgeon says she may have to have several operations. It is very difficult to think about my poor little daughter in the operating room. She was out playing with some other children when it happened. You know how roughly children sometimes play with each other. It's really amazing that they don't have more injuries. Why, just last week, my son . . .

JEAN: Of course I'm very sorry to hear about little Marianna, but I'm sure everything will go well with the surgery. Now, shall we start work on the production schedule?

JUAN: Oh, yes, of course, we must get started on the production schedule.

JEAN: Fred and I thought that June 1 would be a good cutoff date for the first phase of the schedule. And we also thought that 100 A-type computers would be a reasonable goal for that phase. We know that you have some new assemblers whom you are training, and that you've had some problems getting parts from your suppliers in the past few months. But we're sure you have all those problems worked out by now and that you are back to full production capability. So, what do you think? Is 100 A-type computers produced by June 1 a reasonable goal for your people?

JUAN: (hesitates a few seconds before replying): You want us to produce 100 of the newly designed A-type computers by June 1? Will we also be producing our usual number of Z-type computers, too?

JEAN: Oh, yes. Your regular production schedule would remain the same as it's always been. The only difference is that you would be producing the new A-type computers, too. I mean, after all, you have a lot of new employees, and you have all the new manufacturing and assembling equipment that we have in Dayton. So, you're as ready to make the new product as we are.

JUAN: Yes, that's true. We have the new equipment, and we've just hired a lot of new assemblers who will be working on the A-type computer. I guess there's no reason we can't meet the production schedule you and Fred have come up with.

JEAN: Great, great. I'll tell Fred you agree with our decision and will meet the goal of 100 A-type computers by June 1. He'll be delighted to know that you can deliver what he was hoping for. And, of course, Juan, that means that you'll be doing just as well as the Dayton plant.

Scene II: May 1, San Juan, Puerto Rico

JEAN: Hello, Juan. How are things here in Puerto Rico? I'm glad to have the chance to come back and see how things are going.

JUAN: Welcome, Jean. It's good to have you here. How is your family?

JEAN: Oh, they're fine, just fine. You know, Juan, Fred is really excited about that big order we just got from the Defense Department for 50 A-type computers. They want them by June 10, so we will ship them directly to Washington from San Juan as the computers come off

your assembly line. Looks like it's a good thing we set your production goal at 100 A-type computers by June 1, isn't it?

JUAN: Um, yes, that was certainly a good idea.

JEAN: So, tell me, have you had any problems with the new model? How are your new assemblers working out? Do you have any suggestions for changes in the manufacturing specs? How is the new quality control program working with this model? We're always looking for ways to improve, you know, and we appreciate any ideas you can give us.

JUAN: Well, Jean, there is one thing . . .

JEAN: Yes? What is that?

JUAN: Well, Jean, we have had a few problems with the new assemblers. Three of them have had serious illnesses in their families and have had to take off several days at a time to nurse a sick child or elderly parent. And another one was involved in a car accident and was in the hospital for several days. And you remember my daughter's surgery? Well, her arm didn't mend properly, and we had to take her to Houston for additional consultations and therapy. But, of course, you and Fred knew about that.

JEAN: Yes, we were aware that you had had some personnel problems and that you and your wife had had to go to Houston with Marianna. But what does that have to do with the 50 A-type computers for the Defense Department?

JUAN: Well, Jean, because of all these problems, we have had a few delays in the production schedule. Nothing serious, but we are a little bit behind our schedule.

JEAN: How far behind is "a little bit"? What are you trying to tell me, Juan? Will you have 50 more A-type computers by June 1 to ship to Washington to fill the Defense Department order?

JUAN: Well, I certainly hope we will have that number ready to ship. You know how difficult it can be to predict a precise number for manufacturing, Jean. You probably have many of these same problems in the Dayton plant, don't you?

Source: L. Catlin and T. White, *International Business: Cultural Sourcebook and Case Studies* (Cincinnati, Ohio: South-Western, 1994), used with permission.

Exercise Questions

1. Drawing from this chapter, explain in detail what went wrong for Jean in Puerto Rico. Could this have been avoided? What should she have done differently?

2. Replay the role of Jean and Juan during their conversation, establishing a more constructive communication and management style than Jean did previously.

Internet Resources

Visit the Deresky Companion Website at www.pearsonhighered.com/deresky for this chapter's Internet resources.

CASE STUDY

Elizabeth Visits GPC's French Subsidiary

Elizabeth Moreno is looking out the window from her business-class seat somewhere over the Indian Ocean on Thai Air en route to Paris's Orly International Airport from the Philippines, where she has just spent a week of meetings and problem solving in a pharmaceutical subsidiary of the Global Pharmaceutical Company (GPC).

GPC has the lion's share of the worldwide market in ethical pharmaceutical products. Ethical drugs are those that can be purchased only through a physician's prescription. In the United States, GPC has research and manufacturing sites in New York, New Jersey, Pennsylvania, and Michigan. The company also has subsidiaries in Canada, Puerto Rico, Australia, the Philippines, Brazil, England, and France. GPC has its administrative headquarters in Pennsylvania.

Because of the geographically dispersed locations of its subsidiaries, GPC's top scientists and key managers log thousands of jet miles a year visiting various offices and plants. Its top specialists and executives regularly engage in multisite real-time video and telephone conferences, and they also use electronic mail, faxes, modems, and traditional mail to keep in touch with key personnel.

Despite these technological advances, face-to-face meetings and on-site consultations are used widely. In the case of the French subsidiary, nothing can take the place of face-to-face consultations. The French manager is suspicious of figures in the balance sheet, of the telephone, of his subordinates, of what he reads in the newspaper, and of what Americans tell him in confidence. In contrast, the American trusts all these. This is the reason GPC regularly sends its scientists and executives to France.

Elizabeth Moreno is one of the key specialists within GPC. Her expertise in chemical processing is widely known not only within her company but also in the pharmaceutical industry worldwide. She has been working at GPC for more than twelve years since finishing her advanced degree in chemistry from a university in the Midwest. While working for GPC, she has been given more and more responsibilities leading to her current position as vice president of chemical development and processing.

From a hectic visit in the Philippines, her next assignment is to visit the French subsidiary plant for one week to study a problem with shelf-life testing of one of its newest anti-allergy capsules. It seems that the product's active ingredient is degrading sooner than the expiration date. During her stay, she will conduct training for chemists in state-of-the-art techniques for testing and for training local managers in product statistical quality control. These techniques are now currently used in other GPC locations.

To prepare for her foreign assignments, Elizabeth attended a standard three-hour course given by her company's human resource management department on dealing with cross-cultural issues. Moreover, she recalls reading from a book on French management about the impersonal nature of French business relations. This was so much in contrast with what she just has experienced during her visit to the Philippine subsidiary. The French tend to regard authority as residing in the role and not in the person. It is by the power of the position that a French manager gets things done. With this knowledge, she knows that her expertise and her position as vice president will see her through the technical aspects of the meetings that are lined up for the few days she will be in Paris.

French managers view their work as an intellectual challenge that requires application of individual brainpower. What matters to them is the opportunity to show one's ability to grasp complex issues, analyze problems, manipulate ideas, and evaluate solutions.

There are a few challenges for Elizabeth on this assignment. She is not fluent in French. Her only exposure to France and the language was a two-week vacation with her husband in Paris a couple of years ago. However, in her highly technical field, the universal language is English. Thus, she believes she will not have much difficulty communicating with the French management to get her assignment successfully completed.

Americans place high value on training and education. In the United States, the field of management has principles that are generally applicable and can be taught and learned. In contrast, the French place more emphasis on the person who can adapt to any situation by virtue of his intellectual quality. Expertise and intellectual ability are inherent in the individual and cannot be acquired simply through training or education.

It appears that Elizabeth will be encountering very different ways of doing business in France. While she thought about the challenges ahead, her plane landed at Orly International Airport. She whisked through customs and immigration without any delays. No limousine was waiting for her curbside at the arrival. Instead she took the train to downtown Paris and checked into an apartment hotel that was reserved for her in advance of her arrival.

After a week in Paris, she is expected back in her home office to prepare reports to GPC management about her foreign assignments.

Case Questions

1. Drawing from your understanding of verbal and nonverbal communication patterns from this chapter, explain what Elizabeth Moreno can do to establish her position in front of French managers. How can she get them to help her accomplish her assignment in five days?
2. What should Elizabeth know about high-context versus low-context cultures in Europe? How can this knowledge help her be successful there?
3. What should Elizabeth include in her report, and what should be the manner in which it is communicated, so that future executives and scientists avoid communications pitfalls?
4. How can technical language differ from everyday language in corporate communications? Explain.

Source: This case was prepared by Edwin J. Portugal, MBA, Ph.D., who teaches multinational management at State University of New York–Potsdam. It is intended to be used as a basis for discussion on the complexity of multicultural management and not to illustrate effective versus ineffective management styles. Copyright © 2004 by Edwin J. Portugal.

Cross-cultural Negotiation and Decision Making

OBJECTIVES:

1. To learn how to prepare for cross-cultural business negotiations.
2. To recognize the need to build trusting relationships as a prerequisite for successful negotiations and long-term commitments.
3. To be aware of the role of culturally-based behavioral differences, values and agendas of the negotiating parties.
4. To learn the complexities of negotiating with the Chinese.
5. To appreciate the variables in the decision-making process and understand the influence of culture on decision making.
6. To become familiar with the Japanese decision-making process and how it is influenced by their cultural norms.

Opening Profile: BP's Troubled Joint Venture in Russia[1]

Country-specific restrictions and problems in cross-cultural negotiations and decision making styles are major contributing factors in the demise of international JVs. In global business, disputes between states and MNCs are common and often take the form of restrictions and interference on the part of host governments, resulting in regulatory hurdles and resource nationalism. One such case took place between 2007 and 2009 when British Petroleum (BP) was asked to renegotiate and surrender its control and ownership of oil and gas fields in Russia. BP formed a $6.7 billion joint venture (JV) called TNK-BP in August 2003 with pomp and circumstance. In the Western world, the JV received extensive media coverage because of its future viability and long-term foreign direct investment (FDI) prospects in Russia. Interestingly, the JV was majority-controlled by the British company.

At the time of signing, the JV was hailed as a major project since it brought tangible FDI to Russia. In the post-Soviet Union era, Russia was facing financial difficulties and desperately needed the Western FDI to seek stable economic conditions. BP's FDI was seen as a viable solution in Russia. TNK-BP's Russian partners included Alfa Group, Access and Renova (AAR). Robert Dudley, TNK-BP President commented in 2003: "I believe the structure we have developed for TNK-BP through an exhaustive and co-operative integration process has created a very strong foundation for the future success of TNK-BP" (*TNK-BP*, 2009, p. 1).

Many politicians, including then-Russian President Vladimir Putin and former British Prime Minister Tony Blair, hailed the JV as a major milestone in the relations between Russia and the UK. In 1997, BP had entered into Russia when it acquired a 10 percent stake in a Russian oil company Sidanco for $500 million. In 2006–07, global oil prices started to rise, bringing significant revenues to the Russian government and its economic prowess. During the same period, BP started to witness state interference in the TNK-BP project that came in the forms of ownership disputes and raids by the FSB (Russian Secret Service) on the offices of BP. Because of these frequent altercations with Russian authorities, TNK-BP ended up losing its control in the Kovykta gas field to Gazprom, a state-controlled gas company.

In early 2008, state interventions and investigations took the forms of visa hassles encountered by 148 foreign staff of BP, tax evasions, and environmental-related investigations of TNK-BP's oil fields. Other allegations surfaced regarding labor and employment-related inquiries that pressured BP to hire more Russian staff. TNK-BP was asked to relieve Dudley of his daily duties but BP refused to comply. In 2008, the situation became so acute that the British Foreign and Commonwealth Office got involved in negotiations to help seek an acceptable solution. In June 2008, Peter Mendelson, the European Union's Trade Commissioner accused TNK-BP's Russian shareholders of their "menacing behavior" (Timesonline, 2008, p. 2). In July 2008, BP filed a $365 million law suit against its Russian shareholders in London. Dudley was forced to leave Russia in July 2008 and started working from an undisclosed location. Later Tony Hayward, CEO of BP arranged a meeting with the AAR shareholder Mikhail Fridman in Prague. In September 2008, BP ended up signing a memorandum of understanding with the JV's Russian partners that led to Dudley's resignation from the JV.

As of April 2009, TNK-BP continued to struggle with its board's appointments and selection of a CEO. The governance structure of the JV has been stabilized but relationship-building and cooperation between BP and its Russian partners is far from healthy. Since the TNK-BP JV became so much embroiled in Russian politics, resource nationalism, and partners' cross-cultural misunderstandings, it is useful to note the following lessons for similar future ventures:

1. Restrictions and interference on the part of host governments are common in those countries where resource nationalism is prevalent and the rule of law is weak (Buchanan and Anwar, 2009).
2. Multinational corporations often become victims of JV-related disputes and operational hassles.
3. Shareholder disputes are common in international JVs and often culminate from cross-cultural misunderstandings, decision making styles, weak relationships, and governance issues which could have been better resolved in the negotiation phases.
4. By not speaking the Russian language, Dudley was separated from the mainstream Russian corporate culture.
5. There is a risk in doing business in the former socialist countries. This was evidenced by the statement "Boardroom brawl roils BP's Russia venture." which appeared in the *Wall Street Journal* (June 12, 2008, p. A1) The *Financial Times* (June 5, 2008, p. 9) equally corroborated and observed: "Russian roulette: How BP is falling out with its parents at TNK." Looking at the TNK-BP JV, we witness a multitude of cultural and political hurdles that MNCs face when negotiating and doing business with other corporate cultures and regulatory authorities.

** Written exclusively for this book by Syed Tariq Anwar, West Texas A&M University. Copyright © 2009 by Syed Tariq Anwar. Used with permission.

As illustrated in the opening profile, global managers negotiate with parties in other countries to make specific plans for strategies (exporting, joint ventures, acquisitions, etc.) and for continuing operations. While the complexities of cross-cultural negotiations among firms around the world present challenge enough, managers such as those for BP may also be faced with negotiating with government-owned companies. Google's negotiations with the Chinese government, as another example, ended in a compromise that to enter the Chinese market the company had to obey China's censorship laws and agree to purge its search results of any websites disapproved of by the Chinese government.[2]

Managers must prepare for strategic negotiations. Next the operational details must be negotiated—the staffing of key positions, the sourcing of raw materials or component parts, and the repatriating of profits, to name a few. As globalism burgeons, the ability to conduct successful cross-cultural negotiations cannot be overemphasized. Failure to negotiate productively will result in lost potential alliances and lost business at worst, and confusion and delays at best.

During the process of negotiation—whether before, during, or after negotiating sessions—all kinds of decisions are made, both explicitly and implicitly. A consideration of cross-cultural negotiations must therefore include the various decision-making processes that occur around the world. Negotiations cannot be conducted without decisions being made.

This chapter examines the processes of negotiation and decision making as they apply to international and domestic cross-cultural contexts. The objective is a better understanding of successful management.

NEGOTIATION

Implementing strategy depends on management's ability to negotiate productively—a skill widely considered one of the most important in international business. In the global arena, cultural differences produce great difficulties in the negotiation process. Ignorance of native bargaining rituals, more than any other single factor, accounts for unimpressive sales efforts.[3] Important differences in the negotiation process from country to country include (1) the amount and type of preparation for a negotiation, (2) the relative emphasis on tasks versus interpersonal relationships, (3) the reliance on general principles rather than specific issues, and (4) the number of people present and the extent of their influence.[4] In every instance, managers must familiarize themselves with the cultural background and underlying motivations of the negotiators—and the tactics and procedures they use—to control the process, make progress, and therefore maximize company goals.

The term **negotiation** describes the process of discussion by which two or more parties aim to reach a mutually acceptable agreement. For long-term positive relations, the goal should be to set up a win-win situation—that is, to bring about a settlement beneficial to all parties concerned. This process, difficult enough when it takes place among people of similar backgrounds, is even more complex in international negotiations because of differences in cultural values, lifestyles, expectations, verbal and nonverbal language, approaches to formal procedures, and problem-solving techniques. The complexity is heightened when negotiating across borders because of the greater number of stakeholders involved. These stakeholders are illustrated in Exhibit 5-1. In preparing for negotiations, it is critical to avoid projective cognitive similarity—that is, the

EXHIBIT 5-1   Stakeholders in Cross-cultural Negotiations

assumption that others perceive, judge, think, and reason in the same way when, in fact, they do not because of differential cultural and practical influences. Instead, astute negotiators empathetically enter into the private world or cultural space of their counterparts, while willingly sharing their own view of the situation.[5]

THE NEGOTIATION PROCESS

The negotiation process comprises five stages, the ordering of which may vary according to the cultural norms; for most people, relationship building is part of a continuous process in any event: (1) preparation, (2) relationship building, (3) the exchange of task-related information, (4) persuasion, and (5) concessions and agreement.[6] Of course, in reality these are seldom distinct stages but rather tend to overlap; negotiators may also temporarily revert to an earlier stage. With that in mind, it is useful to break down the negotiation process into stages to discuss the issues relevant to each stage and what international managers might expect, so that they might more successfully manage this process. These stages are shown in Exhibit 5-2 and discussed in the following sections.

Stage One: Preparation

The importance of careful preparation for cross-cultural negotiations cannot be overstated. To the extent that time permits, a distinct advantage can be gained if negotiators familiarize themselves with the entire context and background of their counterparts (no matter where the meetings will take place) in addition to the specific subjects to be negotiated. Because most negotiation problems are caused by differences in culture, language, and environment, hours or days of tactical preparation for negotiation can be wasted if these factors are not carefully considered.[7]

To understand cultural differences in negotiating styles, managers first must understand their own styles and then determine how they differ from the norm in other countries. They can do this by comparing profiles of those perceived to be successful negotiators in different countries. Such profiles reflect the value system, attitudes, and expected behaviors inherent in a given society. Other sections of this chapter describe and compare negotiating styles around the world.

VARIABLES IN THE NEGOTIATING PROCESS   Adept negotiators conduct research to develop a profile of their counterparts so that they know, in most situations, what to expect, how to prepare, and how to react. Exhibit 5-3 shows 12 variables to consider when preparing to negotiate. These variables can, to a great degree, help managers understand the deep-rooted cultural and national motivations and traditional processes underlying negotiations with people from other countries.

EXHIBIT 5-2   **The Negotiation Process**

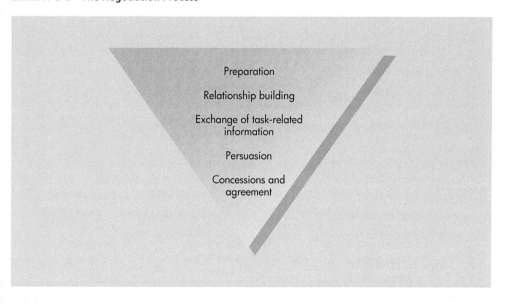

Preparation

Relationship building

Exchange of task-related information

Persuasion

Concessions and agreement

EXHIBIT 5-3   Variables in the Negotiation Process[8]

1. *Basic conception of negotiation process:* Is it a competitive process or a problem-solving approach?
2. *Negotiator selection criteria:* Is selection based on experience, status, expertise, personal attributes, or some other characteristic?
3. *Significance of type of issues:* Is it specific, such as price, or is the focus on relationships or the format of talks?
4. *Concern with protocol:* What is the importance of procedures, social behaviors, and so forth in the negotiation process?
5. *Complexity of communicative context:* What degree of reliance is placed on nonverbal cues to interpret information?
6. *Nature of persuasive arguments:* How do the parties attempt to influence each other? Do they rely on rational arguments, on accepted tradition, or on emotion?
7. *Role of individuals' aspirations:* Are motivations based on individual, company, or community goals?
8. *Bases of trust:* Is trust based on past experience, intuition, or rules?
9. *Risk-taking propensity:* How much do the parties try to avoid uncertainty in trading information or making a contract?
10. *Value of time:* What is each party's attitude toward time? How fast should negotiations proceed, and what degree of flexibility is there?
11. *Decision-making system:* How does each team reach decisions—by individual determination, by majority opinion, or by group consensus?
12. *Form of satisfactory agreement:* Is agreement based on trust (perhaps just a handshake), the credibility of the parties, commitment, or a legally binding contract?

After developing thoughtful profiles of the other party or parties, managers can plan for the actual negotiation meetings, at the same time remaining open to realizing that specific people may not fit the assumed cultural prototype. Prior to the meetings, they should find out as much as possible about (1) the kinds of demands that might be made, (2) the composition of the "opposing" team, and (3) the relative authority that the members possess. After this, the managers can gear their negotiation strategy specifically to the other side's firm, allocate roles to different team members, decide on concessions, and prepare an alternative action plan in case a negotiated solution cannot be found.[9]

Following the preparation and planning stage, which is usually done at the home office, the core of the actual negotiation takes place on-site in the foreign location (or at the manager's home office if the other team has decided to travel there). In some cases, a compromise on the location for negotiations can signal a cooperative strategy, which Weiss calls "Improvise an Approach: Effect Symphony"—a strategy available to negotiators familiar with each other's culture and willing to put negotiation on an equal footing. Weiss gives the following example of this negotiation strategy:

> *For their negotiations over construction of the tunnel under the English Channel, British and French representatives agreed to partition talks and alternate the site between Paris and London. At each site, the negotiators were to use established, local ways, including the language . . . thus punctuating approaches by time and space.*[10]

In this way, each side was put into the context and the script of the other culture about half the time.

The next stage of negotiation—often given short shrift by Westerners—is that of relationship building. In most parts of the world, this stage usually has already taken place or is concurrent with other preparations.

Stage Two: Relationship Building

Relationship building is the process of getting to know one's contacts in a host country and building mutual trust before embarking on business discussions and transactions. This process is regarded with much more significance in most parts of the world than it is in the United States. U.S. negotiators are, generally speaking, objective about the specific matter at hand and usually want to waste no time in getting down to business and making progress. This approach, well understood in the United States, can be disastrous if the foreign negotiators want to take enough time to build trust and respect as a basis for negotiating contracts. In such cases, American efficiency interferes with the patient development of a mutually trusting relationship—the very cornerstone of an Asian business agreement.[11]

In many countries, such as Mexico and China, personal commitments to individuals, rather than the legal system, form the basis for the enforcement of contracts. Effective negotiators allow plenty of time in their schedules for such relationship building with bargaining partners. This process usually takes the form of social events, tours, and ceremonies, along with much **nontask sounding**—general, polite conversation and informal communication before meetings—while all parties get to know one another. In such cultures, one patiently waits for the other party to start actual business negotiations, aware that relationship building is, in fact, the first phase of negotiations.[12] It is usually recommended that managers new to such scenarios use an intermediary—someone who already has the trust and respect of the foreign managers and who therefore acts as a "relationship bridge." Middle Easterners, in particular, prefer to negotiate through a trusted intermediary, and for them as well, initial meetings are only for the purpose of getting acquainted. Arabs do business with the person, not the company, and therefore mutual trust must be established.

In their best seller on negotiation, *Getting to Yes,* Fisher and Ury point out the dangers of not preparing well for negotiations:

> *In Persian, the word "compromise" does not have the English meaning of a midway solution which both sides can accept, but only the negative meaning of surrendering one's principles. Also, "mediator" means "meddler," someone who is barging in uninvited. In 1980, United Nations Secretary-General Kurt Waldheim flew to Iran to deal with the hostage situation. National Iranian radio and television broadcast in Persian a comment he was said to have made upon his arrival in Tehran: "I have come as a mediator to work out a compromise." Less than an hour later, his car was being stoned by angry Iranians.[13]*

As a bridge to the more formal stages of negotiations, such relationship building is followed by posturing—that is, general discussion that sets the tone for the meetings. This phase should result in a spirit of cooperation. To help ensure this result, negotiators must use words like "respect" and "mutual benefit" rather than language that would suggest arrogance, superiority, or urgency.

STAGE THREE: EXCHANGING TASK-RELATED INFORMATION   In the next stage—exchanging task-related information—each side typically makes a presentation and states its position; a question-and-answer session usually ensues, and alternatives are discussed. From an American perspective, this represents a straightforward, objective, efficient, and understandable stage. However, negotiators from other countries continue to take a more indirect approach at this stage. Mexican negotiators are usually suspicious and indirect, presenting little substantive material and more lengthy, evasive conversation. French negotiators enjoy debate and conflict and will often interrupt presentations to argue about an issue even if it has little relevance to the topic being presented. The Chinese also ask many questions of their counterparts, and delve specifically and repeatedly into the details at hand; conversely, Chinese presentations contain only vague and ambiguous material. For instance, after about 20 Boeing officials spent six weeks presenting masses of literature and technical demonstrations to the Chinese, the Chinese said, "Thank you for your introduction."[14]

The Russians also enter negotiations well prepared and well versed in the specific details of the matter being presented. To answer their (or any other side's) questions, it is generally a good idea to bring along someone with expertise to answer any grueling technical inquiries. Russians also put a lot of emphasis on protocol and expect to deal only with top executives.

Adler suggests that negotiators should focus not only on presenting their situation and needs but also on showing an understanding of their opponents' viewpoint. Focusing on the entire situation confronting each party encourages the negotiators to assess a wider range of alternatives for resolution, rather than limiting themselves to their preconceived, static positions. She suggests that to be most effective, negotiators should prepare for meetings by practicing role reversal.[15]

Stage Four: Persuasion

In the next phase of negotiations—persuasion—the hard bargaining starts. Typically, both parties try to persuade the other to accept more of their position and to give up some of their own. Often, some persuasion has already taken place beforehand in social settings and through mutual contacts. In the Far East, details are likely to be worked out ahead of time through the backdoor approach (*houmani*). For the most part, however, the majority of the persuasion takes place over one or more negotiating sessions. International managers usually find that this process of bargaining and making concessions is fraught with difficulties because of the different uses and interpretations of verbal and nonverbal behaviors. Although variations in such behaviors influence every stage of the negotiation process, they can play a particularly powerful role in persuasion, especially if they are not anticipated.

Studies of negotiating behavior have revealed the use of certain tactics, which skilled negotiators recognize and use, such as promises, threats, and so on. Other, less savory tactics are sometimes used in international negotiations. Often called "dirty tricks," these tactics, according to Fisher and Ury, include efforts to mislead "opponents" deliberately.[16] Some negotiators may give wrong or distorted factual information or use the excuse of ambiguous authority—giving conflicting impressions about who in their party has the power to make a commitment. In the midst of hard bargaining, the prudent international manager will follow up on possibly misleading information before taking action based on trust.

Other rough tactics are designed to put opposing negotiators in a stressful situation physically or psychologically so that their giving in is more likely. These include uncomfortable room temperatures, too-bright lighting, rudeness, interruptions, and other irritations. International negotiators must keep in mind, however, that what might seem like dirty tricks to Americans is simply the way other cultures conduct negotiations. In some South American countries, for example, it is common to start negotiations with misleading or false information.

The most subtle behaviors in the negotiation process, and often the most difficult to deal with, are usually the nonverbal messages—the use of voice intonation, facial and body expressions, eye contact, dress, and the timing of the discussions. Nonverbal behaviors, discussed in previous chapters, are ingrained aspects of culture used by people in their daily lives; they are not specifically changed for the purposes of negotiation. Among those behaviors impacting negotiations is the direct communication style, such as with Germans, compared with the indirect style, such as with Japanese. Clearly, also, the individualism-collectivism cultural dimension is one which greatly guides negotiation because of the relative motivation of personal self-interest in individualistic societies, such as the United States; this compares with the group-interest in Asian cultures, so that negotiators will likely give more importance to their social obligations and the needs of the group.[17]

Although persuasion has been discussed as if it were always a distinct stage, it is really the primary purpose underlying all stages of the negotiation process. In particular, persuasion is an integral part of the process of making concessions and arriving at an agreement.

Stage Five: Concessions and Agreement

In the last stage of negotiation—concessions and agreement—tactics vary greatly across cultures. Well-prepared negotiators are aware of various concession strategies and have decided ahead of time what their own concession strategy will be. Familiar with the typical initial positions that various parties are likely to take, they know that Russians and Chinese generally open their bargaining with extreme positions, asking for more than they hope to gain, whereas Swedes usually start with what they are prepared to accept.

Research in the United States indicates that better end results are attained by starting with extreme positions. With this approach, the process of reaching an agreement involves careful timing of the disclosure information and of concessions. Most people who have studied negotiations believe that negotiators should disclose only the information that is necessary at a given point and that they should try to obtain information piece by piece to gradually get the whole picture without giving away their goals or concession strategy. These guidelines will not always work in intercultural negotiations because the American process of addressing issues one at a time, in a linear fashion, is not common in other countries or cultures. Negotiators in the Far East, for example, approach issues in a holistic manner, deciding on the whole deal at the end, rather than making incremental concessions.

Again, at the final stage of agreement and contract, local practices determine how these agreements will be honored. Whereas Americans take contracts very seriously, Russians often renege on their contracts. The Japanese, on the other hand, consider a formal contract to be somewhat of an insult and a waste of time and money in legal costs, since they prefer to operate on the basis of understanding and social trust.[18] More attention to this and all the negotiation phases might have led to better results in the French-Chinese joint venture discussed in the management focus.

MANAGEMENT FOCUS

Cultural Misunderstanding—The Danone-Wahaha Joint Venture in China[19]

Many cross-border joint ventures encounter problems because the partners' differences in management styles, corporate control, and cross-cultural issues do not get recognized and resolved during the negotiation phase, and so continue to fester during the operations phase. One such JV is the Sino-French collaboration that was formed by Groupe Danone (hereafter Danone), and Hangzhou Wahaha Group Co. (hereafter WHH). Danone is one of the largest food conglomerates from France. Wahaha is China's largest beverage company that was started in 1987 and was controlled by the government of Hangzhou's Shangcheng District. From its inception, Zong Qinghou ran the operations of WHH. When the company converted itself into a private entity, Qinghou took the role of a minority shareholder.

The Danone-WHH joint venture was established in March 1996 and took the trademark name of Wahaha because of its strong brand visibility in the Chinese market. In emerging markets, Danone grew by creating a multitude of profitable JVs in India, Pakistan, Vietnam, Columbia, and other countries. On the other hand, WHH achieved its market expansion and corporate growth in China by turning itself into a national brand and highly successful food and beverage company. The Danone-Wahaha JV dealt with the areas of food and beverages and grew at a respectable rate. For Danone, this was a good strategy to enter into China. For WHH, the JV helped the company to make a linkage with a well known global brand.

Negotiations resulted in the following salient features of the JV:

1. Ownership of the JV included foreign partners (51 percent), WHH (39 percent), and employees (10 percent).
2. The JV encompassed five entities: Hangzhou Wahaha Baili Foods, Hangzhou Wahaha Health Foods, Hangzhou Wahaha Foods Co., Hangzhou Wahaha Beverages Co., and Hangzhou Wahaha Quick Frozen Foods. Danone and Peregine collectively invested $70 million in the five entities of the JV.
3. As agreed by Danone, the day-to-day operations of the JV resided with Qinghou.

As the JV's business operations expanded in China, activities of Danone and WHH also became intertwined and complex leading to differences in opinion, corporate control, and management styles. Between 1996 and 2006, the following changes took place in the structure and operations of the Danone-WHH JV:

1. Because of consumer demand and market growth, the JV's operations in China witnessed the emergence of 37 business entities. Danone attempted to buy out Qinghou but the negotiations were unsuccessful.
2. Public rows erupted between the two companies when they kept on blaming each other for breach of contract. Danone blamed Qinghou for going outside of the contract and profiting from 80 unauthorized businesses. This included misusing the Danone brand and its distribution system in China.

3. The dispute between Danone and Qinghou became even more personal when Danone filed a law suit against Qinghou's wife and daughter in a Los Angeles court regarding their business interests and unauthorized JV-related dealings outside of China.
4. Danone filed for arbitration proceedings in Stockholm in May 2007.
5. During the dispute, Danone also filed legal claims against ten business entities that were believed to be controlled by WHH in Samoa and the British Virgin Island.
6. The Danone-WHH case became so much embroiled that Chinese and French governments asked the companies to negotiate an "amicable" resolution.

From this highly publicized dispute between Danone and WHH, we learn the following lessons:

1. Cross-cultural misunderstandings and unfamiliarity with the JV partners were at the heart of this dispute. Qinghou's entrepreneurial style and WHH's consistent growth in China could have been one of the causes of this dispute since Danone management was alienated in the process.
2. Both partners used media and public relations campaigns in China and Western markets to justify their arguments, instead of having open negotiations.
3. In any JV, relationship-building and exchange of project-related information is critical in the post-negotiation phase that is based on concessions and agreement.
4. It seems that Danone and WHH lacked open communication in their day-to-day management of the JV. Also important was the area of trust that happened to be missing in the partners' dealings.
5. According to *China Economic Review*, Chinese companies often become an extension of their founders' personal goals regarding day-to-day business operations. Most Chinese businesses do not see a major difference between 51/49 ownership and enforcement of rights. Foreign partners must make sure that their designated managers and staff members are included in the day-to-day management of the JV. In international markets, JV-related contracts can be abused and could lead to cross-cultural misunderstands and operational disruptions.
6. Finally, in JVs, relationship-building takes time and a good amount of interaction is needed between the partners. In the case of Danone-WHH JV, partner conflict, face-saving problems, blame-game, and accusations could have been avoided had the two companies communicated openly during the negotiation phase and afterwards. Also it seems that Danone and WHH did not understand their low-context and high-context cultures and management styles that eventually led to this conflict.

** Written exclusively for this book by Syed Tariq Anwar, West Texas A&M University. Copyright © 2009 by Syed Tariq Anwar. Used with permission.

UNDERSTANDING NEGOTIATION STYLES

Global managers can benefit from studying differences in negotiating behaviors (and the underlying reasons for them), which can help them recognize what is happening in the negotiating process. Exhibit 5-4 shows some examples of differences among North American, Japanese, and Latin American styles. Brazilians, for example, generally have a spontaneous, passionate, and dynamic style. They are very talkative and particularly use the word "no" extensively—more than 40 times per half-hour compared with 4.7 times for Americans, and only 1.9 times for the Japanese. They also differ markedly from Americans and the Japanese by their use of extensive physical contact.[20]

The Japanese are typically skillful negotiators. They have spent a great deal more time and effort studying U.S. culture and business practices than Americans have spent studying Japanese practices. A typical example of this contrast was apparent when Charlene Barshefsky—a tough American international lawyer who had never visited Japan before—was sent there as a trade negotiator and had little knowledge of its counterparts. But Mr. Okamatsu, like most Japanese negotiators, was very familiar with America. He had lived with his family in New York for three years and had spent many years handling bilateral trade disputes between the two countries. The different styles of the two negotiators were apparent in the negotiations. Ms. Barshefsky wanted specific import goals. Mr. Okamatsu wanted to talk more about the causes of trade problems rather than set specific targets, which he called the "cooperative

EXHIBIT 5-4   Comparison of Negotiation Styles—Japanese, North American, and Latin American[22]

Japanese	North American	Latin American
Emotional sensitivity highly valued	Emotional sensitivity not highly valued	Emotional sensitivity Valued
Hiding of emotions	Dealing straightforwardly or Impersonally	Emotionally passionate
Subtle power plays; conciliation	Litigation not so much as conciliation	Great power plays; use of weakness
Loyalty to employer; employer takes care of employees	Lack of commitment to employer; breaking of ties by either if necessary	Loyalty to employer (who is often family)
Face-saving crucial; decisions often on basis of saving someone from embarrassment	Decisions made on a cost-benefit basis; face-saving does not always matter	Face-saving crucial in decision making to preserve honor, dignity
Decision makers openly influenced by special interests	Decision makers influenced by special interests but often not considered ethical	Execution of special interests of decision expected, condoned
Not argumentative; quiet when Right	Argumentative when right or wrong, but impersonal	Argumentative when right or wrong; passionate
What is down in writing must be accurate, valid	Great importance given to documentation as evidential proof	Impatient with documentation as obstacle to understanding general principles
Step-by-step approach to decision making	Methodically organized decision making	Impulsive, spontaneous decision making
Good of group is the ultimate aim	Profit motive or good of individual is the ultimate aim	What is good for group is good for the individual
Cultivate a good emotional social setting for decision making; get to know decision makers	Decision making impersonal; avoid involvements, conflict of interest	Personalism necessary for good decision making

approach." Ms. Barshefsky snapped that the approach was nonsense and "would analyze the past to death, with no link to future change."[21]

Such differences in philosophy and style between the two countries reflect ten years of anger and feelings of betrayal in trade negotiations. John Graham, a California professor who has studied international negotiating styles, says that the differences between United States and Japanese styles are well illustrated by their respective proverbs: the Americans believe that "The squeaking wheel gets the grease," and the Japanese say that "The pheasant would not be shot but for its cry."[23] The Japanese are calm, quiet, patient negotiators; they are accustomed to long, detailed negotiating sessions. Whereas Americans often plunge straight to the matter at hand, the Japanese instead prefer to develop long-term, personal relationships. The Japanese want to get to know those on the other side and will spend some time in nontask sounding.

In negotiations, the Japanese culture of politeness and hiding of emotions can be disconcerting to Americans when they are unable to make straightforward eye contact or when the Japanese maintain smiling faces in serious situations. It is important that Americans understand what is polite and what is offensive to the Japanese—and vice versa. Americans must avoid anything that resembles boasting because the Japanese value humility, and physical contact or touching of any sort must be avoided.[24] Consistent with the culture-based value of maintaining harmony, the Japanese are likely to be evasive or even leave the room rather than give a direct negative answer.[25] Fundamental to Japanese culture is a concern for the welfare of the group; anything that affects one member or part of society affects the others. Thus, the Japanese view decisions carefully in light of long-term consequences; they use objective, analytic thought patterns; and they take time for reflection.[26]

Further insight into negotiating styles around the world can be gained by comparing the North American, Arab, and Russian styles. Basic cultural values often shed light on the way information is presented, whether and how concessions will be made, and the general nature and duration of the relationship.For North Americans, negotiations are businesslike; their factual appeals are based on what they believe is objective information, presented with the assumption that it is understood by the other side on a logical basis. Arabs use affective appeals based on emotions and subjective feelings. Russians employ axiomatic appeals—that is, their appeals are based on the ideals generally accepted in their society. The Russians are tough negotiators; they stall for time until they unnerve Western negotiators by continuously delaying and haggling. Much of this approach is based on the Russians' different attitude toward time. Because Russians traditionally do not subscribe to the Western belief that "time is money," they are more patient, more determined, and more dogged negotiators. They try to keep smiles and other expressions of emotion to a minimum to present a calm exterior.[27]

In contrast to the Russians, Arabs are more interested in long-term relationships and are, therefore, more likely to make concessions. Compared with Westerners, Arabs have a casual approach to deadlines, and frequently the negotiators lack the authority to finalize a deal.[28]

Successful Negotiators Around the World

Following are selected profiles of what it takes to be a successful negotiator, as perceived by people in their home countries. These are profiles of American, Indian, Arab, Swedish, and Italian negotiators, according to Pierre Casse, and give some insight into what to expect from different negotiators and what they expect from others.[29]

AMERICAN NEGOTIATORS   According to Casse, a successful American negotiator acts as follows:

1. Knows when to compromise
2. Takes a firm stand at the beginning of the negotiation
3. Refuses to make concessions beforehand
4. Keeps his or her cards close to his or her chest
5. Accepts compromises only when the negotiation is deadlocked
6. Sets up the general principles and delegates the detail work to associates
7. Keeps a maximum of options open before negotiation
8. Operates in good faith
9. Respects the "opponents"
10. States his or her position as clearly as possible
11. Knows when he or she wishes a negotiation to move on
12. Is fully briefed about the negotiated issues
13. Has a good sense of timing and is consistent
14. Makes the other party reveal his or her position while keeping his or her own position hidden as long as possible
15. Lets the other negotiator come forward first and looks for the best deal

INDIAN NEGOTIATORS   Indians, says Casse, often follow Gandhi's approach to negotiation, which Gandhi called *satyagraha*, "firmness in a good cause." This approach combines strength with the love of truth. The successful Indian negotiator thus acts as follows:

1. Looks for and says the truth
2. Is not afraid of speaking up and has no fears
3. Exercises self-control ("The weapons of the *satyagraha* are within him.")
4. Seeks solutions that will please all the parties involved ("*Satyagraha* aims to exalt both sides.")
5. Respects the other party ("The opponent must be weaned from error by patience and sympathy. Weaned, not crushed; converted, not annihilated.")
6. Neither uses violence nor insults

7. Is ready to change his or her mind and differ with himself or herself at the risk of being seen as inconsistent and unpredictable
8. Puts things into perspective and switches easily from the small picture to the big one
9. Is humble and trusts the opponent
10. Is able to withdraw, use silence, and learn from within
11. Relies on himself or herself, his or her own resources and strengths
12. Appeals to the other party's spiritual identity ("To communicate, the West moves or talks. The East sits, contemplates, suffers.")
13. Is tenacious, patient, and persistent
14. Learns from the opponent and avoids the use of secrets
15. Goes beyond logical reasoning and trusts his or her instinct as well as faith

ARAB NEGOTIATORS Many Arab negotiators, following Islamic tradition, use mediators to settle disputes. A successful Arab mediator acts in the following way:

1. Protects all the parties' honor, self-respect, and dignity
2. Avoids direct confrontations between opponents
3. Is respected and trusted by all
4. Does not put the parties involved in a situation where they have to show weakness or admit defeat
5. Has the necessary prestige to be listened to
6. Is creative enough to come up with honorable solutions for all parties
7. Is impartial and can understand the positions of the various parties without leaning toward one or the other
8. Is able to resist any kind of pressure that the opponents could try to exercise on him
9. Uses references to people who are highly respected by the opponents to persuade them to change their minds on some issues ("Do it for the sake of your father.")
10. Can keep secrets and in so doing gains the confidence of the negotiating parties
11. Controls his temper and emotions (or loses it when and where necessary)
12. Can use conferences as mediating devices
13. Knows that the opponents will have problems in carrying out the decisions made during the negotiation
14. Is able to cope with the Arab disregard for time
15. Understands the impact of Islam on the opponents who believe that they possess the truth, follow the Right Path, and are going to "win" because their cause is just

SWEDISH NEGOTIATORS Swedish negotiators, according to Casse, are:

1. Very quiet and thoughtful
2. Punctual (concerned with time)
3. Extremely polite
4. Straightforward (they get straight down to business)
5. Eager to be productive and efficient
6. Heavy going
7. Down to earth and overcautious
8. Rather flexible
9. Able to and quite good at holding emotions and feelings
10. Slow at reacting to new (unexpected) proposals
11. Informal and familiar
12. Conceited
13. Perfectionist
14. Afraid of confrontations
15. Very private

ITALIAN NEGOTIATORS Italians, says Casse, value a negotiator who acts as follows:

1. Has a sense of drama (acting is a main part of the culture)
2. Does not hide his or her emotions (which are partly sincere and partly feigned)

3. Reads facial expressions and gestures very well
4. Has a feeling for history
5. Does not trust anybody
6. Is concerned about the *bella figura*—the "good impression"—he or she can create among those who watch his or her behavior
7. Believes in the individual's initiatives, not so much in teamwork
8. Is good at being obliging and simpatico at all times
9. Is always on the *qui vive*—the "lookout"
10. Never embraces definite opinions
11. Is able to come up with new ways to immobilize and eventually destroy his or her opponents
12. Handles confrontations of power with subtlety and tact
13. Has a flair for intrigue
14. Knows how to use flattery
15. Can involve other negotiators in complex combinations

COMPARING PROFILES   Comparing such profiles is useful. Indian negotiators, for example, are humble, patient, respectful of the other parties, and very willing to compromise, compared with Americans, who are firmer about taking stands. An important difference between Arab negotiators and those from most other countries is that the negotiators are mediators, not the parties themselves; hence, direct confrontation is made impossible. Successful Swedish negotiators are conservative and careful, dealing with factual and detailed information. This profile contrasts with Italian negotiators, who are expressive and exuberant but less straightforward than their Swedish counterparts.

MANAGING NEGOTIATION

Skillful global managers must assess many factors when managing negotiations. They must understand the position of the other parties in regard to their goals—whether national or corporate—and whether these goals are represented by principles or specific details. They should have the ability to recognize the relative importance attached to completing the task versus developing interpersonal relationships. Managers also must know the composition of the teams involved, the power allotted to the members, and the extent of the teams' preparation. In addition, they must grasp the significance of personal trust in the relationship. As stated earlier, the culture of the parties involved affects their negotiating styles and behavior and thus the overall process of negotiation. However, whatever the culture, research by Tse, Francis, and Walls has found person-related conflicts to "invite negative, more relation-oriented (versus information-oriented) responses," leading them to conclude that "The software of negotiation—that is, the nature and the appearance of the relationship between the people pursuing common goals—needs to be carefully addressed in the negotiation process.[30]

This is particularly true when representatives of individual-focused cultures (such as the Americans) and group-focused cultures (such as the Chinese) are on opposite sides of the table. Many of these culture-based differences in negotiations came to light in Husted's study on Mexican negotiators' perceptions of the reasons for the failure of their negotiations with U.S. teams.[31] The Mexican managers' interpretations were affected by their high-context culture, with the characteristics of an indirect approach, patience in discussing ideas, and maintenance of dignity. Instead, the low-context Americans conveyed an impatient, cold, blunt communicative style. To maintain the outward dignity of their Mexican counterparts, Americans must approach negotiations with Mexicans with patience and tolerance and refrain from attacking ideas because these attacks may be taken personally. The relationships among the factors of cross-cultural negotiation discussed in this chapter are illustrated in Exhibit 5-5.

The successful management of intercultural negotiations requires that a manager go beyond a generalized understanding of the issues and variables involved. She or he must (1) gain specific knowledge of the parties in the upcoming meeting, (2) prepare accordingly to adjust to and control the situation, and (3) be innovative.[32]

Research has shown that a problem-solving approach is essential to successful cross-cultural negotiations, whether abroad or in the home office, although the approach works

EXHIBIT 5-5   Cross-cultural Negotiation Variables

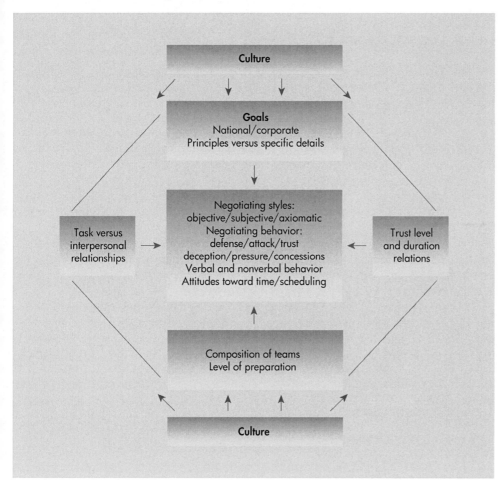

differently in various countries.[33] This problem-solving approach requires that a negotiator treat everyone with respect, avoid making anyone feel uncomfortable, and not criticize or blame the other parties in a personal way that may make someone feel shame—that is, lose face.

Research by the Huthwaite Research Group reveals how successful negotiators, compared to average negotiators, manage the planning process and their face-to-face behavior. The group found that during the planning process, successful negotiators consider a wider range of options and pay greater attention to areas of common ground. Skillful negotiators also tend to make twice as many comments regarding long-term issues and are more likely to set upper and lower limits regarding specific points. In their face-to-face behavior, skillful negotiators make fewer irritating comments—such as "We're making you a generous offer," make counterproposals less frequently, and use fewer reasons to back up arguments. In addition, skilled negotiators practice active listening—asking questions, clarifying their understanding of the issues, and summarizing the issues.[34]

Using the Internet to Support Negotiations

Modern technology can provide support for the negotiating process, though it can't take the place of the essential face-to-face ingredient in many instances. A growing component for electronic commerce is the development of applications to support the negotiation of contracts and resolution of disputes. As Web applications develop, they may provide support for various phases and dimensions, such as "Multiple- issue, multiple- party business transactions of a buy–sell nature; international dispute resolution (business disputes, political disputes); and internal company negotiations and communications, among others."[35]

Negotiation support systems (NSS) can provide support for the negotiation process in the following ways:

- Increasing the likelihood that an agreement is reached when a zone of agreement exists (solutions that both parties would accept)
- Decreasing the direct and indirect costs of negotiations, such as costs caused by time delays (strikes, violence), and attorneys' fees, among others
- Maximizing the chances for optimal outcomes[36]

One Web-based support system, developed at Carleton University in Ottawa, Canada—called INSPIRE—provides applications for preparing and conducting negotiations and for renegotiating options after a settlement. Users can specify preferences and assess offers; the site also has graphical displays of the negotiation process.[37]

E-NEGOTIATIONS   The advantages of electronic communications are well known: speed, less travel, the ability to lay out much objective information to be considered by the other party over time. The disadvantages, however, might kill a deal before it gets off the ground by not being able to build trust and interpersonal relationships over time before getting down to business. In addition, non-verbal nuances are lost, although videoconferencing is a compromise for that purpose.

Rosette et al. noted that "opening offers may be especially aggressive in e-mail as compared to face-to-face negotiations because computer-mediated communications, such as e-mail, loosen inhibitions and cause negotiators to become more competitive and more risk seeking. The increase in competitive and risky behavior occurs because e-mail does not communicate social context cues in the same way as does the presence of another person."[38]

Managing Conflict Resolution

Much of the negotiation process is fraught with conflict—explicit or implicit—and such conflict can often lead to a standoff, or a lose–lose situation. This is regrettable, not only because of the situation at hand, but also because it probably will shut off future opportunities for deals between the parties. Much of the cause of such conflict can be found in cultural differences between the parties—in their expectations, in their behaviors, and particularly in their communication styles—as illustrated in the Comparative Management in Focus, Negotiating with the Chinese.

 COMPARATIVE MANAGEMENT IN FOCUS

Negotiating with the Chinese

The Chinese way of making decisions begins with socialization and initiation of personal guanxi rather than business discussion. The focus is not market research, statistical analysis, facts, PowerPoint presentations, or to-the-point business discussion. My focus must be on fostering guanxi.

SUNNY ZHOU,
*General Manager of Kunming Lida Wood
and Bamboo Products*[39]

When Westerners initiate business negotiations with representatives from the People's Republic of China, cultural barriers confront both sides. However, we should recognize that there are regional cultural differences which may affect negotiations, as detailed in Table 1, as well as regional economic differences. In addition, as concluded in research by Tung et al., there are considerable generational differences, in particular with those younger people who have been educated in the west and are more familiar with western ways and languages, whereas the older generation holds to more traditional culture and negotiation strategies.[40]

MAP 5.1   China

TABLE 1   Generalized Characteristics Associated with Chinese from Beijing, Shanghai, Guangzhou/Shenzhen and Select Cities in Western China

Beijing (capital city, center of political power in the country)	*Shanghai* (commercial center)
• Politically-oriented—everyone talks about politics • Bureaucratic—given the prevalence of state-owned enterprises (SOEs) in Beijing and surrounding areas, people tend to be more bureaucratic • Emphasis on integrity—people place more emphasis on trust and honesty in business dealings • Highly educated—many of the bureaucrats are highly educated • More relationship-focused • More fluid perception of time • Face comparatively more important • More holistic in approaching issues • Focus on general principles • More diversified cultural life • More direct and straightforward	• Business savvy—they are known for their business acumen • Bottom-line oriented • Focus on details—they perform due diligence before meetings and because of this, some people find it difficult to transact business with Shanghainese because they tend to argue over trivial matters • Confident and arrogant—because Shanghai has been an important economic center and is the trendsetter in fashion, Shanghainese tend to look down upon people from other cities, referring to them as "villagers" • Materialistic—Shanghainese are more concerned with brand names and one-upmanship • More tactical, i.e., calculating • Greater admiration of the West • More younger people who have attained high positions • Obsessed with career progression

Guangzhou/Shenzhen (southern city close to Hong Kong)	*Western China* (cities like Chongqing and Chengdu)
• Hard working and highly efficient—in the 1980s, Guangzhou/Shenzhen was recognized for its efficiency in building one entire floor of a skyscraper in three days	• People's mentality more like Beijing, Shanghai, and Guangzhou/Shenzhen 5–6 years ago
• Larger concentration of mass-assembly manufacturing	• More conservative
	• More clannish
• Entrepreneurial—many prefer to start up their own businesses as opposed to working for established corporations	• More traditional
	• Particularistic—emphasize knowing your counterpart first before doing business
• Pride in cuisine and more exotic cuisine	• Socializing (eating, drinking, and smoking) is very important
• Greater deviation from the norm	
• Less concerned about politics	• Greater emphasis on personal relations, i.e., rely on people more than laws or negotiations
• Identify more closely with Hong Kong	
• More concerned with work-life balance issues	• Less experience with international business
• Superstitious—because many businesspeople there are entrepreneurs, they tend to be more superstitious	• More laid back
	• More hardy
	• More emotional
• More informal in protocol and clothing	• In general, westerners find it more difficult to negotiate/do business here
• More risk taking	

Source: Rosalie L. Tung, Verner Worm, and Tony Fang, "Sino-Western Business Negotiations Revisited—30 Years after China's Open Door Policy," *Organizational Dynamics* 37, no 1, January 2008, 60–74; reprinted with permission from Elsevier.

For the most part, however, negotiation process used by the chinese is mystifying to most Westerners. For instance, the chinese put much greate emphasis than Americans and Europeans on respect and friendship, on saving face, and on group goals. Long-term goals are more important to the Chinese than the specific current objectives typical of Western negotiators. Even though market forces now have more influence in China, political and economic agendas are still expected to be considered in negotiations. Research by Xinping Shi of 198 managers in Beijing, 185 in Shanghai, and 189 in Guangzhou shows that prevailing economic conditions, political pervasiveness, and "constituent shadow" (the influence that constituents, such as political and state agencies, have on the negotiating parties in China) are key practical factors that, added to cultural factors, make up the context affecting Chinese negotiations. These antecedent factors, when filtered through the specific negotiator's profile, result in various behaviors, processes, and outcomes from those negotiations. Moreover, little difference in those influence factors was found among the different regions in China. Exhibit 5-6 shows these environmental factors and the relationships among the factors involved in Western–Chinese business negotiation.

Businesspeople report two major areas of conflict in negotiating with the Chinese: (1) The amount of detail the Chinese want about product characteristics, and (2) their apparent insincerity about reaching an agreement. In addition, Chinese negotiators frequently have little authority, frustrating Americans who do have the authority and are ready to conclude a deal.[41] This situation arises because many Chinese companies report to the government trade corporations, which are involved in the negotiations and often have a representative on the team. Often,

EXHIBIT 5-6 Influences on Western–Chinese Business Negotiations

Source: Xinping Shi, "Antecedent Factors of International Business Negotiations in the China Context," *Management International Review*, no. 2 (April 2001): 182.

the goals of Chinese negotiators remain primarily within the framework of state planning and political ideals. Although China is becoming more profit-oriented, most deals are still negotiated within the confines of the state budget allocation for that project rather than on the basis of a project's profitability or value. It is crucial, then, to find out which officials—national, provincial, local—have the power to make, and keep, a deal. According to James Broering of Arthur Andersen, who does much business in China, "companies have negotiated with government people for months, only to discover that they were dealing with the wrong people."[42]

Research shows that for the Chinese, the negotiation process is greatly affected by three cultural norms: their ingrained politeness and emotional restraint, their emphasis on social obligations, and their belief in the interconnection of work, family, and friendship. Because of the Chinese preference for emotional restraint and saving face, aggressive or emotional attempts at persuasion in negotiation are likely to fail. Instead, the Chinese tendency to avoid open conflict will more likely result in negative strategies such as discontinuing or withdrawing from negotiation.[43] The concept of face is at the heart of this kind of response—it is essential for foreigners to recognize the role that face behavior plays in negotiations. There are two components of face—*lien* and *mien-tzu*. *Lien* refers to a person's moral character; it is the most important thing defining that person, and without it one cannot function in society. It can only be earned by fulfilling obligations to others. *Mien-tzu* refers to one's reputation or prestige, earned through accomplishments or through bureaucratic or political power.[44] Giving others one's time, gifts, or praise enhances one's own face. In negotiations, it is vital that you do not make it obvious that you have "won" because that means that the other party has "lost" and will lose face. One must, therefore, make token concessions and other attempts to show that respect must be demonstrated, and modesty and control must be maintained; otherwise anyone who feels he or she has "lost face" will not want to deal with you again. The Chinese will later ignore any dealings or incidents that caused them to lose face, maintaining the expected polite behavior out of social consciousness and concern for others. When encountering an embarrassing situation, they will typically smile or laugh in an attempt to save face, responses that are confusing to Western negotiators.[45]

Research by Kam-hon Lee et al. explored sources of tension felt by Chinese and Americans during negotiations. For the Americans, sources of tension and lack of trust were attributed to what they referred to as Chinese misrepresentations, and to the Chinese not following what the Americans considered normative negotiation procedures. Generally, the Americans felt that the Chinese team was not being truthful with them and were not giving straight answers. From the perspective of the Chinese, tension on the part of the Americans damaged the interpersonal relationships between the parties, which are so important to the Chinese; this resulted in the Chinese not trusting the Americans and having negative expectations about the Americans' cooperativeness in the future. Further, Lee et al. found that intransigence was the most frequent cause of tension in both the Chinese and the American parties.[46]

The emphasis on social obligations underlies the strong orientation of the Chinese toward collective goals. Therefore, appeals to individual members of the Chinese negotiating team, rather than appeals to benefit the group as a whole, will probably backfire. The Confucian emphasis on the kinship system and the hierarchy of work, family, and friends explains the Chinese preference for doing business with familiar, trusted people and trusted companies. "Foreign" negotiators, then, should focus on establishing long-term, trusting relationships, even at the expense of some immediate returns.

Deeply ingrained in the Chinese culture is the importance of harmony for the smooth functioning of society. Harmony is based primarily on personal relationships, trust, and ritual. After the Chinese establish a cordial relationship with foreign negotiators, they use this relationship as a basis for the give-and-take of business discussions. This implicit cultural norm is commonly known as *guanxi*, which refers to the intricate, pervasive network of personal relations that every Chinese carefully cultivates. It is the primary means of getting ahead, in the absence of a proper commercial legal system.[47] In other words, *guanxi* establishes obligations to exchange favors in future business activities.[48] Even within the Chinese bureaucracy, *guanxi* prevails over legal interpretations. Although networking is important anywhere to do business, the difference in China is that "*guanxi* networks are not just commercial, but also social, involving the exchange both of favor and affection."[49] Firms that have special *guanxi* connections and give preferential treatment to one another are known as members of a *guanxihu* network.[50] Sunny Zhou, general manager of Kumming Lida Wood and Bamboo

Products, states that when he shops for lumber, "The lumber price varies drastically, depending on whether one has strong *guanxi* with the local administrators."[51] However, research by Fang, et al indicates some transition to a more business environment, where *guanxi* is still important, but not always decisive, and quotes a Chinese business woman as follows:

> *For example, I started my industrial systems business in Shanghai and Wuhan ten years ago. At that time, if you knew people in the government and had a good guanxi with them you would get your projects irrespective of your nengli (professional ability). Today, nengli becomes more and more important. Without nengli and benshi (professional skills), even your best government guanxi contacts would not let you win the bidding. If he did, he would risk losing his own job.*[52]

FANG ET AL,
International Business Review, 17, April, 2008.

Western managers should thus anticipate extended preliminary visiting (relationship building), in which the Chinese expect to learn more about them and their trustworthiness. The Chinese also use this opportunity to convey their deeply held principles. They attach considerable importance to mutual benefit.[53] The Chinese expect Western firms to sacrifice corporate goals and above-average profits to Chinese national goals and principles, such as meaningful friendship, Chinese national development, and the growth and enhancement of the Chinese people. Misunderstandings occur when Americans show polite acceptance of these general principles without understanding their significance—because they do not have any obvious relationship to American corporate goals, such as profit. Nor do such principles seem relevant to practical decisions on plant locations, employee practices, or sourcing.[54]

Americans often experience two negotiation stages with the Chinese: the technical and the commercial. During the long technical stage, the Chinese want to hammer out every detail of the proposed product specifications and technology. If there are two teams of negotiators, it may be several days before the commercial team is actually called in to deal with aspects of production, marketing, pricing, and so forth. However, the commercial team should sit in on the first stage to become familiar with the Chinese negotiating style.[55] The Chinese negotiating team is usually about twice as large as the Western team; about a third of the time is spent discussing technical specifications, and another third on price negotiations, with the rest devoted to general negotiations and posturing.[56]

The Chinese are among the toughest negotiators in the world. American managers must anticipate various tactics, such as their delaying techniques and their avoidance of direct, specific answers: Both ploys are used to exploit the known impatience of Americans. The Chinese frequently try to put pressure on Americans by "shaming" them, thereby implying that the Americans are trying to renege on the friendship—the basis of the implicit contract. Whereas Westerners come to negotiations with specific and segmented goals and find it easy to compromise, the Chinese are reluctant to negotiate details. They find it difficult to compromise and trade because they have entered negotiations with a broader vision of achieving development goals for China, and they are offended when Westerners don't internalize those goals.[57] Under these circumstances, the Chinese will adopt a rigid posture, and no agreement or contract is final until the negotiated activities have actually been completed.

Successful negotiations with the Chinese depends on many factors. Research by Fang et al. found the top success factors to be sincerity on behalf of the Western team, their team's preparation, technical expertise, patience, knowledge of PC business practices, and good personal relationships.[58] Generally speaking, patience, respect, and experience are necessary prerequisites for anyone negotiating in China. For the best outcomes, older, more experienced people are more acceptable to the Chinese in cross-cultural negotiations. The Chinese want to deal with the top executive of an American company, under the assumption that the highest officer has attained that position by establishing close personal relationships and trust with colleagues and others outside the organization. Western delegation practices are unfamiliar to them, and they are reluctant to come to an agreement without the presence of the Chinese foreign negotiator.[59] From the Western perspective, confusing jurisdictions of government ministries hamper decisions in negotiations.[60] Americans tend to send specific technical personnel with experience in the task at hand; therefore, they have to take care in selecting the most suitable negotiators. In addition, visiting negotiating teams should realize that the Chinese are probably negotiating with other foreign teams, often at the same time, and will use that setup to play one company's offer against the others. On an interpersonal level, Western negotiators must also realize that, while a handshake is polite, physical contact is not acceptable in Chinese social behavior, nor are personal discussion topics such as one's family. However, it is customary to give and take small gifts as tokens of friendship. Pye offers the following additional tips to foreigners conducting business with the Chinese:[61]

- Practice patience
- Accept prolonged periods of stalemate
- Refrain from exaggerated expectations and discount Chinese rhetoric about future prospects
- Expect the Chinese to try to manipulate by shaming
- Resist the temptation to believe that difficulties may have been caused by one's own mistakes
- Try to understand Chinese cultural traits, but realize that a foreigner cannot practice them better than the Chinese

In conclusion, it is evident that China's rapidly changing business environment is evident in more professionalism in the negotiation process. At the same time, research by Fang et al. shows that "one should not underestimate the impact of culture on Chinese business negotiations. Western companies that seek to succeed in China need to demonstrate sincerity and commitment in conducting business in order to gain the Chinese partner's trust as this appears to be the ultimate predictor for success of business relations in China."[62]

As discussed in Chapter 4, much of the difference in communication styles is attributable to whether you belong to a high-context or low-context culture (or somewhere in between, as shown in Exhibit 4-4). In low-context cultures such as that in the United States, conflict is handled directly and explicitly. It is also regarded as separate from the person negotiating—that is, the negotiators draw a distinction between the people involved and the information or opinions they represent. They also tend to negotiate on the basis of factual information and logical analysis. That approach to conflict is called **instrumental-oriented conflict.**[63] In high-context cultures, such as in the Middle East, the approach to conflict is called **expressive-oriented conflict**—that is, the situation is handled indirectly and implicitly, without clear delineation of the situation by the person handling it. Such negotiators do not want to get in a confrontational situation because it is regarded as insulting and would cause a loss of "face," so they tend to use evasion and avoidance if they cannot reach agreement through emotional appeals. Their avoidance and inaction conflict with the expectations of the low-context negotiators who are looking to move ahead with the business at hand and arrive at a solution.

The differences between high- and low-context cultures that often lead to conflict situations are summarized in Exhibit 5-7. Most of these variables were discussed previously in this chapter or in Chapter 4. They overlap because the subjects, culture, and communication are inseparable and because negotiation differences and conflict situations arise from variables in culture and communication.

The point here is, how can a manager from France, Japan, or Brazil, for example, manage conflict situations? The solution, as discussed previously, lies mainly in one's ability to know and understand the people and the situation to be faced. Managers must be prepared by developing an understanding of the cultural contexts in which they will be operating. What are the expectations of the persons with whom they will be negotiating? What kinds of communication styles and negotiating tactics should they expect, and how will they differ from their own? It is important to bear in mind one's own expectations and negotiating style, as well as to be aware of the other parties' expectations. Managers ought to consider in advance what it will take to arrive at a win-win solution. Often it helps to use the services of a host-country adviser or mediator, who may be able to help with early diffusion of a conflict situation.

DECISION MAKING

Negotiation actually represents the outcome of a series of small and large decisions. The decisions include those made by each party before actual negotiations start—for example, in determining the position of the company and what fallback proposals it may suggest or accept.

EXHIBIT 5-7   Sources of Conflict Between Low-Context and High-Context Cultures[64]

Key Questions	Low-Context Conflict	High-Context Conflict
Why	Analytic, linear logic; instrumental oriented; dichotomy between conflict and conflict parties	Synthetic, spiral logic; expressive oriented; integration of conflict and conflict parties
When	Individualistic oriented; low collective normative expectations; violations of individual expectations create conflict potentials	Group oriented; high collective normative expectations; violations of collective expectations create conflict potentials
What	Revealment; direct, confrontational attitude; action and solution oriented	Concealment; indirect nonconfrontational attitude; "face" and relationship oriented
How	Explicit communication codes; line-logic style: rational-factual rhetoric; open, direct strategies	Implicit communication codes; point-logic style: intuitive-effective rhetoric; ambiguous, indirect strategies

The decisions also include incremental decisions, made during the negotiation process, on how to react and proceed, when to concede, and on what to agree or disagree. Negotiation can thus be seen as a series of explicit and implicit decisions, and the subjects of negotiation and decision making become interdependent.

For instance, sometimes just the way a decision is made during the negotiation process can have a profound influence on the outcome, as this example shows:

> In his first loan negotiation, a banker new to Japan met with seven top Japanese bankers who were seeking a substantial amount of money. After hearing their presentation, the American agreed on the spot. The seven Japanese then conferred among themselves and told the American they would get back to him in a couple of days regarding whether they would accept his offer or not. The American banker learned a lesson he never forgot.[65]

The Japanese bankers expected the American to negotiate, to take time to think it over, and to consult with colleagues before giving the final decision. His immediate decision made them suspicious, so they decided to reconsider the deal.

There is no doubt that the speed and manner of decision making affect the negotiation process. In addition, how well negotiated agreements are implemented is affected by the speed and manner of decision making. In that regard, it is clear that the effective use of technology is playing an important role, especially when dealing with complex cross-border agreements in which the hundreds of decision makers involved are separated by time and space.

The role of decision making in management, however, goes far beyond the finite occasions of negotiations. It is part of the manager's daily routine—from operational-level, programmed decisions requiring minimal time and effort to those nonprogrammed decisions of far broader scope and importance, such as the decision to enter into a joint venture in a foreign country.

The Influence of Culture on Decision Making

It is crucial for international managers to understand the influence of culture on decision-making styles and processes. Culture affects decision making both through the broader context of the nation's institutional culture, which produces collective patterns of decision making, and through culturally based value systems that affect each individual decision maker's perception or interpretation of a situation.[66]

The extent to which decision making is influenced by culture varies among countries. For example, Hitt, Tyler, and Park have found a "more culturally homogenizing influence on the Korean executives' cognitive models" than on those of U.S. executives, whose individualistic tendencies lead to different decision patterns.[67] The ways that culture influences an executive's decisions can be studied by looking at the variables involved in each stage of the rational decision-making process. These stages are (1) defining the problem, (2) gathering and analyzing relevant data, (3) considering alternative solutions, (4) deciding on the best solution, and (5) implementing the decision.

One of the major cultural variables affecting decision making is whether a people tend to assume an objective approach or a subjective approach. Whereas the Western approach is based on rationality (managers interpret a situation and consider alternative solutions based on objective information), this approach is not common throughout the world. Latin Americans, among others, are more subjective, basing decisions on emotions.

Another cultural variable that greatly influences the decision-making process is the risk tolerance of those making the decision. Research shows that people from Belgium, Germany, and Austria have a considerably lower tolerance for risk than people from Japan or the Netherlands—whereas American managers have the highest tolerance for risk.[68]

In addition, an often-overlooked but important variable in the decision-making process is the manager's perception of the locus of control over outcomes—whether that locus is internal or external. Some managers feel they can plan on certain outcomes because they are in control of events that will direct the future in the desired way. In contrast, other managers believe that such decisions are of no value because they have little control over the future—which lies in the hands of outside forces, such as fate, God, or nature. American managers believe strongly in self-determination and perceive problem situations as something they can control and should change. However, managers in many other countries, Indonesia and Malaysia among them, are resigned to problem situations and do not feel that they can change them. Obviously, these different value systems will result in a great difference in the stages of consideration of alternative actions and choice of a solution, often because certain situations may or may not be viewed as problems in the first place.

Yet another variable that affects the consideration of alternative solutions is how managers feel about staying with familiar solutions or trying new ones. Many managers, particularly those in Europe, value decisions based on past experiences and tend to emphasize quality. Americans, on the other hand, are more future oriented and look toward new ideas to get them there.

Approaches to Decision Making

In addition to affecting different stages of the decision-making process, value systems influence the overall approach of decision makers from various cultures. The relative level of utilitarianism versus moral idealism in any society affects its overall approach to problems. Generally speaking, utilitarianism strongly guides behavior in the Western world. Research has shown that Canadian executives are more influenced by a short-term, cost–benefit approach to decision making than their Hong Kong counterparts.

Another important variable in companies' overall approach to decision making is that of autocratic versus participative leadership. In other words, who has the authority to make what kinds of decisions? A society's orientation—whether it is individualistic or collectivist (see Chapter 3)—influences the level at which decisions are made. In many countries with hierarchical cultures—Germany, Turkey, and India, among others—authorization for action has to be passed upward through echelons of management before final decisions can be made. Most employees in these countries simply expect the autocrat—the boss—to do most of the decision making and will not be comfortable otherwise. Even in China, which is a highly collectivist society, employees expect autocratic leadership because their value system presupposes the superior to be automatically the most wise. In comparison, decision-making authority in Sweden is very decentralized. Americans talk a lot about the advisability of such participative leadership, but in practice they are probably near the middle between autocratic and participative management styles.

Arab managers have long traditions of consultative decision making, supported by the Qur'an and the sayings of Muhammed. However, such consultation occurs more on a

EXHIBIT 5-8   Cultural Variables in the Decision-Making Process

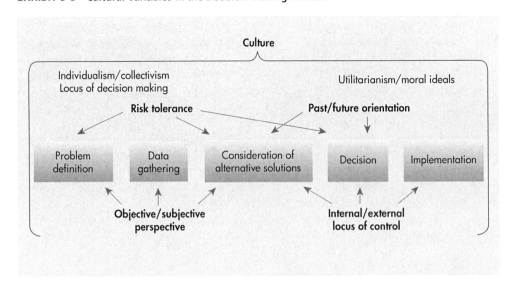

person-to-person basis than during group meetings and thus diffuses potential opposition.[69] Although business in the Middle East tends to be transacted in a highly personalized manner, the final decisions are made by the top leaders, who feel that they must impose their will for the company to be successful. In comparison, in cultures that emphasize collective harmony, such as Japan, participatory or group decision making predominates, and consensus is important. The best-known example is the bottom-up (rather than top-down) decision-making process used in most Japanese companies, described in more detail in the following Comparative Management in Focus section.

One final area of frequent incongruence concerns the relative speed of decision making. A country's culture affects how fast or slow decisions tend to be made. The relative speed may be closely associated with the level of delegation, as just discussed—but not always. The pace at which decisions are made can be very disconcerting for outsiders. North Americans and Europeans pride themselves on being decisive; managers in the Middle East, with a different sense of temporal urgency, associate the importance of the matter at hand with the length of time needed to make a decision. Without knowing this cultural attitude, a hasty American would insult an Egyptian; a quick decision, to the Egyptian, would reflect a low regard for the relationship and the deal.

Exhibit 5-8 illustrates, in summary form, how all the variables just discussed can affect the steps in the decision-making process.

COMPARATIVE MANAGEMENT IN FOCUS

Decision Making in Japanese Companies

Japanese companies are involved in joint ventures throughout the world, especially with U.S. companies. The GM-Toyota joint venture agreement process, for example, was the result of more than two years of negotiation and decision making, and in similar alliances, Americans and Japanese are involved in decision making at all levels on a daily basis. The Japanese decision-making process differs greatly not only from the U.S. process but from that of many other countries—especially at the higher levels of their organizations.

An understanding of the Japanese decision-making process—and indeed of many Japanese management practices—requires an understanding of Japanese national culture. Much of the Japanese culture, and therefore the basis of Japanese working relationships, can be explained by the principle of *wa*, meaning "peace and harmony." This principle is one aspect of the value the Japanese attribute to *amae,* meaning "indulgent love," a concept probably originating in the Shinto religion, which focuses on spiritual and physical harmony. *Amae* results in *shinyo*, which refers to the mutual confidence, faith, and honor required for successful business relationships. The principle of *wa* influences the work group, the basic building block of Japanese work and management. The Japanese strongly identify with their work groups, where the emphasis is on cooperation, participative management, consensus problem solving, and decision making based on a patient, long-term perspective. Open expression of conflict is discouraged, and it is of utmost importance to avoid embarrassment or shame—to lose face—as a result of not fulfilling one's obligations. These elements of work culture generally result in a devotion to work, a collective responsibility for decisions and actions, and a high degree of employee productivity. It is this culture of collectivism and shared responsibility that underlies the Japanese *ringi* system of decision making.

In the *ringi* system, the process works from the bottom up. Americans are used to a centralized system, where major decisions are made by upper-level managers in a top-down approach typical of individualistic societies. The Japanese process, however, is dispersed throughout the organization, relying on group consensus.

The *ringi* process is one of gaining approval on a proposal by circulating documents to those concerned throughout the company. It usually comprises four steps: proposal, circulation, approval, and record.[70] Usually the person who originates the written proposal, which is called a *ringi-sho,* has already worked for some time to gain informal consensus and support for the proposal within the section and then from the department head.[71] The next step is to attain a general consensus in the company from those who would be involved in implementation. To this end, department meetings are held, and if necessary expert opinion is sought. If more information is needed, the proposal goes back to the originator, who finds and adds the required data. In this way, much time and effort—and the input of many people—go into the proposal before it becomes formal.[72]

Up to this point, the process has been an informal one to gain consensus; it is called the *nemawashi* process. Then the more formal authorization procedure begins, called the *ringi* process. The *ringi-sho* is passed up through successive layers of management for approval—the approval made official by seals. In the end, many such seals of approval are gathered, thereby ensuring collective agreement and responsibility and giving the proposal a greater chance of final approval by the president. The whole process is depicted in Exhibit 5-9.

EXHIBIT 5-9   Decision-Making Procedure in Japanese Companies

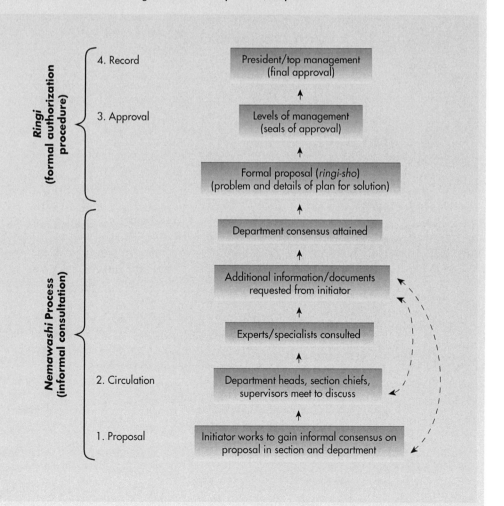

The *ringi* system is cumbersome and very time-consuming prior to the implementation stage, although implementation is facilitated because of the widespread awareness of and support for the proposal already gained throughout the organization. However, its slow progress is problematic when decisions are time-sensitive. This process is the opposite of the Americans' top-down decisions, which are made quite rapidly and without consultation, but which then take time to implement because unforeseen practical or support problems often arise.

Another interesting comparison is often made regarding the planning horizon (aimed at short- or long-term goals) in decision making between the American and Japanese systems. The Japanese spend considerable time in the early stages of the process defining the issue, considering what the issue is all about, and determining whether there is an actual need for a decision. They are more likely than Americans to consider an issue in relation to the overall goals and strategy of the company. In this manner, they prudently look at the "big picture" and consider alternative solutions, instead of rushing into quick decisions for immediate solutions, as Americans tend to do.[73]

Of course, in a rapidly changing environment, quick decisions are often necessary—to respond to competitors' actions, a political uprising, and so forth—and it is in such contexts that the *ringi* system sometimes falls short because of its slow response rate. The system is, in fact, designed to manage continuity and to avoid uncertainty, which is considered a threat to group cohesiveness.[74]

CONCLUSION

It is clear that competitive positioning and long-term successful operations in a global market require a working knowledge of the decision-making and negotiating processes of managers from different countries. These processes are complex and often interdependent. Although managers may make decisions that do not involve negotiating, they cannot negotiate without making decisions, however small, or they would not be negotiating. In addition, managers must understand the behavioral aspects of these processes to work effectively with people in other countries or with a culturally diverse workforce in their own countries.

With an understanding of the environment and cultural context of international management as background, we move next in Part III to planning and implementing strategy for international and global operations.

Summary of Key Points

1. The ability to negotiate successfully is one of the most important in international business. Managers must prepare for certain cultural variables that influence negotiations, including the relative emphasis on task versus interpersonal relationships, the use of general principles versus specific details, the number of people present, and the extent of their influence.

2. The negotiation process typically progresses through the stages of preparation, relationship building, exchange of task-related information, persuasion, and concessions and agreement. The process of building trusting relationships is a prerequisite to doing business in many parts of the world.

3. Culturally based differences in verbal and nonverbal negotiation behavior influence the negotiation process at every stage. Such tactics and actions include promises, threats, initial concessions, silent periods, interruptions,

facial gazing, and touching; some parties resort to various dirty tricks.

4. The effective management of negotiation requires an understanding of the perspectives, values, and agendas of other parties and the use of a problem-solving approach.

5. Decision making is an important part of the negotiation process, as well as an integral part of a manager's daily routine. Culture affects the decision-making process both through a society's institutions and through individuals' risk tolerance, their objective versus subjective perspectives, their perceptions of the locus of control, and their past versus future orientations.

6. The Internet is used increasingly to support the negotiation of contracts and resolution of disputes. Web sites that provide open auctions take away the personal aspects of negotiations, though those aspects are still essential in many instances.

Discussion Questions

1. Discuss the stages in the negotiation process and how culturally-based value systems influence these stages. Specifically, address the following:

   • Explain the role and relative importance of relationship-building in different countries.

• Discuss the various styles and tactics that can be involved in exchanging task-related information.

• Describe differences in culturally-based styles of persuasion.

• Discuss the kinds of concession strategies a negotiator might anticipate in various countries.

2. Discuss the relative use of nonverbal behaviors, such as silent periods, interruptions, facial gazing, and touching, by people from various cultural backgrounds. How does this behavior affect the negotiation process in a cross-cultural context?
3. Describe what you would expect in negotiations with the Chinese and how you would handle various situations.
4. What are some of the differences in risk tolerance around the world? What is the role of risk propensity in the decision-making process?

5. Explain how objective versus subjective perspectives influences the decision-making process. What role do you think this variable has played in all the negotiations conducted and decisions made by Iraq and the United Nations?
6. Explain differences in culturally-based value systems relative to the amount of control a person feels he or she has over future outcomes. How does this belief influence the decision-making process?

Experiential Exercises

EXERCISE 1: MULTICULTURAL NEGOTIATIONS

Goal

To experience, identify, and appreciate the problems associated with negotiating with people of other cultures.

Instructions (Note: Your Professor will give out additional intruction sheets)

1. Eight student volunteers will participate in the role play. Four represent a Japanese automobile manufacturer, and four represent a U.S. team that has come to sell microchips and other components to the Japanese company. The remainder of the class will observe the negotiations.
2. The eight volunteers will divide into the two groups and then separate into different rooms, if possible. At that point, they will be given instruction sheets. Neither team can have access to the other's instructions. After dividing the roles, the teams should meet for 10 to 15 minutes to develop their negotiation strategies based on their instructions.
3. While the teams are preparing, the room will be set up using a rectangular table with four seats on each side. The Japanese side will have three chairs at the table with one chair set up behind the three. The American side of the table will have four chairs side by side.
4. Following these preparations, the Japanese team will be brought in, so they may greet the Americans when they arrive. At this point, the Americans will be brought in and the role play begins. Time for the negotiations should be 20 to 30 minutes. The rest of the class will act as observers and will be expected to provide feedback during the discussion phase.
5. When the negotiations are completed, the student participants from both sides and the observers will complete their feedback questionnaires. Class discussion of the feedback questions will follow.

Feedback Questions for the Japanese Team

1. What was your biggest frustration during the negotiations?
2. What would you say the goal of the American team was?
3. What role (e.g., decider, influencer, etc.) did each member of the American team play?
   Mr. Jones
   Mr./Ms. Smith
   Mr./Ms. Nelson
   Mr./Ms. Frost
4. How would you rate the success of each of the American team members in identifying your team's needs and appealing to them?
   Mr./Ms. Jones, Vice President and Team Leader
   Mr./Ms. Smith, Manufacturing Engineer
   Mr./Ms. Nelson, Marketing Analyst
   Mr./Ms. Frost, Account Executive
5. What strategy should the American team have taken?

Feedback Questions for the American Team

1. What was your biggest frustration during the negotiations?
2. What would you say the goal of the Japanese team was?

3. How would you rate the success of each of the American team members?
   Mr. Jones, Vice President and Team Leader
   Mr./Ms. Smith, Manufacturing Engineer
   Mr./Ms. Nelson, Marketing Analyst
   Mr./Ms. Frost, Account Executive
4. What would you say the goal of the American team was?
5. What role (e.g., decider, influencer, etc.) did each member of the Japanese team play?
   Mr. Ozaka
   Mr. Nishimuro
   Mr. Sheno
   Mr. Kawazaka
6. What strategy should the American team have taken?

Feedback Questions for the Observers

1. What was your biggest frustration during the negotiations?
2. What would you say the goal of the Japanese team was?
3. How would you rate the success of each of the American team members?
   Mr./Ms. Jones, Vice President and Team Leader
   Mr./Ms. Smith, Manufacturing Engineer
   Mr./Ms. Nelson, Marketing Analyst
   Mr./Ms. Frost, Account Executive
4. What would you say the goal of the American team was?
5. What role (e.g., decider, influencer, etc.) did each member of the Japanese team play?
   Mr. Ozaka
   Mr. Nishimuro
   Mr. Sheno
   Mr. Kawazaka
6. What strategy should the American team have taken?

EXERCISE 2: JAPANESE DECISION MAKING

Time: Two class meetings
Goal

To allow students to experience the process and results of solving a problem or initiating a project using the Japanese decision processes of *nemawashi* and *ringi*.

Preparation

Review Chapters 4 and 5 and the Comparative Management in Focus: Decision Making in Japanese Companies.
Note: Instructions for this exercise will be given by your Professor, from the Instructor's Manual.

Source: E. A. Diodati, in C. Harvey and M.J. Allard, *Understanding Diversity* (New York: HarperCollins Publishers, 1995). Used with permission.

Internet Resources

Visit the Deresky Companion Website at www.pearsonhighered.com/
deresky for this chapter's Internet resources.

CASE STUDY
The Alcatel-Lucent Merger—What went wrong?

It did not take long after the merger for things to start going wrong for Alcatel-Lucent CEO Patricia Russo, who opted to leave the vendor last month after admitting she could no longer work with fellow board resignee chairman Serge Tchuruk.

MICROSCOPE,
August 11–17, 2008.[1]

It seems that this deal was not meant to happen. The original merger negotiations between Alcatel of France, the communications equipment maker based in Paris, and Lucent Technologies, the U.S. telecommunications giant, took place in 2001. However, the finely detailed deal collapsed on May 29, 2001, after the two companies could not agree on how much control the French company would have. Lucent's executives apparently wanted the deal as a "merger of equals," rather than a takeover by Alcatel.[2]

The failed deal was regarded as a severe blow to Lucent's image. Industry watchers questioned how Lucent would be able to survive this most recent blow. Although it was not clear which company initiated the negotiations, it was reported that Lucent ended them after much of the senior management detected that the proposed deal would not be a merger of equals.[3]

In 2006, however, renewed negotiations took place, resulting in the transatlantic relationship being consummated. Shareholders in France approved the merger of the telecommunications equipment makers Alcatel and Lucent on September 7, 2006. However, Alcatel investors still had concerns about the leadership and financial health of their new American partner. Alcatel's chief executive, Serge Tchuruk, tried to reassure the 1,500 shareholders gathered in Paris to back the merger, saying the company—to be called Alcatel-Lucent—is "truly global and has no equivalent today and won't in the future."[4] Mr. Tchuruk had agreed in April 2006 to pay 10.6 billion euro ($13.5 billion then) for Lucent, in a deal to create the world's biggest telephone equipment maker, although industry watchers considered the bid as financially inadequate for Alcatel investors. The stock swap was valued at one Alcatel American depository share for every five Lucent shares. Tchuruk said the combined company would realize 1.4 billion euro ($1.8 billion) in cost savings over the following three years, in part by cutting 9,000 jobs, about 10 percent of the combined workforce.[5] He noted that Alcatel-Lucent's revenue would be spread almost equally across Europe, the United States and Asia, offering greater long-term stability. Alcatel does most of its business in Europe, while Lucent does the majority of its business in the United States. Lucent Shareholders also endorsed the deal.

"We are another step closer to creating the first truly global communications solutions provider with the broadest wireless, wireline and services portfolio in the industry," said the chief executive of Lucent, Patricia F. Russo, who was to retain that role in the combined company.

At that time, the company had combined sales of $25 billion.[6] Amid concerns about the potential for cross-cultural conflicts, Tchuruk said that, while cultural issues could arise, "everything is under way to make sure this human factor is dealt with," he said, adding that Alcatel already operated as an international company with a wide mix of nationalities; English is the official language of the company.[7] Other industry commentators cast Alcatel-Lucent as "a Franco-American telecoms behemoth that many regard as a giant transatlantic experiment in multinational diversity."[8]

After the shareholders of both companies endorsed the deal, regulatory hurdles were cleared in both the EU and the U.S.[9]

An Alcatel-Lucent merger provided the combined company a strong position in several categories of equipment sold to the major telecommunications carrier: wireless telecommunications equipment, wireline equipment, wireless infrastructure, Internet routers, equipment for carrying calls over the Internet, etc.[10]

However, success was illusive. Overall, it seemed that "the difficulties of integrating a French company with an American one dominated during Russo's tenure, with analysts suggesting the corporate culture of Lucent clashed with Alcatel's French business model. One source close to the company saw little evidence of cooperation between the two factions from the outside."[11] In July 2008, the Alcatel-Lucent CEO Patricia Russo resigned, citing the inability to get along with Serge Tchuruk, her fellow board member; subsequently he too resigned. Much of the resentment came from Alcatel management because the overall leadership had been handed to the target company, Lucent, an unusual decision; in addition, it became clear that it was a poor decision to appoint leaders based on their nationality rather than skills. Other factors seemed to be against Ms. Russo, however, as she struggled to bring together the vastly different cultures of the two companies amid a tough business climate. As the first woman to run a company listed on the CAC 40, she had to make her way in the clubby, male-dominated world where French business and politics overlap.[12]

In addition, the combined, but still rather weak companies, faced low-cost competition from new Chinese rivals and were struggling in a business that Internet technology was changing beyond recognition. Worse, demand has been weakening across the industry. A *Barron's* article in August 2008 noted that "while it might have been helpful if outgoing CEO Patricia Russo had spoken French, that's not why she and Chairman Serge Tchuruk failed to make a go of the 2006 merger of Alcatel and Lucent Technologies. They were pushed into each other's arms out of desperation as the industry began a painful, necessary consolidation. . . . the telephone-equipment business is brutal and likely to see more attrition. The marriage didn't avert six straight quarterly losses."[13]

The series of quarterly losses ($7 billion loss since the merger) led to a bombardment of negative comment as Alcatel-Lucent initiated restructuring and cut around 16,500 jobs.[14]

In September the new chiefs were announced—a French chairman, who lives in America, and a Dutch chief executive, who will be based in Paris. Both Philippe Camus and Ben Verwaayen were considered to have the personality and experience that could iron out the beleaguered telecoms group's problems. Mr. Verwaayen accepted the new job only when he found he could get along with Mr. Camus, who had already agreed to be chairman. "We share the same sense of humour," he says. "You need to have complete understanding at the top of the house."[15] "We must deliver on the merger," Ben Verwaayen, the former head of BT, who was appointed to succeed Patricia F. Russo as chief executive, said at a meeting with journalists. Acknowledging that there remained "a divided Alcatel-Lucent," Mr. Verwaayen said, "We need to move quickly to become an integrated company."[16] Mr. Verwaayen speaks fluent French and English. Alcatel-Lucent operates in 130 countries, and like many global enterprises, its language of business is English. He was quoted in *The Economist* as saying that he "sees his job as removing barriers within the company and unleashing its talents." But perhaps his biggest advantage in rescuing a failed Franco-American merger is that he is neither French nor American.[17]

References

1. Alex Scroxton, *Microscope*, August 11–17, 2008, 7.
2. A. Sorkin and S. Romero, "Alcatel and Lucent Call Off Negotiations Toward a Merger," *New York Times*, May 30, 2001; S. Shiesel, "Pride and Practicalities Loom Behind Failed Lucent 'Merger'," *New York Times*, May 31, 2001.
3. L. H. LaBarba, "Let's Call the Whole Thing Off," *Telephony* 240, no. 23, June 4, 2001, 14–16.
4. J. Kanter, "Shareholders in Paris Approve Merger of Alcatel and Lucent," *New York Times*, September 6, 2006.
5. Ibid.
6. Ibid.
7. Ibid.
8. I. Austen and V. Bajaj, "A Continental Shift," *New York Times*, March 25, 2006.
9. "EU Clears Proposed Alcatel-Lucent Merger," *Wall Street Journal*, July 25, 2006.
10. Data from Austen and Bajaj.

11. Scroxton, 2008.
12. David Jolly, "New Alcatel-Lucent Leaders Vow to Persist on Integration," *New York Times*, Sep 3, 2008.
13. Mark Veverka. "Chiefs, not Problems, leave Alcatel-Lucent," *Barron's*, Aug 11, 2008, 16.
14. Scroxton, 2008.
15. Anonymous, "Bring down the Barriers: Alcatel-Lucent," *The Economist*, September 6, 2008
16. *Jolly*, 2008.
17. *The Economist*, 2008.

Case Questions

1. Referring to the case and this chapter, discuss what conditions and negotiation factors pushed forth the merger in 2006 that were not present in 2001.
2. Research the status of the merged company at the time of your reading of this case. What has happened in the industry since the merger, and how is the company faring?
3. Evaluate the comment that the merger is "a giant transatlantic experiment in multicultural diversity." What evidence is there that the company has run into cross-cultural problems since the merger took place in 2006?
4. How much of the decline do you attribute to leadership problems, as opposed to industry factors?
5. What, if any, factors should have been negotiated differently?

PART II: Comprehensive Cases

ICMR
Center for
Management Research

CASE 4   MTV NETWORKS: THE ARABIAN CHALLENGE

"[. . .] MTV has a penchant for airing controversial material and making a mockery of convention. And of course, it's an American brand . . . The challenge, therefore, is transforming a notoriously risqué channel into a Middle Eastern-friendly platform for music and creativity without stripping MTV of its edge. It isn't without some irony that a channel known for angering religious, political, and conservative communities is operating in and catering to a region renowned for reacting (and sometimes overreacting) negatively to controversial content."[1]

DANA EL BALTAJI,
Special Projects Manager, Trends magazine in Dubai, in 2008.

"In many ways (MTV Arabia) is the epitome of our localization strategy. It's a different audience (in the Middle East) but this is what we do – we reflect culture and we respect culture. The programming mix on this one is going to be a little more local than normal."[2]

WILLIAM H. ROEDY,
*Vice Chairman for MTV Networks and President
MTVI Network International, in 2007.*

A Litmus Test for MTV's Localization Strategy

MTV Networks (MTVN) launched MTV Arabia on November 17, 2007, in partnership with Arabian Television Network[3] (ATN) as part of its global expansion strategy. According to analysts, MTV's presence in the Middle East would provide the region with an international music brand, which till then, did not have an international music brand though it had clusters of local music channels. On its part, the region promised to offer tremendous growth opportunities to MTVN.

Analysts felt that MTV Arabia was MTVN's most ambitious and challenging venture. The Middle East offered huge growth potential to MTVN given its huge youth populace. However, according to analysts, MTV's success in the Middle East was contingent upon a tactical balancing between deliv-

ery of international quality music and the culturally sensitive environment prevalent in the region. Some analysts felt that the channel was well equipped to achieve this considering MTVN's extensive experience in the global market and its ability to provide localized content without diluting what MTV stood for.

To ensure that its programs won over the hearts of the Arabs and adhered to the local taste and culture without diluting MTV's global brand, MTV Arabia designed a much localized Arabic version of its international music and reality shows. In this connection, Patrick Samaha (Samaha), General Manager of MTV Arabia, said, "We've created programs that are an Arabic version of MTV programs. It is the first time that programs like this will really reflect the youth culture here, but we've been mindful all the way about respecting the local culture."[4]

According to the company, the launch of MTV Arabia was also expected to act as a culturally unifying force by propelling Arabic Music to the global forefront and vice versa. While launching MTV Arabia, William H. Roedy, Vice Chairman for MTV Networks and President of MTVI, said, "Tonight's [November 16, 2007] MTV Arabia launch show celebrates one of the most important landmarks in MTV's 25-year history. MTV Arabia will reach the largest potential audience of any MTV channel outside the United States. MTV is proud to celebrate the voice of the Arab youth and through our global network we can showcase what this rich and diverse culture is all about to new audiences around the world."[5]

Author Information:
This case was written by **Debapratim Purkayastha,** ICMR. It was compiled from published sources, and is intended to be used as a basis for class discussion rather than to illustrate either effective or ineffective handling of a management situation.

[1] Dana El Baltaji, "I Want My MTV," www.arabmediasociety.com, May 11, 2008.
[2] Lynne Roberts, "MTV Set for Middle East Launch," www.arabianbusiness. com, October 17, 2007.
[3] Arabian Television Network (ATN) is a Dubai, United Arab Emirates based broadcast media company, part of the Arab Media Group's Arabian Broadcasting Network (ABN). ABN is a part of the Arab Media Group (AMG). As of 2007, AMG was the largest media group in the UAE, with approximately 1,500 employees. It was an unit of TECOM Investments that was controlled by Dubai's ruler.

[4] Jolanta Chudy, "MTV's Arab Net Thinking Locally," www.hollywoodreporter. com, November 6, 2007.
[5] "Akon and Ludacris Dazzle the Desert in their Middle East Debuts to Celebrate the Launch of MTV Arabia," www.dubaicityguide.com, November 16, 2007.

Background Note

MTV (short for Music Television), which pioneered the concept of a cable music channel, was launched on August 1, 1981, and marked the commencement of the cable TV revolution. It was promoted by Warner Amex Satellite Entertainment Company, a joint venture between Warner Communications and American Express. In 1984, the company was renamed MTV Networks (MTVN) with its operations confined to the US.

At the time of its launch, the MTV channel primarily catered to those in the 12 to 24 age group, airing heavy-metal and rap music. However, over the years, it also launched many sister channels such as VH-1 (short for video hits one) which was formed in 1985 to play light popular music; Rhythm and Blues (R&B, for jazz, country music, and classics targeted at the 18 to 35 age group; and Nickelodeon,[6] which was launched in 1977 keeping children as its target segment. While these sister channels of MTVN continued playing different varieties of music, the core channel MTV began to diversify in 1990.

Besides playing music, it also started airing non-music, reality shows. *The Real World* and *MTV Fear* were some of the popular reality shows aired. Animated cartoon series were also introduced, the most popular of them being *Beavis and Butthead.*

In 1986, MTVN was acquired by Viacom Inc. (Refer to Exhibit I for a note on Viacom). Thereafter, in 1987, MTVN launched its first overseas channel in Europe and this marked the beginning of MTV's global expansion. The international arm of MTVN was known as MTVI. In addition to MTV, MTVI managed a bouquet of channels like VH-1 and Nickelodeon.

By the mid-1990s MTVI realized that to become a successful brand globally, it had to adapt to local conditions. Hence it adopted a strategy of "Think Globally, Act Locally." Thereafter, MTVI became the first international TV network to offer channels like MTV Australia, MTV Asia, MTV India, MTV China, MTV Germany, etc. in local languages with localized content.[7] To penetrate any new market, MTVI initially tied

EXHIBIT I   A Note on Viacom Inc.

Viacom was established as a public company in 1971. In 1985, it acquired a 65 percent stake in MTV Networks, which included MTV, VH-1, and Nickelodeon, and purchased the remaining interest in 1986. In 1991, Viacom completed its purchase of MTV Europe by acquiring a 50 percent stake from British Telecommunications and other parties. In 1994, the Viacom Entertainment Group was formed through a merger with Paramount Communications Inc. In 2000, CBS Corporation, a major media network in the US, merged with Viacom, as a result of which TNN (re-named as Spike TV in 2003) and CMT (Country Music Television) joined the MTV Networks. The BET (Black Entertainment Television) channel was acquired by Viacom in 2001. In the early 2000s, Viacom launched many channels worldwide under MTV Networks and BET.

In 2005, Viacom Corporation split into Viacom Inc. and CBS Corporation. In 2006, Viacom Inc. was one of the world's leading media companies operating in the Cable and Satellite Television Networks (C&S) and film production divisions.

VIACOM INC. BRANDS*
Cable Networks & Digital Media

• MTV Networks (Comedy Central, CMT, LOGO, MTV, MTV 2, MTV U, MTV Networks Digital Suite, **MTV International**, MTV Networks online, Nickelodeon, Nick @ Nite, The N, Noggin, Spike, TV Land, VH-1)

• BET Networks presents the best in Black media and entertainment featuring traditional and digital platforms. Brands including BET, BET J, BET Gospel, BET Hip Hop, BET.com, BET Mobile, BET Event Productions, and BET International deliver relevant and insightful content to consumers of Black culture in more than 84 million households.

Entertainment (Film & Music Publishing)
• Paramount Pictures
• Paramount Home Entertainment
• DreamWorks SKG
• Famous Music

---

* The list is not exhaustive
Source: www.viacom.com

---

[6] Nickelodeon's primarily caters to children in age group 7–11, but along with this it also airs weekend programmes in TEENick catering to children in age group 12–17 and also weekday morning programs aimed at chidren in age group 2–6 and a late-night segment known as Nick at nite aimed at general audiences.

[7] Dirk Smillie, "Tuning in First Global TV Generation," *The Christian Science Monitor,* June 4, 1997.

up with a local music channel and in course of time, it acquired the local company in that region. For instance, in the early 2000s, MTVI entered the Australian market by setting up a joint venture between Austereo (a national commercial radio network in the country) and MTVN. Later on, it acquired Austereo to become MTV Australia.

Initially, some analysts were doubtful as to how far MTVN's global expansion would be successful, given the latent and overt anti-American sentiments in various parts of the world. However, the channel did not face too many difficulties. Commenting on this, Roedy said, "We've had very little resistance once we explain that we're not in the business of exporting American culture."[8] According to some analysts, Roedy was instrumental in taking MTVI across many countries worldwide. To gain an entry into difficult markets such as China, Israel, and Cuba, Roedy even met the political leaders of those countries to explain the network's initiatives to them.

Overall, despite the initial hiccups, the channel's global expansion strategy proved successful. Thus, by following a policy of having a global presence with a local outlook, by mid-2006, MTVI catered to an audience of more than 1 billion and expanded its presence in 179 countries across Europe, Asia, Latin America, and Australia.[9] It operated more than 130 channels in over 25 languages and it comprised MTV Networks Europe (MTVN Europe), MTV Networks Asia-Pacific (MTVN Asia-Pacific), and MTV Networks Latin America (MTVN Latin America). In addition to this, it operated some broadband services and more than 130 websites.[10]

According to analysts, a noteworthy reason behind MTV's global success was that the channel adopted a decentralized structure and gave commercial and creative autonomy to the local staff. This policy of minimal interference in local operations led to innovation and rapid expansion. Commenting on this, Roedy said, "Something we decided early on was to not export just one product for the world but to generate a very different experience for our brands depending on the local cultures."[11]

MTV's impressive growth globally contributed significantly to the revenues of its holding company Viacom over the years and it also became Viacom's core network. As of end 2007, MTVI had more than 140 channels around the world catering to a potential 1.5 billion viewers globally.[12] In the U.S. alone, it reached 87.6 million homes.[13] Its Emerging Markets group was the network's fastest growing business segment.[14] For the year

EXHIBIT II Selected Financials of Viacom

(US$, million)	2008	2007	2006
Revenues	14,625	13,423	11,361
Operating Income	2,523	2,936	2,767
Net Earnings	1,251	1,838	1,592
From Media Networks			
Revenue	8,756	8,101	7,241
Operating Income	2,729	3,048	2,904

Adapted from http://www.viacom.com/news/News_Docs/78157ACL.PDF

ending 2008, Viacom's total revenues (including cable network and entertainment divisions) were US$14,625 million. Out of this, the revenue from Media Network channels (which includes MTVN) was US$8,756 million (Refer to Exhibit II for selected financials of Viacom).

Preparing for the Launch

With the growing popularity of MTV, there was a mushrooming of many similar channels across the world. Though the Arab media was late in adopting this concept, some European and US channels had started offering such programs in this region, analysts pointed out. In the mid-1990s, some Arab music channels too entered the fray. Some of these channels were influenced by MTV. By the mid-2000s, there were a number of Arab music channels (Refer to Exhibit III for a note on major music channel in Saudi Arabia). These channels relied heavily on Arab artists but also aired international numbers by entering into agreements with production houses and other TV networks. MTV was available in the region through a special deal with Showtime Arabia.[15] As part of the deal, Showtime aired Nickelodeon and MTV in English with Arabic subtitles.[16] The channel catered to the middle and upper classes, who had been exposed to the West and had an interest in Western entertainment. Analysts felt that MTV was popular with a section of the audience in the region who were waiting eagerly for its launch there.

The first announcement that MTVI was preparing to launch MTV Arabia came in August 2006. During MTV's 25th anniversary of its first US channel, the company said that it was on the lookout for local partners in the Middle East and would provide the audience in the region content that would be very different from that offered by popular Arab music channels. Dean Possenniskie, Vice President and General Manager for Emerging Markets, MTVI, said, "[MTV is] very interested in the [Arab satellite channel] market and realizes how important it is . . . Hopefully [we] will be in the market in the next 24 months . . . it all depends on finding the right

---

[8] Kerry Capell, Catherine Belton, Tom Lowry, Manjeet Kripalani, Brian Bremner, and Dexter Roberts, "MTV's World," *BusinessWeek*, February 18, 2002.

[9] www.viacom.com/cable.jhtml.

[10] MTVI operated more than 130 websites of its international channels while MTVN, totally, operated more than 150 websites, which included online representations of channels broadcast in the US.

[11] Brad Nemer, "How MTV Channels Innovation," *BusinessWeek*, November 6, 2006.

[12] Tamara Walid, "Finally Got My MTV," www.arabianbusiness.com, November 22, 2007.

[13] "MTV to Launch Music TV Channels in Three Baltic States," www.eubusiness.com, March 6, 2006.

[14] "Arab Media Group and MTV Networks International to Launch Nickelodeon Arabia in 2008," www.media.ameinfo.com, October 20, 2007.

[15] Showtime Arabia is one of the leading subscription-based television networks in the Middle East. It is partly owned by Viacom.

[16] Zeid Nasser, "Showtime Braces for Impact of Free-to-air MTV Arabia & Arabic Nickelodeon," http://mediame.com, October 16, 2007.

EXHIBIT III   Music and Entertainment Channels in Saudi Arabia

As of early 2008, there are 370 Arabic satellite TV networks broadcasting in the Middle East. This is an increase of 270 percent since 2004.[17] Among these, 56 belong to private companies, 54 are music channels, and 38 are state owned. Most of these are headquartered in United Arab Emirates (22 percent), Saudi Arabia (15 percent), and Egypt (11 percent). In Saudi Arabia alone, there are more than 200 free-to-air satcasters and 50 music channels in the region. Some of the important music and entertainment channels are:

Mazzika, which offers a variety of music and light entertainment programs.

Melody Hits, which is a music channel airing Arabic and international music videos.

MBC, headquartered in Dubai, which is a pan-Arab news and entertainment television channel. MBC 2 is a non-stop premium movie channel. MBC 3 is a children's channel and it broadcasts famous animated kids' shows, including exclusive translated titles and live action and animated feature films. It also airs family shows and family movies for younger audiences as well as the adult audience. MBC 4 broadcasts specifically American programs.

Nojoom, which is a music channel airing Arabic and international music videos.

Rotana TV network, which broadcasts Arabic music and films. It has six channels under its wings—Mousica, Rotana Clip, Rotana Tarab, Rotana Khalijiyya, Rotana Cinema, and Rotana Zaman. The channels are dedicated to Arabic pop music, Arabic classical music, interactive games, Gulf music, cinema, featuring the biggest and latest blockbuster releases, and old classical movies.

Saudi Arabian TV, which features live coverage of Ramadan, Hajj, and Eid prayers. It also shows popular movies and news programs.

Shada channel—a part of the Al Majd Group—which is a channel totally devoted to Islamic songs (Anasheed).

Wanasah TV channel, which broadcasts music videos and some variety programs. All its programs are in Arabic.

Panorama FM, which is a music radio channel in Arabic.

Radio Rotana FM, which broadcasts customized programs and the latest Arabic hits fifteen days ahead of any of its competitors due to an exclusive deal with Rotana Music.

Radio Fann FM, which broadcasts a mix of the latest Arabic, English, and International music hits, along with hourly news broadcasts and various customized programs.

Al-Ikhbariya channel, which broadcasts news and current affairs.

* The list is not exhaustive
Compiled from various sources.

local partners."[18] By the end of the year, it was announced that MTVI would launch the channel in the region in partnership with Arabian Television Network (ATN), which was a part of the Arabian Broadcasting Network (ABN).[19]

MTVI's venturing into the Middle East was a result of the combined efforts of innovative and enthusiastic personalities such as Roedy, Bhavneet Singh,[20] Senior Vice President and Managing Director of MTVNI Emerging Markets group, and Abdullatif Al Sayegh, CEO and Chairman of ABN.

Analysts felt that it would have been very difficult for a western company like MTVI to venture into the highly regulated and complex business arena of the Middle East on its own. In this regard, Singh said, "A market such as the Middle East, however, also brings a level of complexity in the way business is done and regulatory challenges which mean it takes a western media company a long time to get its head around it."[21] Hence, it entered the Middle East by tying up with a local partner, the Arab Media Group (AMG), an established player in the Arab media industry with eight radio stations and three daily newspapers. The channel MTV Arabia was formed as a result of a licensing arrangement between MTV and AMG. MTV would earn an estimated US$10 million annually in licensing fees from AMG for 10 years.[22]

[17]"Arab Satellite TV channels Rapidly Expanding," www.xrdarabia.org, November 14, 2007.
[18] Faisal Abbas, "MTV Eyes Middle East Market," www.asharq-e.com, August 8, 2006.
[19] "Arabian Television Network Partners with MTV to Launch MTV Arabiya," http://mediame.com, December 27, 2006.
[20] On April 23, 2007, Bhavneet Singh was promoted to Senior Vice President and Managing Director of MTVNI's Emerging Markets group.

[21] Andrew Edgecliffe-Johnson, "MTV Tunes in to a Local Audience," www.us.ft.com, October 26, 2007.
[22] Sarah Raper Larenaudie, "MTV's Arab Prizefight," www.time.com, November 2, 2007.

On the other hand, an alliance with MTV was a winning deal for AMG too as it could access the former's world class resources to enhance its visibility in the Arab media as well as across the globe. "We found it very good to start our TV business with MTV Arabia because it's a great name to start with. Great team, great people; they provided us with a lot of resources. We believe that MTV is the beginning of a new era in television in this part of the world,"[23] said Sayegh.

However, the tie-up with a local partner was not enough to guarantee the success of MTV's launch in the Middle East given the conflict between the hip-hop explicit music culture portrayed by MTV and the conservative social culture prevalent in the Middle East. Hence, before launching the channel, Samaha conducted an extensive survey of the region to understand what people wanted. The survey team targeted people in the 18–24 age group and travelled around the region to schools and universities canvassing opinions. They also spoke to the elderly and figures of authority to assure them that they were there to entertain people within the limits of Arab traditions and had no intention of showing disrespect to the local culture. On this Samaha commented, "We also spoke to the governments, leaders, and parents and said, 'Don't worry, it will be nice,' so they know what's going on,"[24] said Samaha.

Accordingly, MTV Arabia's programming team decided to air MTVN's globally successful music shows but with a local flavor that would suit the Arab mindset and this laid the foundation for a planned launch of MTV in Arabia. The launch team comprised a mix of Saudis, Palestinians, Emiratis, Iraqis, and Lebanese.[25] "MTV first launched in 1981 when cable television was in its infancy. Since then we've grown into the world's largest TV network by becoming part of the fabric of youth culture, and by respecting audience diversity and different cultures. We're delighted to be launching MTV Arabiya and looking forward to working with our partners to provide the best youth programming,"[26] said Singh.

MTV commissioned ad agencies TBWA\Raad and Fortune Promoseven to handle the launch of the Channel in the Middle East.[27] "We're targeting normal Arabs. We're not targeting educated, private school people. Those are Arab society's niche. They are not more than 10 percent of the population. We are trying to appeal to the masses,"[28] said Samer Al Marzouqi, channel manager, MTV Arabia.

MTV Enters the Middle East

MTV Arabia was considered by experts as the biggest launch in MTVI's history in terms of potential audience at launch.[29] An exclusive, star-studded preview event marked the launch of MTV in the Middle East. The launch featured performances by eminent stars such as Akon, Ludacris, and Karl Wolf along with local hip hop group Desert Heat. The channel was formally launched on November 17, 2007, as a 24-hour, free-to-air television channel, having a target audience in Saudi Arabia, Egypt, United Arab Emirates, Lebanon, Bahrain, Jordan, Kuwait, Oman, Qatar, Yemen, Palestine, and Syria. MTVa.com, an Arabic and English language website, complemented the channel and provided users with a wide range of online community and interactive elements.

In line with its mixed-content strategy, MTV Arabia was to showcase 60 percent international music and 40 percent Arabic music, along with the local version of the channel's popular international non-music shows. About 45 percent of MTV Arabia's content was to be produced locally, with the rest translated. In this regard, Roedy commented, "The key is that the packaging, attitude, and obviously the language, should reflect the country. There is already great music there."[30] The channel's programming was to have a mix of music videos, music-based programming, general lifestyle and animated programs, reality shows, comedy and dramatic series, news specials, interviews, and documentaries. Besides international MTV shows, MTV Arabia was also to design new shows in Arabic to cater to pan-Arab youth audiences.

The company also said that the channel could act as a cultural unifying force in a region known for its political tensions. "The launch of MTV's 60th channel is a chance to correct misconceptions of the region . . . This part of the world has been associated with stresses and tensions . . . the one thing music can do is act as a unifying cultural force across regions,"[31] Roedy said.

Rationale Behind the Venture

Favorable demographics had been one of the key rationales behind MTV's commercial launch in the Middle East. About 65 percent of the Arab population consisted of youth under the age of 25, and the launch of MTV Arabia would provide MTV an opportunity to cater to a 190 million audience.[32] Further, though the Arab market was crowded with more than 50 channels, none of them provided a global platform to export the musical talent of the local youth. In this regard, Sayegh said, "Through our network, we now have more platforms to talk to our youth and in ways that have never been done before in the Middle East." Since young people "represent 65% of the population in the Middle East, it's time they were heard . . . Understanding the next generation is a key priority."[33] MTV being an international brand, had global reach and this became its key selling proposition for gaining critical mass in the Arab music world. Singh commented,

[23] Tamara Walid, "Finally Got my MTV," www.arabianbusiness.com, November 22, 2007.

[24] Matt Pomroy, "The Revolution Will be Televised," www.arabianbusiness.com, November 15, 2007.

[25] Sarah Raper Larenaudie, "MTV's Arab Prizefight," www.time.com, November 2, 2007.

[26] "Arabian Television Network Partners with MTV to Launch MTV Arabia," www.mediame.com, December 27, 2006.

[27] Iain Akerman, "MTV Hires Two Agencies for Launch of MTV Arabiya," www.brandrepublic.com, May 23, 2007.

[28] Dana El Baltaji, "I Want My MTV," www.arabmediasociety.com, May 2008.

[29] Irene Lew, "MTVNI Ups Singh," www.worldscreen.com, April 30, 2008.

[30] Lynne Roberts, "MTV Set for Middle East Launch," www.arabianbusiness.com, October 17, 2007.

[31] Simeon Kerr and Peter Aspden, "MTV Arabia Beams 'Bling' to Gulf," www.ft.com, November 17, 2007.

[32] "MTV Arabia to launch November 17," www.mediame.com, October 28, 2007.

[33] Ali Jaafar, "MTV Arabia Announces Lineup," www.variety.com, October 28, 2007.

"The fact that there has been no real youth platform, no real brand out there for the kids, makes us [feel] there is an opportunity for us."[34]

Moreover, the Middle East had the potential to offer MTV not only lucrative ad revenues but also numerous media like mobiles and the Internet to reach its end consumers. Singh said, "There are 37 million mobile subscribers in the wider Middle East, which is phenomenal and the average revenue per user is comparable to Western Europe. We believe that's where the future is—the ability to watch content wherever and however you want. We want to provide Middle East youth with the opportunity to watch MTV on mobile, on broadband, and on television. We're in discussions with mobile operators in the UAE, Kuwait, and Egypt, to look at how to distribute MTV content. There's been a huge amount of interest in that."[35] Products such as MTV Overdrive in which the user could download the video at broadband speed, and MTV Flux in which the online users could create their own TV channel were expected to help in luring the various Internet service providers in the region to MTV and to become major sources of its revenue.

The existence of various communication media with mass reach was expected to act as a catalyst in augmenting the channel's penetration rate in the Arabic region. In times to come if the channel validated its success in the Middle East, it would become a major revenue contributor to the MTV group.

Key Challenges and Success Strategy

MTV was known for airing sexually explicit and provocative programmes. In other words, it carried with it an image of open Western culture. This explicit Western culture projected by MTV went contrary to the socially conservative culture of the Middle East and could be a key bottleneck to the channel's acceptance in the Arab region, according to analysts. "As a brand, one would think that MTV is the ultimate example of what the religious, conservative cultures of the Middle East would most revile about Western pop culture,"[36] according to leading brand portal brandchannel.com. Adapting content to suit local tastes too could prove challenging because of many different countries comprising the region. What was acceptable in Dubai may not be acceptable in other parts of Saudi Arabia; what was acceptable in Egypt may not be acceptable in Jeddah (in Saudi Arabia). Analysts felt that the company also had to maintain what it stood for and too much localization could dilute its brand. And to complicate matters, there were strong anti-American sentiments prevalent among a large section of the population. Issues such as the US invasion of Iraq and its support to arch enemy Isreal had left many Arabs angry.

However the channel seemed well prepared to overcome such impediments to its growth plans in the Arab market. Though MTV Arabia would air its popular international programs, the network said that music videos and reality shows like "HIP Hop Na" and "Pimp my Ride" would be appropriately edited to ensure their alignment with the cultural ethos prevailing in the Middle East. Commenting on this, Sayegh said, "when we come to people's homes, we want to earn their respect."[37] He explained that there would be "culturally sensitive editors going through content of the programming."[38] In short, the channel expected to respect the local culture without diluting its brand. The channel aimed to prove that despite being a global brand, it would be a channel for the Arabs and made by Arabs—by people just like them.

Analysts said that MTVN's entry into the Middle East, which already had more than 50 local music channels operating, would be marked by stiff competition. In other words, unlike its past forays into India and Europe, MTV would not be entering a virgin music industry when it came to the Middle East. If on the one hand, the existence of a youth population was a business opportunity for MTVN, the same favorable demographic factor had also led to the explosion of dozens of local music channels which had a better understanding of the local audience's taste and could pose a formidable threat to MTVN's growth in the Middle East.

Also channels such as Rotana and Melody, which had already created a niche for themselves in the region, could pose a big competitive threat to MTVN. These channels had been functioning taking into account the tastes of the youth and had been able to attract a huge chunk of their target segment by offering creative concepts like games that allowed viewers to be part of the action from home along with interesting programs, music videos, and various artist albums and concerts. Moreover, some popular Arab music stars had already signed exclusive deals with some local channels. The challenge for MTV would be to not only find the right content but also ways to connect and captivate the Arabian youth, who were habituated to log on to any number of sites and enjoy music channel and videos according to their whims and fancies.

However, MTV Arabia was confident of scoring over its competitors and posting an impressive growth in the years to come. To overcome competition, the channel planned to project itself as unique and different from the existing lot. It proposed to establish itself as a platform wherefrom the Arab youth could voice their local concerns as well as advertise their music talent. For instance, MTV Arabia's flagship show "HIP Hop Na" would audition the best local hip-hop acts in seven different Middle Eastern cities. Thereafter, the winner from each city would get a chance to record a track for a compilation CD produced by Fred Wrecks.[39]

In a nutshell, MTV Arabia would not only provide entertainment but would also leverage on its global reach to advertise the musical talent of Arab youths. In this connection, Samaha said, "We are not only a music channel, we are an

[34] Von Andrew Edgecliffe Johnson, "MTV Tunes in to a Local Audience," www.ftd.de, October 26, 2007.
[35] "MTV Arabia to be Launched Soon," www.oceancreep.com, October 8, 2007.
[36] "Will the MTV Brand Change the Middle East?" www.brandchannel.com, December 3, 2007.

[37] "MTV Aims to Win over Middle East," www.cnn.com, November 19, 2007.
[38] "MTV Aims to Win over Middle East," www.cnn.com, November 19, 2007.
[39] Fred Wrecks is a Palestinian-born hip-hop producer who has worked under some of the eminent record label such as Dogghouse Records, Virgin Records, etc. He has also worked with many distinguished rap stars like 50 Cent and Snoop Dogg.

entertainment channel where young Arabs will get a voice."[40] He added, "MTV Arabia is a fresh take on MTV the brand, made by Arabs for Arab youth, and is dedicated to their self-expression. We've done extensive research to listen to our audiences, and MTV Arabia will be the first free-to-air channel to celebrate young people and their lives and talents from across this dynamic, vibrant region. We'll also offer audiences a window to the world of global youth culture, bringing top international entertainment to the region and showcasing the Arab region in the context of what's happening around the world. Through MTV's global network, we'll also be able to export Arabic music and culture to the international stage."[41]

Also, the programming line-up would feature more local content (Refer to Exhibit IV for a note on local production program to be aired on MTV Arabia) in comparison to other localized MTV ventures. There would be a localized version of popular shows such as "MADE" (al Helm) and "Boiling Point" (Akher Takka), which would constitute 40 percent of the content to be aired on MTV Arabia.

The company also said it did not expect anti-American sentiments to affect its chances in the region. MTV said that it expected to win over the target segment with content relevant to them. Moreover, it said that its research before the launch had shown that the majority of respondents thought that MTV was a European or Indian brand.[42]

The Road Ahead

MTVN catered to a huge market segment of nearly 2 billion people worldwide and was expected to provide a global platform for Arabic music and culture. It had influenced young people all over the world and given them a voice and it would try to do the same in the Middle East. An Arabic category was already added in MTV Europe Music Awards 2007, giving Arabic music the much needed global platform.

The MTV-AMG combine would not only provide entertainment to the region but would also take up social issues and try to contribute to Arab society, according to the network. In this regard, Sayegh commented, "We are going to encourage education and look for solutions to problems such as unemployment. These are all causes on our agenda."[43]

MTVN, along with AMG, planned to expand its operations in the Middle East. It had already announced the launch of Nickelodeon Arabia in 2008. It would be the first free-to-air channel for children in Arabic. Roedy commented, "Adding the voices of Arab children to our worldwide Nickelodeon family is a significant milestone in our history, and advances our ambitious strategy to build a portfolio of integrated kids businesses across the region. The Middle East is a dynamic, thriving market with vast growth opportunities, and we look forward to launching even more MTVNI brands and businesses through our successful partnership

EXHIBIT IV   Local Productions to be Aired on MTV Arabia

The flagship local show :

Hip Hop Na, a twelve-episode series which follows auditions to uncover the best local hip hop acts in four different Middle Eastern cities

Music Related Shows:

Waslati, viewers with webcams become VJs and introduce three of their favorite videos.

Baqbeeq is a music trivia show with a twist, where interesting and hilarious bits of trivia pop up through the most popular videos in the world.

Introducing Block goes behind the scenes in the music industry, with exclusive interviews and performances by the biggest international and Arab stars.

Other Programs:

Al Helm, based on MTV's *MADE* format, follows the journey of aspiring teenagers looking to fulfill their dreams with the help of an MTV Arabia-supplied "coach."

Al Hara tours the Middle East's street scene, and features previously unknown artists displaying innovative talent in skills like beat-boxing, break-dancing, or magic acts. The show is based on MTV's international program format, *Barrio 19*.

In *Akher Takka*, based on MTV's hit format, *Boiling Point*, actors antagonize stressed-out "victims" who can win a cash prize if they manage to keep their cool in extremely annoying situations.

Compiled from various sources.

[40] "MTV Looks to Conquer Middle East Market," www.aol.in, November 18, 2007.

[41] "MTV Arabia to Launch November 17," www.middleeastevents.com, October 27, 2007.

[42] Adam Sherwin, "MTV Arabia to Feature Regional Talent and Tone Down Network's Risque Content," www.business.timesonline.co.uk, November 16, 2007.

[43] Simeon Kerr and Peter Aspden, "MTV Arabia Beams 'Bling' to Gulf," www.ft.com, November 17, 2007.

with AMG."[44] Singh added, "The launch of Nickelodeon Arabia is a part of our wider, ongoing multi-platform strategy encompassing consumer products, digital media, hotels and theme parks, which we hope will establish Nickelodeon as the premier destination for kids in the region."[45]

Thus far, MTVN's model of entering a market in partnership with a local partner and following a localization strategy had worked well for the company. Analysts felt that only time would tell whether the company would succeed in the Middle East. But Singh had a rather philosophical take on what success meant. To him, the venture would be a success when people in the smallest cities of the Middle East came up to him and professed their love for MTV. "After all, it's not about how many eyeballs you reach, it's about how many people relate to you," he said.[46]

Case Questions

1. Experts felt that one of the biggest challenges faced by MTV while launching MTV Arabia was the prevalent culture in the Arab world. Discuss the Arab culture. How is it expected to pose a challenge to MTV?

2. Critically analyze MTV's strategy in the Middle East. Comment on its entry strategy and also its strategy of providing mixed content to the market. Do you think MTV will be able to succeed in this market?

References and Suggested Readings:

1. Dirk Smillie, "**Tuning in First Global TV Generation,**" *The Christian Science Monitor*, June 4, 1997.
2. Kerry Capell, Catherine Belton, Tom Lowry, Manjeet Kripalani, Brian Bremner, and Dexter Roberts, "**MTV's World,**" *BusinessWeek*, February 18, 2002.
3. "**MTV to Launch Music TV Channels in Three Baltic States,**" www.eubusiness.com, March 6, 2006.
4. Faisal Abbas, "**Q&A with Showtime Arabia's CEO Peter Einstein,**" www.asharq-e.com, June 29, 2006.
5. Faisal Abbas, "**MTV Eyes Middle East Market,**" www.asharq-e. com, August 8, 2006.
6. Brad Nemer, "**How MTV Channels Innovation,**" *BusinessWeek*, November 6, 2006.
7. "**Arabian Television Network Partners with MTV to Launch MTV Arabiya,**" www.mediame.com, December 27, 2006.
8. Michael Learmonth, "**MTV Maps Mideast Move,**" www.variety. com, December 27, 2006.
9. Iain Akerman, "**MTV Hires Two Agencies for Launch of MTV Arabiya,**" www.brandrepublic.com, May 23, 2007.
10. Salman Dossari, "**A Talk With MTV Vice Chairman Bill Roedy,**" www.asharq-e.com, July 23, 2007.
11. Ali Jaafar, "**MTV Arabia Ready to Rock Middle East,**" www. variety.com, September 25, 2007.
12. "**MTV Arabia to be Launched Soon,**" www.oceancreep.com, October 8, 2007.
13. Kerry Capell, "**The Arab World Wants Its MTV,**" www. businessweek.com, October 11, 2007.
14. Lynne Roberts, "**MTV Set for Middle East launch,**" www. arabianbusiness.com, October 17, 2007.
15. Stuart Kemp, "**MTV, Arab Media to Launch Nickelodeon Arabia,**" www.hollywoodreporter.com, October 17, 2007.
16. Andrew Edgecliffe Johnson, "**MTV Targets Muslim Countries as it Tunes in to Local Audiences,**" www.theaustralian.news.com, October 18, 2007.
17. "**Arab Media Group and MTV Networks International to Launch Nickelodeon Arabia in 2008,**" www.ameinfo.com, October 20, 2007.
18. Von Andrew Edgecliffe Johnson, "**MTV Tunes in to a Local Audience,**" www.ftd.de, October 26, 2007,
19. "**MTV Arabia to Launch November 17,**" www.middle eastevents.com, October 27, 2007.
20. Ali Jaafar, "**MTV Arabia Announces Lineup,**" www.variety. com, October 28, 2007.
21. "**MTV Arabia to Launch November 17,**" www.mediame.com, October 28, 2007.
22. Irene Lew, "**MTV Arabia to Launch in November,**" www.world-screen.com, October 29, 2007.
23. Sarah Raper Larenaudie, "**MTV's Arab Prizefight,**" www.time. com, November 2, 2007.
24. Jolanta Chudy, "**MTV's Arab Net Thinking Locally,**" www. hollywoodreporter.com, November 6, 2007.
25. Matt Pomroy, "**The Revolution Will be Televised,**" www.arabian-business.com, November 15, 2007.
26. "**Akon and Ludacris Dazzle The Desert in their Middle East Debuts to Celebrate the Launch of MTV Arabia,**" www. dubaicityguide.com, November 16, 2007.
27. Adam Sherwin, "**MTV Arabia to Feature Regional Talent and Tone Down Network's Risque Content,**" www.timesonline.co. uk, November 16, 2007.
28. Simeon Kerr and Peter Aspden, "**MTV Arabia Beams 'Bling' to Gulf,**" www.ft.com, November 17, 2007.
29. "**MTV Launches New Arabic Service,**" www.news.bbc.co.uk, November 18, 2007.
30. "**MTV Looks to Conquer Middle East Market,**" www.aol.in, November 18, 2007.
31. "**"MTV Arabia": Will It Work?**" www.scopical.com, November 19, 2007.
32. "**MTV Aims to Win over Middle East,**" www.cnn.com, November 19, 2007.

---

[44] "Arab Media Group and MTV Networks International to Launch Nickelodeon Arabia in 2008," www.ameinfo.com, October 20, 2007.
[45] Stuart Kemp, "MTV, Arab Media to Launch Nickelodeon Arabia," www. hollywoodreporter.com, October 17, 2007.

[46] Tamara Walid, "Finally Got My MTV," www.arabianbusiness.com, November 22, 2007.

33. **"Muslim Hip-hop Turban Wrote, That's Good,"** www.reuters. donga.com, November 19, 2007.

34. Barbara Surk, **"MTV for Young Arab is Less Naughty,"** www. cincinnati.com, November 21, 2007.

35. Barbara Surk, **"MTV Launches Arab Music Video Channel,"** www.theeagle.com, November 22, 2007.

36. Tamara Walid, **"Finally Got My MTV,"** www.arabianbusiness. com, November 22, 2007.

37. **"Will the MTV Brand Change the Middle East?"** www. brandchannel.com, December 2, 2007.

38. Irene Lew, **"MTVNI Ups Singh,"** www.worldscreen.com, April 30, 2008.

39. Dana El Baltaji, **"I Want My MTV,"** www.arabmediasociety.com, May 11, 2008.

40. www.topfive.com

41. www.en.wikipedia.org

42. www.mtva.com

43. www.viacom.com

CASE 5 GOOGLE'S COUNTRY EXPERIENCES: FRANCE, GERMANY, JAPAN

"We must take up the global challenge of the American giants Yahoo! and Google." "Culture is not merchandise and cannot be left to blind market forces." "We must staunchly defend the world's cultural diversity against the looming threat of uniformity."[1]

–JACQUES CHIRAC,
French President

"Search engine users aren't terribly loyal, so a better or more targeted technology could make headway."[2]

– CHARLENE LI,
Analyst at Forrester Research Inc., a technology and market research company

"It would be interesting to see if we're about to have a trade war emerge in the search space over government backing, similar to the arguments that are made about government support given to aircraft makers Airbus in Europe and Boeing in the US."[3]

– DANNY SULLIVAN,
Editor, Search Engine Watch, a site providing analysis of the search engine industry

Google Inc.—founded in September 1998 by Stanford graduates Sergey Brin and Larry Page—by June 2000, became the world's largest search engine with its introduction of a billion-page index.[4] Web search was increasingly used as a way to find products and services. In August 2007 alone, there were more than 61 billion individual searches worldwide. Google, based in the US, became widely popular because it could provide simple, fast and relevant search results. It used PageRank technology to display results by not only looking for keywords inside web pages, but also gauging the importance of a search result based on the number and popularity of other sites that linked to the page. The search results were algorithmically determined, with no hand-editing of the results. Over the years, Google perfected its technology to display results that were more accurate and relevant. Google did not follow the practice of paid inclusion, i.e., one could not buy their way into the search results. Paid results were shown outside regular search results.

Google's business was split between advertising on its website and selling its technology to other sites. Its business model (Exhibit I) of AdWords allowed companies to purchase keywords for advertising purposes. An Internet user searching on that keyword would get the organic (unsponsored) results as well as the advertisements (sponsored links).

Google's advertising revenues rose steadily and stood at $21.1 billion in 2008 (Exhibit II).

A key component in Google's strategy was to expand its reach into new international markets. By 2000, Google users could search for content in 10 different languages. Google's new search index released in 2000 included a large collection of international websites signifying Google's plans to expand into new international markets. Google saw its revenues going up, more from its international forays (Exhibit III).

By 2007, Internet users could use the Google search interface in almost 120 languages and it was available in almost 160 local domains.[5] For a query, originating outside the US, the location of the surfer would be determined and google.com would automatically assume the local domain. Messages in the local language and custom-tailored results for that location were shown. For instance, if a user in the UK made a Google search, the results would be served up by google.co.uk.

As the Internet grew bigger, Google got better. It launched its IPO in 2004, with an offer price of $85 that rose to $670 by November 2007, giving it a market capitalisation of $211.70 billion.[6] In a survey released by comScore Inc., a global Internet information provider, Google sites ranked as the top worldwide search property in August 2007 with 37.1 billion searches.[7] Apart from search, Google expanded its portfolio by introducing an array of new software and added services. It sought ways to import offline media, such as books and television shows, into its search engine. Through 2001 to July 2007,

This case was written by Shanul Jain, under the direction of R. Muthukumar, Icfai Business School Case Development Centre. It is intended to be used as the basis for class discussion rather than to illustrate either effective or ineffective handling of a management situation. This case was compiled from published sources.

[1] "Attack of the Eurogoogle", http://www.economist.com/research/articles BySubject/displaystory.cfm?subjectid= 10009611&story_id=E1_VVSTQJG, March 19th 2006
[2] Regan Keith, "Japanese Government May start Rival Search Engine", http://www.ecommercetimes.com/story/AUhp9eKd2SP8AX/Japanese-Government-May-Start-Rival-Search- Engine.xhtml, December 20th 2005
[3] Ibid.
[4] "Google Milestones", http://www.google.com/corporate/history.html
[5] "Language Tools", http://www.google.com/language_tools?hl=EN, 2007
[6] "61 billion searches conducted worldwide in August", http://www.comscore.com/press/release.asp?press=1802, October 10th 2007
[7] "Google Inc.", http://finance.google.com/finance?q=GOOG

EXHIBIT I   How Google Earns its Revenues

> Google's original business model was licensing its search engine services to other websites. In the first quarter of 2000, it introduced its first advertising programme— premium sponsorships. Through its direct sales force, it offered advertisers the ability to place text-based ads on its websites targeted to the user's search queries. Advertisers paid based on the number of times their ads were displayed on search results pages. It launched AdWords in the fourth quarter of 2000 that enabled advertisers to place targeted text-based ads on Google's sites. Here advertisers paid on a Cost-Per-Click basis—only when a user clicked on one of its ads. In the first quarter of 2002, Google released its AdSense service that distributed relevant ads from advertisers, for display with search results on the Google Network members' sites, which was a large group of websites and other products such as e-mail programs and blogs, who had partnered with Google to display AdWords ads.

Compiled by the author

EXHIBIT II   Select Google Financials ($ million)

Year	Revenues	Net Income	Advertising Revenues	Spend on R&D
2008	21,795.5	4,226.8	21,128.5	2,793.2
2007	16,593.9	4,203.7	16,412.6	2,119.9
2006	10,604.9	3,077.4	10,492.6	1,228.6
2005	6,138.6	1,465.4	6,065.0	599.5
2004	3,189.2	399.1	3,143.3	395.2
2003	1,465.9	105.6	1,420.7	229.6
2002	439.5	99.7	410.9	40.5
2001	86.4	7.0	Not Available	16.5

Compiled by the author from "Financial Tables", http://investor.google.com/fin_data.html

EXHIBIT III   Google Quarterly Revenues ($ billion)

Year	Q1	IR*	Q2	IR	Q3	IR	Q4	IR
2008	5.18	51%	5.36	52%	5.54	51%	5.70	50%
2007	3.66	47%	3.87	48%	4.23	48%	4.82	48%
2006	2.25	42%	2.46	42%	2.69	44%	3.21	44%
2005	1.26	39%	1.38	39%	1.58	39%	1.92	38%
2004	N/A	N/A	N/A	N/A	0.8058	N/A	1.032	N/A

*IR: International Revenues, i.e., the % of revenues from outside the US
N/A: Not Available
Compiled by the author from "Financial Tables", http://investor.google.com/fin_data.html

the company made about 44 acquisitions, including the video sharing service YouTube and online advertising company DoubleClick.[8] Google's rapid rise and its dominance in search and other web areas, prompted concerns in a number of countries. The nature of Google's services and its AdWords programme saw Google defending itself in a number of lawsuits against it for copyright infringement.

Action against Google was sparked by fear of US dominance over the local cultures, to the kind of information that Google provided. There were demands that Google censor its search results according to government regulations. Google, for instance, in France and Germany, removed links to pro-Nazi, anti-semitic and other controversial sites. Its AdWords model attracted a number of lawsuits. More and more companies sought control over their brand names and trademarked search in paid terms.

Google France

Europe was a surging market for Internet advertising and Google's multi-language search service, started in 2000, included the French and German versions. The same year, Google launched a webpage with a French domain name—

[8] "Google acquisitions by year, 2001–2007", http://mashable.com/2007/07/03/google-acquisitions/, July 3rd 2007

google.fr. Given its rapid growth in the country, it opened its sales office in 2002 to facilitate a direct point of contact to the French businesses and incorporate targeting by language, by country, and by keyword in its advertising programmes. Google soon became the dominant search engine in France and offered services in regional French dialects like Breton, Basque and Corsican.

However, Europe's patchwork of languages and cultures was seen as an advantage by companies, seeking to break into the search market to compete with Google, by entertaining demand for locally focused search. Nate Elliott, an analyst for JupiterResearch, remarked, "Europe's diversity can play toward exploiting niches."[9] Aiming for this niche were search engines like Paris-based Exalead and international media groups like Oslo-based Schibsted, that saw Google as the prime competitor in the media industry. To challenge Google, the French and German governments reacted with plans to develop their country-specific search engines.

To many French companies, Google's business model of displaying sponsored links amounted to trademark counterfeiting. Numerous advertisers sued Google and the French courts ruled mostly in favour of copyright holders. The court ruling called into question the legality of the search system. It stated that Google should "find the means to block advertisements by third parties who have no right to these trademarks."[10] Google paid €75,000 in damages and costs to Luteciel and Viaticum, two French travel companies. Louis Vuitton, French luxury goods maker, too filed a suit for trademark infringement, saying that handbag producers could pay to ensure that their ads would pop up when someone googled for Louis Vuitton. A court ruling ordered Google to cease the practice and pay fines. In another ruling, Google was ordered to stop linking ads to the trademarks of European resort chain Le Meridien Hotels and Resorts. Even the French news service, Agence France-Presse (AFP) alleged that Google had stolen its copyrighted material by including it on the Google News website. Similar lawsuits against Google in US had either been dismissed or gone in Google's favour. Google spokeswoman Myriam Boublil said, "French law is just very protective of trademarks."[11]

There was further uproar when Google announced its plans to digitise books and documents, from a handful of US and British university libraries. Google would spend between $150 million and $200 million over a decade to digitise collections of Harvard, Stanford, the University of Michigan, the New York Public Library and Oxford University. This caused alarm, as it was felt that the initiative—rather than democratising knowledge—would further strengthen US power to set a global cultural agenda. Of the Google-Print (renamed Google Book Search) project, the French chief librarian Jean-Noël Jeanneney said, "The libraries that are taking part in this enterprise are of course themselves generously open to the civilisations and works of other countries, but still, their criteria for selection

will be profoundly marked by the Anglo-Saxon outlook."[12] In response, in March 2005, the French president Jacques Chirac announced that the country would start its own digital-book project. The culture minister, Renaud Donnedieu de Vabres and Jeanneney were asked to digitise French texts. Even Google's criterion to rank results was condemned. "I do not believe that the only key to access our culture should be the automatic ranking by popularity, which has been behind Google's success,"[13] stated de Vabres. Jeanneney believed that Europe should not only convert its books into digital files, but should also control the page rankings of responses to searches, "European ranking should reflect a European vision of history and culture."[14] The question was how to manage the digitised knowledge? For this, Europe could either have its own search engine or reach an agreement with Google or other Internet search providers.

In April 2005, President Chirac and the German chancellor Gerhard Schröder endorsed a plan to build a Franco-German multimedia search engine—*Quaero*, meaning, "I seek" in Latin. The project was a public-private consortium including among others Thomson and France Telecom in France, Siemens and Deutsche Telekom in Germany— with the government as the main financier and developer of the search engine. The Agency for Industrial Innovation (AII) was created in Paris to oversee the project. AII got an initial endowment of €1.7 billion ($2 billion), to be spent on *Quaero* and other centrally directed high-tech initiatives. Out of this, €250 million ($294 million) would go for *Quaero*.

Quaero would be superior to existing search engine technology. Search engines displayed results by matching the user's keywords with the text, image, audio and video files. *Quaero* would enable keywords search in the usual way, but would also allow users to query using pictures and sounds. The process was 'image mining', where the software would recognise shapes and colours and then retrieve still images and video clips quite similar to the query image. Researchers at the University of Karlsruhe, Germany would develop voice recognition and translation technology. The software would find audio files, automatically transcribe and translate them into a number of European languages. In short, it would offer multimedia search features. Marie-Vincente Pasdeloup of Thomson remarked, "It's beyond Google."[15]

The European Union however had to rule whether the money earmarked for the project amounted to unfair subsidy— something stringently forbidden by European law. Observers stated *Quaero*'s main aims as being cultural and political, rather than commercial. Alexander Waibel, a member of *Quaero*'s steering committee, said, "Europe wants to secure access that does not have to be channelled through American technology."[16]

[9] Crampton Thomas, "European search engines take on Google", http://www.iht.com/articles/2006/12/17/business/search.php, December 17th 2006

[10] "Handbag maker Vuitton sues Google", http://edition.cnn.com/2003/TECH/biztech/10/24/france.google.ap/, October 24th 2003

[11] Lamb Scott, "What does France have against Google?", http://journalism.nyu.edu/portfolio/bestof/2005/001617.html

[12] "Why Google Scares Jacques Chirac", http://www.expatica.com/actual/article.asp?subchannel_id=58&story_id=18407, March 2005

[13] "Google à la française", http://www.economist.com/research/articles By Subject/displaystory.cfm?subjectid=10009611&story_id=E1_PRTJTGJ, March 31st 2005

[14] Riding Alan, "Entr'acte: A French call to arms over Google challenge", http://www.iht.com/articles/2005/03/30/news/entracte.php, March 31st 2005

[15] "Attack of the Eurogoogle", op.cit.

[16] Ibid.

Hal Varian, an Internet economics specialist at the University of California at Berkley, opined that the European desire for "search parity" was understandable and that "it was not so long ago that the US was paranoid about Japanese super-computer initiatives for pretty much the same reason: control of a critical piece of infrastructure."[17]

The *Quaero* alliance included companies like Exalead, for search technology; France Telecom, for communications; Jouve, for scanning and other digital publishing expertise and Thompson, for information technology. Alongside, there would be German counterparts including Deutsche Telekom and the publishing giant, Bertelsmann. The French side would look at the image search research and Germany at the voice clip and sound media searches and the subsequent translation into text and other languages.

Google Germany

In 2000, Google launched the google.de domain. In Germany, Google's free e-mail (Gmail) came under the court scanner. Daniel Giersch, a German-born venture capitalist, insisted that Google had infringed on his trademark registration of Gmail, the name by which his electronic postal delivery service went. He remarked, "Google's behaviour is very threatening, very aggressive and very unfaithful, and to me, it's very evil."[18] Google lost the courtroom battle and was asked to remove all 'Gmail' references from its German service and cease handing out gmail.com aliases to users within the geographic area. Google stopped the use of Gmail in Germany and instead adopted google mail.

In 2006, Angela Merkel took over from Schröder as the new German chancellor. Under the new government, the Germans did not officially commit to the *Quaero* project. In January 2007, Germany pulled out to set up its alternative development project—*Theseus*—named after a legendary Greek hero who found his way out of a labyrinth inhabited by a monster. Hendrik Luchtmeier, a spokesman for Germany's Economics Ministry, said, "We will still see cooperation, but in another form, such as work groups. The consortium between the German and French governments is over."[19]

This decision underscored the difficulty of cross-border projects, mostly because of the personal differences between project managers. Some argued that the Germans were fed up with the French need to develop a Google killer. Francois Bourdoncle, a French participant in the project, remarked, "The truth is that the German and French projects were only remotely connected. We wanted to develop multimedia search and the Germans wanted to develop text search. Part of the problem is talk of a European challenge to Google exaggerated expectations."[20]

The European Union gave Germany the go-ahead to spend €120 million ($167 million) on *Theseus*. An additional €90 million would be chipped in, by the companies and institutes involved in the research. There were in all 22 partner organisations, companies and universities—including SAP, Siemens and Deutsche Thompson. The German Economic Minister Michael Glos opined, "With Theseus we want to improve Germany and Europe's ability to compete and reach a top position in IT and communication technology."[21]

Google Japan

Along with Europe, the Asia-Pacific was another important region on Google's global expansion list and it built additional search services for Asian character-based languages like Japanese, Korean and Chinese. Google's Japanese subsidiary, established in 2002, was its fourth business venture outside the US. Considering the significance of overseas markets to its revenues, Google opened an R&D centre in Tokyo in 2004, the third such one outside the US. It was meant to blend Japan's advanced technology in broadband and mobile phone services, into Google's corporate activities.

In 2005, Japan's Ministry of Economy, Trade and Industry organised a study group consisting of about 20 Japanese electronics companies and universities. The group was to consider the merits of creating a search tool specifically for the Japanese users. Fumihiro Kajikawa, a Ministry Official, said, "The group will look into issues including whether Japan will start its own search engine."[22] The government would spend up to $885 million on the plan. The search engine technology would be developed to compete with search companies like AJ Japan, Google Japan, Yahoo Japan and others. The trigger for a Japanese project came from concerns that the country's pre-eminence in consumer electronics had faded and value in the technology industry was moving away from hardware. There were fears that the country's manufacturers were falling behind in innovation. The government wanted a Japan-centric search engine that would likely wrest back some of the domestic market share and advertising revenue that the large search firms were getting.

In 2007, Japan launched its project to counter Google's and Yahoo!'s dominance of searching. The state-led project comprised 10 partnerships, each tasked with a specific next-generation search function. The country hoped to use its strength in developing devices such as mobile phones and car navigation systems, to create proprietary search and information retrieval functions. As a part of the initiative in '2008 information Grand Voyage Project'[23]

'Laddering search service' was included. Toshihide Yahiro, director of the information service industry division at the Ministry of Trade, said, "The key to Japan's competitiveness has been our core technology but we need to create a new value-added service that is personalised."[24]

[17] Ross E. Philip, "Loser: What's the Latin for 'Delusional'?", http://sepctrum.ieee.org/print/4842

[18] Broache Anne, "Behind Google's German courtroom battle", http://news.zdnet.com/2100-9588_22-6115056.html, September 14th 2006

[19] Spongenberg Helena, "Germany Quits Quaero Web Search Project", http://www.businessweek.com/globalbiz/content/jan2007/gb20070104_427008.htm?chan=search, January 4th 2007

[20] Ibid.

[21] "Germany to fund rival to Google search engine", http://www.dw-world.de/dw/article/0,2144,2698176,00.html, July 20th 2007

[22] Wearden Graeme, "Japan may create its own search engine", http://www.sakshay.in/news/technologynews4.html, December 21st 2005

[23] It enables users to find what they are looking for on the web through dialogues with a computer. It was jointly developed by OKi Electric Industry Co. and Recruit Co., Ltd.

[24] Sanchanta Mariko and Waters Richard, "Japan to fight Google search dominance", http://www.ft.com/cms/s/0/b3046d5c-5b1d-11dc-8c32-0000779fd2ac.html, September 4th 2007

Google: Understanding the Competition

All these countries stressed on search not only because it was crucial, but also they were wary of US dominance in information business. Google on its part focused on strengthening its R&D efforts in Europe. In January 2007, it opened another R&D centre in Poland. It also worked to bolster its presence in Japan. It considered the possibility of partnering with Japan's largest mobile carrier, NTT DoCoMo, to provide search and e-mail services to mobile handsets. Google's market share in 2007 reached 85.8% and 88.5% of the French and German markets (Exhibit IV); whereas the government search engines are yet to be rolled out. Can these search engines, backed by the national governments, overhaul Google? Will Google's country experiences question the exportability of its business model?

Google, as it expands to emerging economies in the Asia-Pacific, has to tackle competition from the local search engines. China, with one of the highest and fastest growing Internet population, is an attractive and important market for all search companies, but there, Google has a tough contender in the local search engine, Baidu. China's cultural differences could also question Google's ability to serve overseas markets. In its international growth, Google is in the unenviable position of deciding who poses a bigger threat to its dominance—the international search companies as Yahoo! and Microsoft, the local search engines as Baidu or the unfinished government-backed country search engines.

EXHIBIT IV   Search Engine Market Share (%): July 2007 and July 2008

Year		US	France	Germany	Japan
2008	Google	61.9	–	79.8	39.0[**]
	Yahoo!	20.5	–	0.9	51.2[**]
2007	Google	55.2	85.8	88.5[*]	35.0
	Yahoo!	23.5	3.8	3.4[*]	47.4

[*] German Market Share figures are for August 2007 and [**] Japanese Market Share figures are for September 2008

Compiled by the author from comScore Inc. press releases

Assignment Questions

1. How does a search engine work and make money? What is the exportability of a search engine's technology and business model?
2. Why did many governments appear threatened by Google? How did they counter this threat? Discuss each country separately
3. Is the threat, from the government-sponsored search engines, real or imagined? What can Google do to secure its dominance in those countries? What can Google learn from those experiences to guide its entry strategy for other countries?

16

Hiring and Managing Employees

◀ A LOOK **BACK**

Chapter 15 examined how companies launch and manage their international production efforts. We also explored briefly how companies finance their various international business operations.

■ A LOOK **AT THIS CHAPTER**

This final chapter examines how a company acquires and manages its most important resource—its employees. The topics we explore include international staffing policies, recruitment and selection, training and development, compensation, and labor–management relations. We also learn about culture shock and how employees can deal with its effects.

Learning Objectives

After studying this chapter, you should be able to

1 Explain the three different types of staffing policies used by international companies.

2 Describe the recruitment and selection issues facing international companies.

3 Discuss the importance of training and development programs, especially cultural training.

4 Explain how companies compensate managers and workers in international markets.

5 Describe the importance of labor–management relations and how they differ around the world.

Leaping Cultures

CHENGDU, China — Intel (www.intel.com) created the world's first microprocessor in 1971. Today, annual revenue is $38 billion, around 75 percent of which is earned outside the United States. Intel is the world's largest maker of computer chips and a leading manufacturer of computer, networking, and communications products.

With around 100,000 employees worldwide, Intel must deal with many issues when managing people. The company must answer some important questions when selecting people to manage each local office in 45 countries. Can a qualified manager be found locally? If so, what salary should Intel pay the local manager? Or, will a manager need to be sent from the United States or from an office in another nation? If so, what should Intel pay that individual? Intel's compensation and benefits packages vary greatly from one country to another because of different practices around the world.

There is also the issue of culture. Although the depth of cultural knowledge required of various employees differs, Intel wants all its employees to be culturally astute. Its culture-specific training courses teach its employees how business differs across cultures. Intel says its training is designed "to develop the knowledge, awareness, and skills to ensure effectiveness and productivity and to identify strategies for successfully doing business in other countries and with people from other countries."

Source: China Photos/Getty Images.

From tech-support reps working long-distance with customers abroad to globetrotting executives, many Intel employees regularly rely on their cross-cultural communication skills. Chairman of the Board, Craig Barrett (above right), gets a hero's welcome as he greets employees at the opening of Intel's new assembly plant in Chengdu, China. As you read this chapter, consider all the human resource issues that arise when international companies manage their employees around the world.[1]

Perhaps the most important resource of any successful business is the people who comprise it. If a company gives its human resource management practices the importance they deserve, it can have a profound impact on performance. Highly trained and productive employees who are proficient in their duties allow a company to achieve its business goals both domestically and internationally. **Human resource management (HRM)** is the process of staffing a company and ensuring that employees are as productive as possible. It requires managers to be effective in recruiting, selecting, training, developing, evaluating, and compensating employees and in forming good relationships with them.

International HRM differs considerably from HRM in a domestic setting because of differences in national business environments. There are concerns over the employment of **expatriates**—citizens of one country who are living and working in another. Companies must deal with many issues when they have expatriate employees on job assignments that could last several years. Some of these issues are related to the inconvenience and stress of living in an unfamiliar culture. In the company profile at the start of this chapter, we saw how Intel (www.intel.com) enrolls its employees in culture-specific training courses to prepare them for doing business internationally.

Training and development programs must often be tailored to local practices. Some countries, such as Germany and Japan, have extensive vocational-training schools that turn out graduates ready to perform their jobs proficiently. Finding well-qualified nonmanagerial workers in those markets is relatively easy. By contrast, developing a production facility in many emerging markets requires far more basic training of workers. For example, workers in China work hard and tend to be well educated. But because China lacks an advanced vocational training system like those in Germany and Japan, Chinese workers tend to require more intensive on-the-job training. Recruitment and selection practices must also be adapted to the host nation's hiring laws. Hiring practices regarding nondiscrimination among job candidates must be carefully monitored so that the company does not violate such laws. And companies that go abroad to lower labor expenses then adjust pay scales and advancement criteria to suit local customs.

Because culture is so important to international business, we studied culture early (Chapter 2) and returned repeatedly to the topic throughout this book. Culture is also central to this final chapter's discussion of how international companies manage their employees. We begin by discussing the different types of human resource staffing policies that international companies use. Then, we learn about the important factors that have an effect on recruitment and selection practices internationally. We explore the many different types of training and development programs companies can use to improve the effectiveness of their employees. We also examine the compensation policies of international companies. We close the chapter with a discussion of the importance of labor–management relations around the world.

International Staffing Policy

The customary means by which a company staffs its offices is called its **staffing policy**. Staffing policy is greatly influenced by the extent of a firm's international involvement. There are three main approaches to the staffing of international business operations—*ethnocentric*, *polycentric*, and *geocentric*. Although we discuss each of these approaches as being distinct from one another, companies often blend different aspects of each staffing policy in practice. The result is an almost infinite variety of international staffing policies among international companies.

Ethnocentric Staffing

In **ethnocentric staffing**, individuals from the home country manage operations abroad. This policy tends to appeal to companies that want to maintain tight control over decision making in branch offices abroad. Accordingly, those companies work to formulate policies designed to work in every country in which they operate. But note that firms generally pursue this policy in their international operations for top managerial posts—implementing it at lower levels is often impractical.

---

human resource management (HRM)
Process of staffing a company and ensuring that employees are as productive as possible.

expatriates
Citizens of one country who are living and working in another.

staffing policy
The customary means by which a company staffs its offices.

ethnocentric staffing
Staffing policy in which individuals from the home country manage operations abroad.

Advantages of Ethnocentric Staffing   Firms pursue this policy for several reasons. First, locally qualified people are not always available. In developing and newly industrialized countries, there is often a shortage of qualified personnel that creates a highly competitive local labor market.

Second, companies use ethnocentric staffing to re-create local operations in the image of home-country operations. Especially if they have climbed the corporate ladder in the home office, expatriate managers tend to infuse branch offices with the corporate culture. This policy is important for companies that need a strong set of shared values among the people in each international office—such as firms implementing global strategies. For example, Mihir Doshi was born in Bombay but his family moved to the United States in 1978. Doshi graduated from New York University and became a naturalized U.S. citizen in 1988. In 1995 he became executive director of Morgan Stanley's (www.ms.com) operations in India. "Mentally," he reports, "I'm very American. Here, I can be Indian. What the firm gets is somebody to indoctrinate Morgan Stanley culture. I provide the link."[2]

By the same token, a system of shared values is important when a company's international units are highly interdependent. For instance, fashioning branch operations in the image of home-office operations can also ease the transfer of special know-how. This advantage is particularly valuable when that know-how is rooted in the expertise and experience of home-country managers.

Finally, some companies feel that managers sent from the home country will look out for the company's interests more earnestly than will host-country natives. Japanese companies are notorious for their reluctance to place non-Japanese managers at the helm of international offices. And when they do appoint a foreigner, they often place a Japanese manager in the office to monitor important decisions and report back to the home office. Companies that operate in highly nationalistic markets and those worried about industrial espionage also typically find an ethnocentric approach appealing.

Disadvantages of Ethnocentric Staffing   Despite its advantages, ethnocentric staffing has its negative aspects. First, relocating managers from the home country is expensive. The bonuses that managers often receive for relocating plus relocation expenses for entire families can increase the cost of a manager several times over. Likewise, the pressure of cultural differences and long periods away from relatives and friends can contribute to the failure of managers on international assignments.

Second, an ethnocentric policy can create barriers for the host-country office. The presence of home-country managers in the host country might encourage a "foreign" image of the business. Lower-level employees might feel that managers do not really understand their needs because they come from another culture. Occasionally they are right: Expatriate managers sometimes fail to integrate themselves into the local culture. And if they fail to overcome cultural barriers, they typically fail to understand the needs of their local employees and those of their local customers.

Polycentric Staffing

In **polycentric staffing**, individuals from the host country manage operations abroad. Companies can implement a polycentric approach for top and mid-level managers, for lower-level staff, or for nonmanagerial workers. It is well suited to companies who want to give national units a degree of autonomy in decision making. This policy does not mean that host-country managers are left to run operations in any way they see fit. Large international companies usually conduct extensive training programs in which host-country managers visit home offices for extended periods. This exposes them to the company's culture and specific business practices. Small and medium-sized companies can find this policy expensive, but being able to depend on local managers who fully understand what is expected of them can far outweigh any costs.

polycentric staffing
Staffing policy in which individuals from the host country manage operations abroad.

Advantages and Disadvantages of Polycentric Staffing   Polycentric staffing places managerial responsibility in the hands of people intimately familiar with the local business environment. Managers with deep cultural understanding of the local market can

According to Microsoft (www.microsoft.com) founder Bill Gates, when opening an international office, "It sends the wrong message to have a foreigner come in to run things." So when Microsoft opened a branch in India, it hired native Indian Rajiv Nair to see that legitimate copies of Microsoft software went into the hundreds of thousands of PCs built in India each year. Five years later, Indian operations were promoted to a full-fledged subsidiary, with Nair as its general manager.

Source: Dilip Mehta/Contact Press Images Inc.

be an enormous advantage. They are familiar with local business practices and can read the subtle cues of both verbal and nonverbal language. They need not overcome any cultural barriers created by an image of being an outsider, and they tend to have a better feel for the needs of employees, customers, and suppliers.

Another important advantage of polycentric staffing is elimination of the high cost of relocating expatriate managers and families. This benefit can be extremely helpful for small and medium-sized businesses that cannot afford the expenses associated with expatriate employees.

The major drawback of polycentric staffing is the potential for losing control of the host-country operation. When a company employs natives of each country to manage local operations, it runs the risk of becoming a collection of discrete national businesses. This situation might not be a problem when a firm's strategy calls for treating each national market differently. It is not a good policy, however, for companies that are following global strategies. If these companies lack integration, knowledge sharing, and a common image, performance will surely suffer.

Geocentric Staffing

geocentric staffing
Staffing policy in which the best-qualified individuals, regardless of nationality, manage operations abroad.

In **geocentric staffing**, the best-qualified individuals, regardless of nationality, manage operations abroad. The local operation may choose managers from the host country, from the home country, or from a third country. The choice depends on the operation's specific needs. This policy is typically reserved for top-level managers.

Advantages and Disadvantages of Geocentric Staffing Geocentric staffing helps a company develop global managers who can adjust easily to any business environment—particularly to cultural differences. This advantage is especially useful for global companies trying to break down nationalistic barriers, whether between managers in a single office or between different offices. One hope of companies using this policy is that a global perspective among its managers will help them seize opportunities that may otherwise be overlooked.

The downside of geocentric staffing is the expense. Understandably, top managers who are capable both of fitting into different cultures and being effective at their jobs are highly prized among international companies. The combination of high demand for their skills and their short supply inflates their salaries. Moreover, there is the expense of relocating managers and their families—sometimes every year or two.

Quick Study

1. List several ways in which *human resource management* differs in the international versus domestic environment.

2. What are the three different types of international *staffing policies* that companies can implement?

3. Identify the advantages and disadvantages of each type of international staffing policy.

Recruiting and Selecting Human Resources

Naturally, companies try to recruit and select qualified managers and nonmanagerial workers who are well-suited to their tasks and responsibilities. But how does a company know the number of managers and workers it needs? How does it recruit the best available individuals? How does it select from the pool of available candidates? In this section, we explore some answers to these and other important questions about recruiting and selecting employees.

Human Resource Planning

Recruiting and selecting managers and workers requires **human resource planning**—the process of forecasting a company's human resource needs and its supply. The first phase of HR planning involves taking an inventory of a company's current human resources—that is, collecting data on every employee, including educational background, special job skills, previous jobs, language skills, and experience living abroad.

human resource planning Process of forecasting a company's human resource needs and its supply.

The second phase of HR planning is estimating the company's future HR needs. For example, consider a firm that plans to sell its products directly to buyers in a new market abroad. Will it create a new operation abroad and staff it with managers from the home office, or will it train local managers? Will it hire its own local sales force, or will it hire a distributor? Likewise, manufacturing or assembling products in an international market requires factory workers. A company must decide whether to hire these people itself or to subcontract production to other producers—thus eliminating the need for it to hire factory workers. These issues are extremely important to small and medium-sized businesses that have far more limited budgets than do global companies. For additional issues that small companies should consider when staffing internationally, see the Entrepreneur's Toolkit titled, "Growing Global."

As we noted in previous chapters, this decision frequently raises ethical questions. The general public is becoming increasingly well informed about the fact that global companies make extensive use of subcontractors in low-wage nations. Of particular concern is the question of whether subcontractors are taking advantage of "sweatshop labor." But publicity generated by allegations of workplace abuse caused many firms to establish codes of conduct, and they stepped up efforts to ensure compliance. For example, Apple (www.apple.com) sent a team of investigators to China to look into charges of sweatshop-like conditions at a company manufacturing Apple's iPod. The company that Apple investigated was a division of the world's largest contract electronics manufacturer, Hon Hai Precision Industry.[3]

Another example on this topic involves Levi Strauss (www.levistrauss.com). When apparel contractors in Bangladesh admitted that they hired children, Levi Strauss demanded that they comply with local regulations. Unfortunately, it turned out that many of the underage workers were their families' sole sources of support. So Levi's struck a deal: Contractors agreed to continue paying wages to the youngsters while they went to school and then they would be rehired when they reached age 14. Levi's paid for them to attend school until they came of age.

In the third phase of HR planning, managers develop a plan for recruiting and selecting people to fill vacant and anticipated new positions, both managerial and nonmanagerial. Sometimes, a firm must also make plans for reducing its workforce—a process called *decruitment*—when current HR levels are greater than anticipated needs. Planning for decruitment normally occurs when a company decides to discontinue manufacturing or selling in a market. Unfortunately, the decision by global companies to shift the location of manufacturing from one country to another can also result in lost jobs. Let's now take a closer look at the recruitment and selection processes.

Growing Global

For an entrepreneur or small business, going global can strain resources of time, money, and people. Here is some advice on important human resource issues to consider when expanding internationally.

- **Don't Rely Solely on Home-Country Expatriates.** "While they understand the company and the product, they don't understand the local practices and culture and don't have the relationships," said Joseph Monti, a partner at Grant Thornton (www.gt.com). "The best strategy is to have a local general manager with a support staff that could be seeded with U.S. expatriates."

- **Contacts Don't Guarantee Contracts.** "Relationships matter more than mere contacts," said Virginia Kamsky, CEO of Kamsky Associates (www.kamsky.com). "Don't assume that hiring the son of a government official will automatically get you business. It's more important to hire a person with a good attitude and strong relationship-building skills," she added.

- **Treat Your Employees Abroad as You Want to be Treated.** "People are basically the same worldwide; it doesn't matter where you are," notes Jeff Dzuira, director of international sales at Ferris Manufacturing (www.polymem.com). "Awareness and respect of cultural protocol demonstrates honesty and goodwill, and this leads to trust, which in turn leads to mutually profitable relationships."

- **Employ the Web in Your Search.** One of the largest employment Web sites is Monster (www.monster.com). It has branches in 22 countries and literally millions of résumés. Another popular Web site for international job seekers is at (www.hotjobs.yahoo.com). Employers can also post job announcements on the Web site at (www.overseasjobs.com). Of course, there are many more Web sites out there, and undertaking an aggressive job search or recruitment drive on the Internet is becoming increasingly common.

Recruiting Human Resources

recruitment
Process of identifying and attracting a qualified pool of applicants for vacant positions.

The process of identifying and attracting a qualified pool of applicants for vacant positions is called **recruitment**. Companies can recruit internally from among their current employees or look to external sources.

Current Employees   Finding an international manager among current employees is easiest for a large company with an abundance of internal managers. Likely candidates within the company are managers who were involved in previous stages of an international project—say, in *identifying* the new production site or potential market. It is likely that these individuals have already made important contacts inside the host country, and they have already been exposed to its culture.

Recent College Graduates   Companies also recruit from among recent college graduates who have come from other countries to attend college in the firm's home country. This is a particularly common practice among companies in the United States. Over a one-year period, these new hires receive general and specialized training and then are given positions in their native countries. As a rule, they learn about the organization's culture and the way in which it conducts business. Most important, perhaps, is their familiarity with the culture of the target market, including its customs, traditions, and language.

Local Managerial Talent   Companies can also recruit local managerial talent. Hiring local managers is common when cultural understanding is a key job requirement. Hiring local managers with government contacts can speed the process of getting approvals for local operations. In some cases, governments force companies to recruit local managers so that they can develop their own internal pools of managerial talent. Governments sometimes also restrict the number of international managers that can work in the host country.

Nonmanagerial Workers   Companies typically recruit locally for nonmanagerial positions because there is often little need for highly specialized skills or training. However, a specialist from the home country is typically brought in to train people chosen for more demanding positions.

Firms also turn to the local labor market when governments restrict the number of people allowed into the host country for work purposes. Such efforts are usually designed to reduce unemployment among the local population. On the other hand, countries sometimes permit the importation of nonmanagerial workers. Kuwait, a wealthy oil-producing country in the Middle East, has brought in large numbers of nonmanagerial workers for its blue-collar and technical jobs. Many of these workers come from Egypt, India, Lebanon, Pakistan, and the Philippines in search of jobs or higher wages.

Selecting Human Resources

The process of screening and hiring the best-qualified applicants with the greatest performance potential is called **selection**. The process for international assignments includes measuring a person's ability to bridge cultural differences. Expatriate managers must be able to adapt to a new way of life in the host country. Conversely, native host-country managers must be able to work effectively with superiors who have different cultural backgrounds.

In the case of expatriate managers, cultural differences between home country and host country are important factors in their potential success. Culturally sensitive managers increase the likelihood that a company will achieve its international business goals. Recruiters can assess cultural sensitivity by asking candidates questions about their receptiveness to new ways of doing things and questions about racial and ethnic issues. They can also use global aptitude tests such as the one mentioned in the Web Site Report exercise at the end of this chapter.

It is also important to examine the cultural sensitivity of each family member who will be going to the host country. The ability of a family member (particularly a spouse) to adapt to a new culture can be a key factor in the success or failure of an expatriate manager.

selection
Process of screening and hiring the best-qualified applicants with the greatest performance potential.

Culture Shock

Successful international managers typically do not mind, and often enjoy, living and working outside their native lands. In extreme cases, they might even be required to relocate every year or so. These individuals are capable of adapting quickly to local conditions and business practices. Such managers are becoming increasingly valuable with the emergence of markets in Asia, Central and Eastern Europe, and Latin America. They are also helping to create a global pool of managers who are ready and willing to go practically anywhere on short notice. The size of this pool, however, remains limited because of the difficulties that many people experience in relocating to unfamiliar cultures.

Living in another culture can be a stressful experience. Selecting managers comfortable traveling to and living in unfamiliar cultures, therefore, is an extremely important factor when recruiting for international posts. Set down in the midst of new cultures, many expatriates experience **culture shock**—a psychological process affecting people living abroad that is characterized by homesickness, irritability, confusion, aggravation, and depression. In other words, they have trouble adjusting to the new environment in which they find themselves. *Expatriate failure*—the early return by an employee from an international assignment because of inadequate job performance—often results from cultural stress. The higher cost of expatriate failure is convincing many companies to invest in cultural-training programs for employees sent abroad. For a detailed look at the culture-shock process and how to reduce its effects, see the Global Manager's Briefcase titled, "A Shocking Ordeal."

culture shock
Psychological process affecting people living abroad that is characterized by homesickness, irritability, confusion, aggravation, and depression.

Reverse Culture Shock

Ironically, expatriates who successfully adapt to new cultures often undergo an experience called **reverse culture shock**—the psychological process of readapting to one's home culture. Because values and behavior that once seemed so natural now seem so strange, reverse culture shock may be even more disturbing than culture shock. Returning managers often find that either no position or merely a "standby" position awaits them in

reverse culture shock
Psychological process of readapting to one's home culture.

GLOBAL MANAGER'S BRIEFCASE
A Shocking Ordeal

Culture shock typically occurs during stays of a few months or longer in an unfamiliar culture. It begins on arrival and normally occurs in four stages (although not all people go through every stage):

- **Stage 1:** The "honeymoon" typically lasts from a few days to a few weeks. New arrivals are fascinated by local sights, pleasant hospitality, and interesting habits. They are thrilled about their opportunity and are optimistic about prospects for success. Yet this sense of security is often false because, so far, interactions with locals are similar to those of a tourist.
- **Stage 2:** This stage lasts from a few weeks to a few months; in fact, some people never move on to Stage 3. Unpredictable quirks of the culture become annoying, even maddening. Visitors begin mocking the locals and regarding the ways of their native cultures as superior. Relationships with spouses and children suffer, and depression, perhaps even despair, sets in.
- **Stage 3:** Emotions hit bottom and recovery begins. Cynical remarks cease as visitors begin to learn more about the local culture, interact more with locals, and form friendships.
- **Stage 4:** Visitors not only better understand local customs and behavior but actually appreciate many of them. They now treat differences as "unique" solutions to familiar problems in different cultural contexts. Reaching this stage is a sign that the expatriate has adapted well and that success in his or her international assignment is likely.

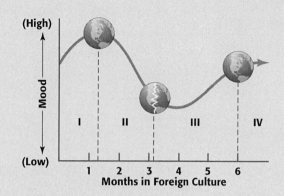

Here are some steps that prospective expatriates can take to reduce the burden of culture shock during an international assignment:

- Undergo extensive psychological assessment to ensure that both you and your family members are emotionally able to handle the assignment.
- Obtain knowledge of the local culture (especially its language) and critically examine your own culture biases before leaving home.
- If possible, visit the assigned country, mingling with local people and getting a feel for your future assignment. Ask about local educational, financial, and health-care services.
- After you are inside a culture, meet with others—both natives and expatriates—to discuss your negative and positive experiences.
- Most important: Relax, be adventurous, take a worldly perspective, and keep your sense of humor.

the home office. Companies often do not know how to take full advantage of the cross-cultural abilities developed by managers who have spent several potentially valuable years abroad. It is not uncommon for expatriates to leave their companies within a year of returning home because of difficulties blending back into the company culture.

Moreover, spouses and children often have difficulty leaving the adopted culture and returning home. For many Japanese employees and their families, reentry into Japanese culture after a work assignment in the United States can be particularly difficult. The fast pace of business and social life in the United States, plus the relatively high degree of freedom and independence for women, contrasts with life in Japan. Returning Japanese expatriates can find it difficult to adjust back to life in Japan after years of living in the United States.

Dealing with Reverse Culture Shock The effects of reverse culture shock can be reduced. Home-culture reorientation programs and career-counseling sessions for returning managers and their families can be highly effective. For example, the employer might bring the entire family home for a short stay several weeks before the official return. This kind of trip allows returnees to prepare for at least some of the reverse culture shock that may await them.

Good career development programs can help companies retain valuable managers. Ideally, the career development plan was worked out before the employee went abroad and revised before his or her return. Some companies work with employees before they go abroad to plan career paths of up to 20 years within the company. Mentors who have previously gone abroad and had to adjust on returning home can also be assigned to returning managers. The mentor becomes a confidant with whom the expatriate manager can discuss particular problems related to work, family, and readjusting to the home culture.

Quick Study

1. Why is *human resources planning* important? Identify its three phases.

2. What are the main sources from which companies *recruit* their international managers?

3. What is meant by the term *culture shock*? Describe its four stages and how its effects can be reduced.

4. Under what circumstances might someone experience *reverse culture shock*?

Training and Development

After a company recruits and selects its managers and other employees, it normally identifies the skills and knowledge that employees have and those that they need to perform their duties. Employees who lack the necessary skills or knowledge can then be directed into specific training or development programs.

Approximately 300,000 U.S. citizens live outside the United States on international assignments, in addition to hundreds of thousands more who travel abroad on business for stays of up to several weeks. Some of the many costs of relocating an employee for a long-term international assignment include moving expenses and ongoing costs for things such as housing, education, and cost-of-living adjustments. That is why many companies realize the need for in-depth training and development programs if they are to get the maximum productivity from managers posted abroad.

As companies increasingly reach out to the world to obtain services, they are turning to online training (eTraining) programs that teach skills immediately relevant to employees' jobs. These include administrative training, human resources training, compliance training, and frontline issues such as the consumer benefits of a new product. The appeal of eTraining to international companies is its consistency: eTraining delivers a consistent message in the same way to an infinite number of employees. By contrast, employees receiving other types of training in diverse settings worldwide can go away with many different perceptions or biases. Workplace eTraining is not perfect: it can be difficult to engage people online and to teach soft skills, such as appropriate facial expressions and tone of voice. But its ability to flexibly train large groups cost-effectively makes it a viable alternative to traditional training methods.[4]

Methods of Cultural Training

Ideally, everyone involved in business should be culturally literate and prepared to go anywhere in the world at a moment's notice. Realistically, many employees and many companies do not need or cannot afford to be entirely literate in another culture. The extent of a company's international involvement demands a corresponding level of cultural knowledge from its employees. Companies whose activities are highly international need employees with language fluency and in-depth experience in other countries. Meanwhile, small companies or those new to international business can begin with some basic cultural training. As a company increases its international involvement and cross-cultural contact, employees' cultural knowledge must keep pace.

As we see in Figure 16.1, companies use many methods to prepare managers for an international assignment. These methods tend to reflect a manager's level of international involvement. The goal is to create informed, open-minded, flexible managers with a level of cultural training appropriate to the duties required of them.

FIGURE 16.1

International Assignment Preparation Methods

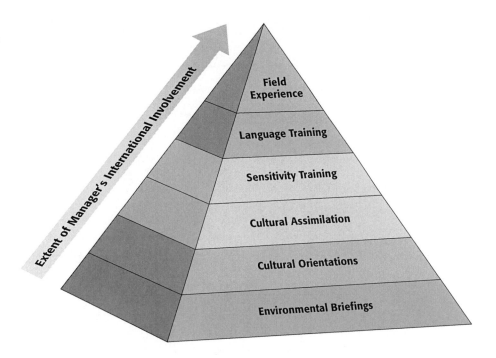

Environmental Briefings and Cultural Orientations *Environmental (area) briefings* constitute the most basic level of training—often the starting point for studying other cultures. Briefings include information on local housing, health care, transportation, schools, and climate. Such knowledge is normally obtained from books, films, and lectures. *Cultural orientations* offer insight into social, political, legal, and economic institutions. Their purpose is to add depth and substance to environmental briefings.

Cultural Assimilation and Sensitivity Training *Cultural assimilation* teaches the culture's values, attitudes, manners, and customs. So-called guerrilla linguistics, which involves learning some phrases in the local language, is often used at this stage. It also typically includes role-play exercises: The trainee responds to a specific situation to be evaluated by a team of judges. This method is often used when someone is given little notice of a short stay abroad and wishes to take a crash course in social and business etiquette and communication. *Sensitivity training* teaches people to be considerate and understanding of other people's feelings and emotions. It gets the trainee "under the skin" of the local people.

Language Training The need for more thorough cultural preparedness brings us to intensive *language training*. This level of training entails more than memorizing phrases for ordering dinner or asking directions. It gets a trainee "into the mind" of local people. The trainee learns more about why local people behave as they do. This is perhaps the most critical part of cultural training for long-term assignments.

A survey of top executives found that foreign-language skills topped the list of skills needed to maintain a competitive edge. According to the survey, 31 percent of male employees and 27 percent of female employees lacked foreign-language skills. To remedy this situation, many companies either employ outside agencies that specialize in language training or they develop their own programs. Employees at 3M Corporation (www.3m.com) developed a third way. They created an all-volunteer "Language Society" composed of current and retired employees and family members. About 1,000 people are members, and the group offers classes in 17 languages taught by 70 volunteer employee teachers. The society meets 45 minutes per week and charges a nominal $5 membership fee. Officials at 3M say that the society nicely complements the company's formal language education program.[5]

Field Experience *Field experience* means visiting the culture, walking the streets of its cities and villages, and becoming absorbed by it for a short time. The trainee gets to enjoy some of the unique cultural traits and feel some of the stresses inherent in living in the culture.

Finally, remember that spouses and children also need cultural training. Training for them is a good investment because the alternatives—an international "commuter marriage" or expatriate failure—are both psychologically and financially expensive options.

Compiling a Cultural Profile

Cultural profiles can be quite helpful in deciding whether to accept an international assignment. The following are some excellent sources for constructing a cultural profile:

- **CultureGrams.**   Published by ProQuest, this guide can be found in the reference section of many libraries. Frequent updates make *CultureGrams* (www.culturegrams.com) a timely source of information. Individual sections profile each culture's background and its people, customs, courtesies, and society. A section titled "For the Traveler" covers details such as required entry visas and vaccinations.
- **Country Studies Area Handbooks.**   This series explains how politics, economics, society, and national security issues are related to one another and shaped by culture in more than 70 countries. Handbooks tend to be politically oriented because they are designed for U.S. military personnel. The *Country Studies Area Handbooks* are available on the Web at http://lcweb2.loc.gov/frd/cs/cshome.html.
- **Background Notes.**   These notes contain much relevant factual information on human rights and related issues in various countries. Yet because they are published by the U.S. Department of State (www.state.gov), they take a U.S. political perspective.

Information can also be obtained by contacting the embassies of other countries in your home nation. People with firsthand knowledge and specific books and films are also good sources of information. After you're inside a country, you'll find your home country's embassy a good source of further cultural advice. Embassies maintain networks of home-nation professionals who work in the local culture, some with many years of experience on which you can draw.

Nonmanagerial Worker Training

Nonmanagerial workers also have training and development needs. This is especially true in some developing and newly industrialized countries where people have not even completed primary school. Even if the workforce is fairly well-educated, workers may lack experience working in industry. In such cases, companies that do business abroad can train local workers in how to work on an assembly line or cultivate business leads to make sales. The need for such basic-skills training continues to grow as companies increasingly explore opportunities in emerging markets.

In many countries, national governments cooperate with businesses to train nonmanagerial workers. Japan and Germany lead the world in vocational training and apprenticeship programs for nonmanagerial workers. Students who are unable or unwilling to enter college can enter programs paid for by the government and private industry. They undergo extensive practical training that exposes them to the cutting-edge technologies used by the country's leading companies. For example, Germany's Mittelstand is a network of three million small and medium-sized companies that account for about two-thirds of the country's jobs. Mittelstand companies provide 80 percent of Germany's apprenticeships. Although they typically employ fewer than 100 people, many Mittelstand companies are export powerhouses.

Employee Compensation

Essential to good international HRM is a fair and effective compensation (reward) system. Such a system is designed to attract and retain the best and brightest employees and to reward them for their performance. Because a country's compensation practices are rooted in its culture and legal and economic systems, determining compensation can be complicated. For example, base pay accounts for nearly all employee compensation in some countries. In others, bonuses and fringe benefits account for more than half of a person's compensation.

Managerial Employees

Naturally, compensation packages for managers differ from company to company and from country to country. Good packages are fairly complicated to design, for several reasons. Consider the effect of *cost of living*, which includes factors such as the cost of groceries, dining out, clothing, housing, schooling, health care, transportation, and utilities. Quite simply, it costs more to live in some countries than in others. Moreover, within a given country, the cost of living typically varies from large cities to rural towns and villages. Most companies add a certain amount to an expatriate manager's pay to cover greater cost-of-living expenses. On the other hand, managers who are relocating to lower cost-of-living countries are typically paid the same amount that they were receiving at the home office—otherwise they would be financially penalized for accepting an international job assignment.

Companies must cover other costs incurred by expatriate managers even when the cost of living abroad is lower than at home. One important concern for relocating managers is the quality of local education. In many cases, children cannot immediately enter local classes because they do not speak the local language. In such instances, most companies pay for private-school education.

Bonus and Tax Incentives   Companies commonly offer managers inducements to accept international postings. The most common is a financial bonus. This bonus can be in the form of a one-time payment or an add-on to regular pay—generally 15 to 20 percent. Bonuses for managers who are asked to go into a particularly unstable country or one with a very low standard of living often receive *hardship pay*.

Managers can also be attracted by another income-related factor. For example, the U.S. government permits citizens working abroad to exclude $82,000 of "foreign-earned income" from their taxable income in the United States—even if it was earned in a country with no income tax. But earnings over that amount are subject to income tax, as are employee benefits such as free housing.[6]

Cultural and Social Contributors to Cost   Culture also plays an important role in the compensation of expatriate managers. Some nations offer more paid holidays than others. Many offer free medical care to everyone living and working there. Granted, the quality of locally available medical care is not always good. Many companies, therefore, have plans to take seriously ill expatriates and family members home or to nearby countries where medical care is equal to that available in the home country.

Companies that hire managers in the local market might encounter additional costs engendered by social attitudes. For instance, in some countries employers are expected to provide free or subsidized housing. In others the government obliges employers to provide paid maternity leaves of up to one and a half years. Government-mandated maternity leaves vary significantly across European countries. Although not all such costs need to be absorbed by companies, they do tend to raise a country's cost of doing business.

Managers recruited from within the host country generally receive the same pay as managers who work for local companies. Yet they often receive perks not offered by local firms. And some managers are required to visit the home office at least several times per year. If time allows, many managers will make these into short vacations by taking along their families and adding a few extra days onto the length of the trip.

Nonmanagerial Workers

Two main factors influence the wages of nonmanagerial workers. First, their compensation is strongly influenced by increased cross-border business investment. Employers can relocate fairly easily to nations where wages are lower. In the home country, meanwhile, workers must often accept lower wages when an employer gives them a choice of accepting the reduction or watching their jobs move abroad. This situation is causing a trend toward greater equality in workers' pay around the world. This equalizing effect encourages economic development and improvement in workers' lives in some nations at the expense of workers in other nations.

The freedom with which an employer can relocate differs from country to country, however. Although firms in some countries are allowed to move with little notice, in others they are highly restricted. Some countries force companies to compensate workers who lose their jobs because of relocation. This policy is common in European countries that have erected extensive social safety nets for unemployed workers.

Second, the greater mobility of labor today affects wages. Although labor laws in Europe are still more stringent than in the United States, the countries of the European Union are abolishing the requirement that workers from one EU nation must obtain visas to work in another. If workers in Spain cannot find work at home or if they feel that their current pay is inadequate, they are free to move to another EU country where unemployment is lower (say, Britain). A problem that plagues some European countries today is that they seem to be creating a group of people who are permanently unemployed.

Quick Study

1. Identify the types of training and development used for: (a) international managers and (b) nonmanagerial workers.

2. Describe each type of cultural training used to prepare managers for international assignments.

2. What variables are involved in decisions regarding employee compensation for: (a) managers and (b) nonmanagerial workers?

Labor–Management Relations

The positive or negative condition of relations between a company's management and its workers (labor) is referred to as **labor–management relations**. Cooperative relations between labor and management can give a firm a tremendous competitive advantage. When management and workers realize they depend on one another, the company is often better prepared to meet its goals and surmount unexpected obstacles that may crop up. Giving workers a greater stake in the company—say, through profit-sharing plans—is one way to increase morale and generate commitment to improved quality and customer service.

Because relations between laborers and managers are human relations, they are rooted in culture and are often affected by political movements in a market. Large international companies tend to make high-level labor decisions at the home office because it gives them greater control over their network of production operations around the world—yet lower-level decisions are often left to managers in each country. In effect, this policy places decisions that have a direct impact on workers' lives in the hands of experts in the local market.

labor–management relations
Positive or negative condition of relations between a company's management and its workers.

Workers in Germany and France are typically protected by very powerful labor unions. In fact, German workers have a direct influence on company decisions through a plan called *codetermination*. Here German metalworkers shout slogans during a rally at a car factory in Sindelfingen, Germany. Why do you think countries around the world differ in the amount of influence that they give labor unions?

Source: © Michael Dalder/Reuters/ CORBIS. All Rights Reserved.

Such decisions might include the number of annual paid holidays, the length of maternity leave, and the provision of day-care facilities. Localizing such management decisions tends to contribute to better labor–management relations because managers familiar with local practices are better equipped to handle matters that affect workers personally.

Importance of Labor Unions

The strength of labor unions in a country where a company has operations is important to its performance and can even affect the selection of a location. Developing and emerging markets in Asia are a popular location for international companies. Some Asian governments appeal to international companies to locate facilities in their nations by promising to keep labor unions in check. But companies also find developed nations attractive if, for whatever reason, a cooperative atmosphere exists between company management and labor unions. In some Asian countries, especially Japan, a cultural emphasis on harmony and balanced interests discourages confrontation between labor and management.

Ireland became a favorite location for a toehold in the European Union (EU). The main attractions are productive labor, lower wages, and a reduced likelihood of disruptive strikes. Labor unions are not as strong there as they are on the continent, particularly in France and Germany. Nevertheless, Germany has not been immune to the trend of falling union membership. Union membership has dropped off in Germany over the past decade from about 12 million to about 8 million workers. The main reason for the decline is the lack of interest in union membership in the former East German territories. By contrast, labor unions comprise only about 9 percent of the labor force in the United States today, compared with 36 percent 50 years ago.

Despite declines in union membership, labor in Germany exercises a good deal of power over management decisions. In fact, under a plan called *codetermination*, German workers enjoy a direct say in the strategies and policies of their employers. This plan allows labor representatives to participate in high-level company meetings by actually voting on proposed actions.

International Labor Movements   The global activities of unions are making progress in areas such as improving the treatment of workers and reducing incidents involving child labor. But the efforts of separate national unions to increase their cooperation are somewhat less successful. Although unions in one nation might want to support their counterparts in another country, generating grassroots support is difficult for two reasons. First, events taking place in another country are difficult for many people to comprehend. Distance and cultural difference make it hard for people to understand others who live and work elsewhere.

Second, whether they realize it or not, workers in different countries sometimes compete against one another. For example, today firms can relocate internationally rather easily. Thus, labor unions in one country might offer concessions to attract the jobs that will be created by a new production facility. In this way, unions in different nations can wind up competing against one another. Some observers argue that this phenomenon creates downward pressure on both wages and union power worldwide.

Quick Study

1. What is meant by the term *labor–management relations*?
2. Explain how labor–management relations differ around the world.

A Final Word

This chapter has concluded our survey of international business. We studied how firms, ranging from small and medium-sized businesses to large global companies, hire and manage their most important resource—their employees. We covered a great deal of territory in our tour of international business. We hope we piqued your interest in the global marketplace and in the activities of all types of international companies. Yet our learning does not end here. Each of us will continue to be exposed to international business in our daily lives—whether as consumers or as current or future business managers. We will continue to expand our knowledge of other national cultures, the international business environment, and how companies manage their international operations. We wish you well on your continued journey through this fascinating and dynamic subject!

Chapter Summary

1. Explain the three different types of staffing policies used by international companies.
   - *Ethnocentric staffing* means staffing operations outside the home country with home-country nationals; it can give a company tight control over subsidiary decision making.
   - *Polycentric staffing* means staffing operations with host-country natives; it can give subsidiaries some autonomy in decision making.
   - *Geocentric staffing* means staffing operations with the best-qualified individuals, regardless of nationality; it is typically reserved for top-level managers.
2. Describe the recruitment and selection issues facing international companies.
   - Large companies often recruit international managers from within the ranks of existing employees, but smaller companies may need to hire outside managers.
   - International students who have graduated from colleges abroad can be hired, trained locally, and posted in their home countries.
   - Local managerial talent may be recruited in the host country to obtain people with an understanding of the local culture and political system; oftentimes required when manufacturing or marketing extensively abroad.
3. Discuss the importance of training and development programs, especially cultural training.
   - *Culture shock* refers to the psychological difficulties experienced when living in an unfamiliar culture; it is characterized by homesickness, irritability, confusion, aggravation, and depression.
   - *Reverse culture shock* is the psychological process of readapting to one's home culture.
   - *Cultural training* can reduce the effects of culture shock and reverse culture shock.

   - *Environmental briefings* and *cultural orientations* provide insight on local housing, health care, and the political, economic, and social institutions.
   - *Cultural assimilation* and *sensitivity training* explain the local values, attitudes, and customs, and stress understanding local feelings and emotions.
   - *Language training* provides specific, practical skills that allow employees to communicate in the local language.
   - *Field experience* means visiting the culture for a brief period to begin growing accustomed to it.
4. Explain how companies compensate managers and workers in international markets.
   - An effective compensation policy takes into account local cultures, laws, and practices; key issues are base pay, bonuses, and fringe benefits.
   - Managerial compensation packages may need adjustment to reflect the local cost of living and, perhaps, the cost of education.
   - *Bonus payments* or hardship pay may be needed to entice managers to accept international assignments.
   - Nonmanagerial compensation levels can be influenced by wage rates in other countries.
5. Describe the importance of labor–management relations and how they differ around the world.
   - *Labor–management relations* are the positive or negative condition of relations between company management and its workers.
   - Good labor–management relations can help a company meet its goals and surmount unexpected obstacles.
   - Labor–management relations are rooted in culture and are often affected by political movements in the local market.
   - The strength of labor unions where a company operates can affect its performance and can affect site-selection decisions.

Talk It Over

1. Many Japanese companies use ethnocentric staffing policies in international operations. Why do you think Japanese companies prefer to have Japanese in top management positions? Would you recommend a change in this policy?

2. Did you ever experience culture shock? If so, in which country did it occur? What, if anything, did you do to overcome it? Did your methods work? Did you experience reverse culture shock on returning home?

Teaming Up

1. **Labor–Relations Project.** Suppose you and several of your classmates are the senior management team for a major automobile manufacturer. Among your company's worldwide operations are plants in Spain and Germany. Your company is considering closing these two plants and moving production to Poland in order to take advantage of lower wages. As a group, write a short report explaining how easy (or difficult) it will be for your company to close the plant and lay off workers in both Spain and Germany.

2. **Research Project.** Small and medium-sized businesses sometimes face significant obstacles when expanding operations abroad. Write a group report on the obstacles they face in the area of recruiting and selecting employees when first venturing internationally. Address specific issues such as financial constraints, a lack of contacts, cultural differences, legal issues, geographical distance, and so on.

Key Terms

culture shock
ethnocentric staffing
expatriates
geocentric staffing
human resource management (HRM)

human resource planning
labor–management relations
polycentric staffing
recruitment

reverse culture shock
selection
staffing policy

Take It to the Web

1. **Video Report.** Visit this book's channel on YouTube (YouTube.com/MyIBvideos). Click on "Playlists" near the top of the page and click on the set of videos labeled "Ch 16: Hiring and Managing Employees." Watch one video from the list and summarize it in a half-page report. Reflecting on the contents of this chapter, which aspects of hiring and managing employees can you identify in the video? How might a company engaged in international business act on the information contained in the video?

2. **Web Site Report.** Visit the Web site of the Intercultural Business Center (www.ib-c.com) and read about the cultural training services of this top-ranked company. One evaluative technique the firm offers is called the Global Mentality Test that measures a person's aptitude of doing business globally.

A British company recently found that the top three reasons people quit or underperform are rooted in personality rather than skill, knowledge, or qualification. What do you think are the aspects of a person's personality that cause this to occur? Explain your answer. What advantages do you think global aptitude tests might offer companies doing business internationally?

Personality testing in the workplace is widespread in Australia, Europe, and the United States, but is just starting to catch on in Asia. Why do you think this is? Do you think the reason could be rooted in Asian societies and culture? Explain your answer.

What personal characteristics do you think make someone better suited to doing business globally? Be specific. Do you think these characteristics are innate or can they be learned?

Ethical Challenges

1. You are the manager of a publishing company in China, whose focus is on developing English language learning books for people from non-English-speaking countries. As part of the content development phase, you have decided to hire some native English speakers to work on the project. After these employees have worked with you for two weeks, you notice that several of them are not performing well at work and seem to be depressed and lacking motivation. When you confront them about this, they inform you that they are homesick and do not feel comfortable with Chinese culture. They are suffering from culture shock. Do you fire these employees or take measures to make

them more comfortable? If you choose to keep them on staff, what steps do you take to ensure their happiness and assimilation into Chinese culture?

2. You are an expatriate manager at a manufacturing facility in the Middle East on your first assignment abroad. You are aware of increasing concern among your employees about low wages that barely allow them to live at sustenance level. The plant is not unionized, and you know that your superiors in your home country are not particularly supportive of efforts to organize workers. You also know that if workers vote to form a union and then demand higher wages, corporate headquarters is likely to shut down the facility and shift production elsewhere. If the plant were to be shut down, you would be transferred and your employees would lose their jobs, going from making low wages to no wages. Should you encourage or discourage your workers in their efforts to unionize? Explain your decision.

PRACTICING INTERNATIONAL MANAGEMENT CASE

South Korea's Struggle With Poor Workplace Relations

A good rapport between workers and their superiors is essential in maintaining a productive workplace all over the world. If bosses make unreasonable demands or generally ignore the needs of their workers, a company will often face problems. A labor-management relationship crisis occurred in 1996 due to the practices of South Korean businesses and several labor laws passed by the South Korean government.

The Sejin Electronics plant in China, owned and operated by South Koreans, became notorious for its business practices. The rules in the assembly plant were unbelievably strict. Talking, unless work-related, was not permitted on the assembly line at any time, and three violations of this policy led to immediate dismissal. Employees were only permitted to use the bathroom during a ten-minute break, which occurred every two hours. The Chinese press broke the story of an incident in which over 100 workers were required to kneel down before Kim Jin Sun, Korean owner of the plant, after she spotted a few employees falling asleep during their break. Incidents such as this gave South Korean bosses a reputation for treating employees unfairly.

Adding to the climate of worker strife were two labor laws enacted by the South Korean government. The first law made the dismissal of employees easier for employers, and the second law sought to curtail labor-organizing rights. A massive labor strike was started by the automotive and shipbuilding workers in protest against these laws. The Federation of Korean Trade Unions called upon its 1.2 million members to strike as well. In response to the strike, the government attempted to use tear gas and various other forceful tactics to end the strike. Workers held their ground, and the strike finally ended in January of 1997, when the Korean government repealed the harsh labor laws.

Recently, South Korea suffered a major disruption in trade due to a nationwide trucker strike. On June 11, 2008, over 13,000 truckers stopped moving freight in protest of rising fuel costs, demanding higher transport fees and bigger government fuel subsidies. The strike lasted for a week, and cost the South Korean economy an estimated $5.92 million in lost trade. Some of the trucker's demands were met, including a 19 percent increase in hauling fees, and a 50 percent discount on toll gate fees for night drivers.

South Korea experienced the negative consequences that can occur as a result of treating workers poorly and learned a lesson about the proper treatment of workers and the power of unions. Although relations between government and laborers have certainly improved since the 1990s, they are far from perfect, as labor strikes continue to this day. This back-and-forth between the government and unions is a normal part of employee relations and helps maintain a healthy balance in the workplace and ensure that everyone is keeping employees' needs a top priority.

Thinking Globally

1. Do you feel that is even more important for foreign managers of international companies to attempt to develop strong labor-management relations? Why or why not? What problems might arise as a result of major dispute with foreign managers and domestic workers?

2. In your opinion, how effective are labor unions in achieving better working conditions? Do you support workers that go on strike, or do you think that they are merely wasting time and decreasing productivity?

3. If international labor unions were formed, do you think that disputes between countries about labor laws would increase or decrease? Explain your answer.

Source: "South Korean Labor Laws and Regulations," *Wikia Education*, March 27, 2008, http://internationalbusiness.wikia.com/wiki/South_Korean_Labor_Laws_and_Regulations. William Sim, "South Korea Trucker Strike Costs $5.92 Billion, May Slow Growth," *Bloomberg.com*, June 17, 2008, http://www.bloomberg.com/apps/news?pid=20601087&sid=a2v1NYLW95dI&refer=home.

Index